T0021817

The Legend of
Starcrash

by
Dolores Cannon

OZARK
MOUNTAIN
PUBLISHING

P.O. Box 754
Huntsville, AR 72740-0754
ozarkmt.com

Library of Congress Cataloging-in-Publication Data
Cannon, Dolores, 1931-2014
        "The Legend of Starcrash" by Dolores Cannon
Information obtained through regressive hypnosis about an alien spacecraft that crashed in Alaska-Canada thousands of years ago.
1. Hypnosis 2. Reincarnation 3. Extraterrestrials 4. North American Indian Legends
I. Cannon, Dolores, 1931-2014 II. Reincarnation III. Title
Library of Congress Catalog Card Number: 94-065021
ISBN 0-9632776-7-7

Book Design: Kris Kleeberg
Cover Artwork: Lyle Vasser
Cover Design and Layout: enki3d.com
Animal Illustration: Jenelle Johannes
Book set in Adobe Garamond

Published by:

OZARK
MOUNTAIN
PUBLISHING

P.O. Box 754
Huntsville, AR 72740-0754
ozarkmt.com

History is a glorification of fairy tales. There isn't a thing you know that is correct, but still it is better to know something that is wrong than not to know anything.

Joseph Kane
A fact collector and debunker of erroneous history.

Books by Dolores Cannon

Conversations with Nostradamus, Volume I
Conversations with Nostradamus, Volume II
Conversations with Nostradamus, Volume III
Jesus and the Essenes
They Walked with Jesus
Keepers of the Garden
Conversations with a Spirit
A Soul Remembers Hiroshima
The Legend of Starcrash

Conversations with Nostradamus is available
in abridged form on audio tape cassette.

For more information about any
of the above titles, or other titles
in our catalog, write to:

OZARK
MOUNTAIN
PUBLISHERS

P.O. Box 754
Huntsville, AR 72740-0754

Table of Contents

Chapter 1

The Discovery of the Legend

FOR OVER FIFTEEN YEARS I have been exploring history through regressive hypnosis. During that time I have become increasingly convinced that recorded history, the history which we are exposed to in school, may be only minimally accurate. And I am now even suspicious of the small percent that may be based upon fact. History as we know it is dry and lifeless, without form and substance, mostly inanimate facts and figures. Facts that rarely deal with the people who lived during those times and the emotions they felt. I feel history has also been romanticized through our literature, movies, and television, until it bares only the slightest resemblance to what really happened in the past. In my work I regularly take trips through time and space to visit people while they are alive in those bygone time periods and hear history from their own lips as it is being lived. Not *re*-lived through the mind of an author, but actually while it is being experienced. I have found the real substance that history is made of, not that which is found in history books.

I am a regressionist, which is a hypnotist that specializes in past-life therapy, reincarnation, and the research and investigation of this phenomenon. In my work I have discovered that far from being romantic, the past was often filled with hunger, despair and frustration. Before our present day knowledge of hygiene and germs, the world was a place of incredible filth and ignorance. I do not mean this as a put-down on our long-dead ancestors, because I suspect that our descendants a few hundred years in the future may also look back at us with the same dismay. These people did the best with what they had, and could not be expected to have done otherwise, since they were dealing with the knowledge of their time, just as we are utilizing ours. But I do believe that my adventures into the past have revealed a more accurate picture of the lives of these people than the popular romantic novel or television show. Someday I intend to incorporate my findings about history into a book and show the real panorama of time, as told by those who lived it.

But this present book will concentrate of the life of a man who lived so far in the past that *all* knowledge of his time period has been lost totally. The scientists would have us believe that if there were any human beings living during that distant time they must surely have been savages, or primitive cave dwellers. At the very least they would not be anyone we would be able to communicate with. The experts smugly claim that we are far too intellectually superior. To be fair with them I have explored past-lives in prehistoric times when the subjects did relive lives of an animalistic nature, predominated by emotions, natural urges and cravings. I have also examined cases where the subjects were in the prehuman stages of development. I have found that the eternal soul adapts to its environment and learns to function within its limitations. The importance of any life is the lesson that is learned from it. But I feel this story shows that *man* has not really changed that much since the beginning of time. His outer trappings, his world, changes, but not the essential core, the divine spark that makes him a human being. The same feelings and emotions have always been there. Only the way we react to them and learn from them have changed.

History is relevant. It is handed down to us in the manner it was perceived by the reporter, the recorder, the scribe. No human being can ever be expected to be totally objective in reporting an event. He would have to allow his own or his superior's viewpoint or opinions to enter into the narrative. To understand what I mean, one has only to observe how reporters on two different TV stations report the same news event. I have seen this occur time after time in my regression work. The thoughts of the peasant are different from the king's, and the opinions of the soldier are different from the general. Which gives the truest picture of the event? Each view is accurate for the individual that is perceiving it. It is true for them even if it conflicts with the broader view which is recorded as historical fact.

But what about the history that has *not* been passed down to us? Surely we cannot be so naïve as to believe that what is recorded is all that there is. We cannot think that because we have no record of it, it didn't happen. I believe there must have been several huge civilizations containing thousands of people who existed long before the advent of our present history. Someday concrete evidence of them may hopefully be found. With the help of my subjects I have returned to the time of the ancient Aztecs and Mayans living in the dense jungles. I have also explored the lost continent of Atlantis, and relived their terror as their land disappeared beneath the angry tidal waves. Just because they have faded from memory does not mean that these people did not live and love and hope and dream just as we do in our present day.

I believe this story I have uncovered, and am reporting in this book, is one of those small forgotten incidents that predates our known history. Even though it deals with travelers from the stars and has a faint undercurrent reminiscent of science fiction, I believe it is really an unknown tale of people who could well be our own ancestors. People whose presence has been hidden from us until now. It would have continued to remain hidden had it not been brought forth from the dark recesses of a young girl's subconscious mind by the regressive hypnosis technique.

I continually work with many different people who wish to experience regression into past lives for a wide variety of reasons. These reasons can range from simple curiosity to the search for answers to problems in their present life. I have conducted much therapy relating to the causes of phobias, allergies, illnesses, and troubling karmic relationships. Many of these people have heard about my work and contacted me, and others have been referred to me. I have never had to go searching for subjects. The interest in this phenomenon is much more widespread than people would believe. I have traveled hundreds of miles to conduct these sessions in the privacy of the subjects' homes. I always hesitate to turn anyone down because I never know which one will become the excellent subject I am looking for; the one who will provide my next amazing excursion into the unknown. These people are never recognizable by their outward appearances, so I have no way of knowing what knowledge their subconscious possesses until they have been put into trance. The mundane and the common past life is encountered much more frequently than the bizarre. The example in this book demonstrates that I never really know what I am looking for until I find it. I never know what will spark my insatiable curiosity and inspire my research for more knowledge.

I had no idea that an excellent somnambulistic subject would be found in my own back yard, so to speak. I had known Beth for several years because she had attended school at the same time as my own children. She was now approaching 30 years old, and working in an office at the local university. Although I had contact with her all during this time, we had never discussed metaphysical subjects. I had only recently discovered that she was interested in my type of work. She mainly wanted to try a regression out of curiosity. As we set the date for our first appointment I suspected she would follow the pattern which I have found common during first sessions.

I discovered this repetitive pattern among 90 percent of first-time subjects. This is a form of proof to me, especially since the individual does not know what the pattern is, and is not aware of what I am expecting to happen. The other 10 percent that do not follow this pattern are usually looking for something specific and if we are lucky we can zero in on that objective. The majority of my subjects have no such goal in mind, and thus the pattern emerges.

One characteristic of this pattern is that the first time their subconscious allows them to explore their memory files, a dull, boring, mundane life usually emerges. An insignificant life where one day is pretty much like the next, definitely not fantasy-type material. I say it is not significant because it does not mean anything to me. But I am often surprised that the material has some deeper meaning to the person who is reliving it, usually an important relevance that I could never have suspected. I have boxes full of this type of material which would never be important enough for a book unless it were one compiling these people's view of historical times. I sit through hundreds of these mundane lives hopefully awaiting the one subject to emerge with a story worth exploring in more detail.

The somnambulist is the main requirement for the type of research that I need because of their ability to literally become the other personality in *every* detail. This type enters a trance level so deep that they will remember very little upon awakening. As far as they are concerned, they think they have fallen asleep. Their only memories are usually snatches of scenes, similar to dreams. This type of subject is not common, and I consider myself fortunate to have located the ones that I have written about in my books. This ideal type can go into a very deep trance and virtually relive the life. Anything else, especially the life they are living at the present time, ceases to exist. In this respect, it is very similar to journeying through a time tunnel. So I consider myself a time traveler and explorer. As such I feel I must ask every conceivable question I can think of. By doing this I believe I have uncovered much knowledge that is unknown to the average person and possibly also unknown to historical authorities, as well.

In my first session with Beth it became immediately obvious that she was a somnambulist. It was most unusual for such excellent quality of material to come forth during the first session with a subject. Perhaps the reason was because the trust level (which is extremely important) had already been established, since I was not a stranger to her. Normally, before and during the first session, a lot of time is spent creating this type of rapport, which is essential to success. In Beth's case this was not necessary. I was surprised at the ease with which she entered the deep level trance state. She regressed immediately to a past life and began to release buried information. She was clearly an observer during the first five minutes and then totally merged with the other personality, and this waking world ceased to exist for her.

Her first view was of a large field surrounded partially by pine trees. The only sign of life were some oxen yoked together in the field. Then she saw a path and had the desire to follow it. It led into a small village with about 15 or 20 houses. They were houses that were not familiar to her or me. They were built of wood with grass (rush) roofs, and shutters on the windows. One building stood out; it was different because it was the only one with two stories. Its first story was built from rock and the second story of wood. She commented, "It seems to be an inn, perhaps. There's a sign hanging over the front door. I can see the shape of it. But the sun is shining wrong, I can't see what's written."

I asked her to look down at herself and describe her clothing, and she was surprised to discover that she was a man. She was barefooted, wearing beige baggy pants made of undyed wool with a darker brown cloth wrapped several times around her waist. She was also wearing a leather vest that laced up the front. She remarked, "I must be a man. There are no bosoms." It was the body of a young adult with dark skin and short black hair. It is amazing that this seldom disturbs the subject to find themselves in the body of a stranger of the opposite sex. They readily accept it and continue with what they are seeing. She seemed to have a cap on her head, so she went through the motions of pulling it off and examining it. "It's a leather cap. It has a medium-sized crown and a brim that can be turned up or down. And I have the brim turned down in front to help shade my eyes. The sun is shining very brightly. It's a warm day." She then put the cap back on and rubbed her hand across her chin, "And my face is clean-shaven."

During these sessions I must ask many questions to try to discover the time and place before we proceed further. Often even the simplest answer can establish these things. Since his clothing was so nondescript, I asked if he had any ornaments or jewelry. Beth then discovered that she had an amulet of some sort around her neck. It was a small leather bag hanging by a thong. She went through the motions of opening it and examining what was inside of it. She announced in surprise, "There's a rock in there. Some sort of gem, unfinished, sort of rough. I want to say quartz, but it doesn't look like quartz. It has a fire in it. Part of it is cloudy and part of it is a clear black-blue color. You can see into it; the spark in there is blue-white, and the edges of the rock are black-blue. It fits easily into the palm of the hand."

At this point the strange phenomenon which I have observed many times occurred. Her present personality slipped away and she began to merge with the mind and memories of the man. "I found it beside a stream. It was different. It seemed to contain a spark. I am not knowledgeable on this. It was explained to me by the wise man. He told me that it contained a spirit. I could ask for guidance by looking at the rock. It is like a friend to guide you. You look at the rock, ideas come."

When this occurs I know I can proceed to ask more definite questions about the life the personality is leading. I asked if he lived in the village.

"Sometimes. I am a hunter. I stay outside. I do not like being closed in by the roof. I spend most of my time in the hills. I hunt whatever comes. What the village needs. Deer mostly."

He said he used a bow-and-arrow, but the description of the clothes and the house did not suggest a Native American. I asked if he was a good hunter.

"Yes. I am careful. That makes me good. You do not move too quickly or you are as noisy as … as a boar in heat. You be careful. You be patient. Let the stone help you and you wait. You be one with the forest. You be one with the wind. The deer comes. You apologize to the deer for taking its life, but it is needed for the village. You kill the deer. You bring it to the village. We share with all. There is one who is skillful in cutting the deer up. Another is good with working the skin and another carves the bones. It is good for all. There are some who can grow the grain. They grow enough for all. There are others who are good at fishing from the stream. I am the hunter."

The only leader the village had was the wise man. He explained: "He is called the wise man because he can solve problems to the benefit of all. And he is good at communing with the spirits. He knows of things not ordinarily known."

It was obvious now that she had entered a deep level of trance, and I could proceed to ask for names, dates and places. In the lighter states this type of information is more difficult to obtain. He said his name was Tuin. I had her repeat it because it had a strange sound and I had difficulty with it. It was pronounced quickly so the two syllables ran together. I had more difficulty obtaining a name for the location.

He explained, "It is just the village. It is just us with wilderness around. We have some fields cleared. We grow in the fields; it is surrounded by woods and there are mountains nearby. But there is nobody else. It is just 'the land'."

I have received this answer many times when a subject has regressed to a primitive lifetime. They are simple the "people" and where they live is the "land." What could be more natural? Why do they have to have names? They are fully aware of who they are and where they are living.

One way to obtain information that may establish location is to ask about the food eaten. I asked what was grown in the fields.

"Grains ... wheat. I am not sure what the grains are called. I am a hunter. They taste good when they are cooked. As long as I hunt for the village we share everything. There are some other things grown: vegetables, different kinds of beans. Some roots, kind of an orange color, red. They come in different shapes, sometimes long, sometimes round. I do not know what they are called. There are juicy fruits on the trees, very good to eat on a hot summer day. The women prepare the food for all. We have a central site where there are large kettles. They prepare stews that are real good. Each woman has a kitchen garden, I suppose for their herbs."

There was still not enough information to identify locale, so I asked about the women's clothing.

He provided the description, "Most of them have a long skirt. A type of a shirt with sleeves of some sort, that wraps around to support their bosoms, covering them. I do not know how they wear those confining clothes. I have never had to deal with those garments. They are basically various shades of brown, but some women have found some stones that are pretty—bright blue, red, various stones. They sew these into the clothes or they wear on top to add color. Their hair is long and they keep it bound in various ways. They have things stuck in their hair ... kind of like a double-pronged knife. But it is not a knife because it does not cut. It has stones attached to the hilt, so that they stick it through a bundle of hair and it holds the hair in place and it looks pretty. Most of the village people wear shoes of some sort, for they are in the village. When you are hunting you must be barefooted. The women's shoes, they fit close to the feet but they are flexible. They are made out of the leather that I supply with my hunting. They fasten on the side, or sometimes they lace up. The men ... somehow they make the sole stiffer so it will not be punctured when they are in the fields. For women, usually shoes are just up over the ankles so they are protected up to where the skirt goes. The skirt comes down to just above the ankles and their shoes go up under the skirts. I am not sure how far. I might get slapped if I ask. I would not want that to happen."

Where Tuin was living it apparently got very cold in the winter, so he dressed differently during that time. He wore thicker pants and a type of pullover garment with long, loose sleeves. In the colder weather he would also wear a type of hood to keep his head and ears protected. And over it all was a larger loose garment that sounded like some type of poncho. He would then wrap skins around his hands and reluctantly put on fur boots. Although he preferred to go barefooted he said he also did not want to lose his toes during cold weather. All of these clothes were usually made of different kinds of animal skins. The women could make clothes out of some kind of fiber, but he thought the skins were warmer. Since the survival of the village depended upon Tuin's hunting skill he had to be prepared to venture out into the worst of weather, whether he truly wished to or not. "It depends on the food supply," he said. "If we have enough food I stay in and be warm. If we start getting low, then it is my duty to go hunt."

Tuin did not have a regular house to live in such as the others did. He preferred to stay outdoors. But in this climate the winters would get very cold with much snow and he would have to come inside, much to his dislike. So when he needed it he had a small room in the two-story building. There was a large fireplace in this building so it was warm. He had made a bed by sewing and stretching deer skins between poles. This was set on legs and about a foot off the floor, and a cover of bear skin made it quite comfortable. The only other furniture in the room was a table and bench where he usually kept water and a loaf of bread. He explained that there was another drink that was available in the village besides water.

"There is a drink that the farmers make out of the fruit that is very good. It brings you up, in addition to tasting good. If you drink too much, you get very relaxed and you laugh a lot. I do not drink much of it because I like being in harmony, and I do not feel in harmony when I am laughing too much. And some of them complain of having a pain— the head not feeling good the next morning. And that would interfere with hunting." He was obviously describing some type of wine, but the drink seemed to mostly be consumed at celebrations.

It also appeared that Tuin did not have a family.

"No, I am just by myself. I am a hunter. No permanent family. Of course I had parents; everyone does. My mother, she is very old. She may not live much longer. My father, she was not sure who was my father."

When I asked if he had ever married, he did not understand the word. This is another interesting aspect of past-life regression. It shows the complete absorption of the somnambulist into the other personality. I often use words and concepts that are perfectly understandable in our modern world. But if they are alien to or not present in the other entity's time period, then they cannot understand them at all. This displays most graphically that they are not associating with their present personality's mind at all, or they would be able to draw upon that information and apply it. This often puts me into awkward positions. I must try to find a simple definition for a common word so the entity will understand. This is often difficult to do on the spur of the moment.

Dolores: I think you called it "living under a roof." Marriage is when you live with one woman.

Beth: We live with women. You have children, and then if you decide that you need to change your life, or the woman decides that she needs to change her life, then you live under the roof with someone else. And someone else comes to live with the woman.

That was as close to our definition of marriage that he could come.

D: Then you have never done that?

B: No. I do not like staying under the roof. I am outside. There is a young woman that I am friends with. We talk. I can tell her things I cannot tell others. But she wants someone to live in the village and to stay there, and I do not like living under the roof. But it is good to have someone to talk to. Usually I talk with the animals.

I switched my questions to eating utensils, because sometimes answers can be found from that area.

D: *Do the people in the village have any certain things they eat with?*

B: Yes. The carpenter, he gets pieces of wood. They are flat pieces of wood but he has tools to make out a hollow in them to hold what we are eating. So in case there is juice, like with the stew, it will not drip. We use our knives to cut things to the right size. The women have sticks that are hollowed-out at the end for stirring the food so it will not stick. The women tend to use these; I think they are called "spoons."

These answers were not helping me to find the time period or locale. These apparently were a people who lived very simply, but were not primitive.

D: *What are the pots made out of that you cook the food in?*

B: Usually clay. There is one pot that the wise man uses. I do not know where he got it. It is made out of something hard, not stone, but like metal that shines.

This was the first introduction of a strange element into this regression, an indication that all was not as simple and ordinary as it first appeared. This did not sound like the common cooking pot.

D: *It shines? It's not a dark color?*

B: It depends on the spirit. Sometimes it is a shiny reddish-golden color. Sometimes it is black. I suspect he may have two different pots, but they both look alike and he says that the color changes because of the spirits. Perhaps it is like my rock. The legends say that the things we have were brought by the old ones long ago.

I have heard the old ones mentioned in many other regressions. The term has various meanings. It usually refers to ancestors who had much knowledge or who worshipped the old gods. Usually these people had disappeared, died out, or were so few that they were in hiding and being protected. They are considered to be very special, and normally the subject is reluctant to speak of the "old ones." I was expecting this type of protective answer when I asked what he meant by that term. I was really taken off guard by his definition.

B: They came ... the legends say they traveled across the void. It was dark and void, and their ship—they were in a ship—something went wrong and it says they *crashed*, but our stream is not big enough for any boats. I do not understand, but that is what the legends say. This ship had much metal on it, and we used the metal for our knives and for our pots.

This was quite a surprise. I was wondering where they had learned the art of metallurgy, but I never expected this to be the answer.

Up to this point the session had been going as expected for a first time regression: mundane, a simple person living a simple life. I had already collected hundreds of these. With so little information being presented to warrant continuing, it surely would have been a one-time regression, and the tape would have been put into a box with hundreds of others. And Tuin, the hunter, would have receded back into the mists of time and would not have been called forth again. *Except*... except that he made that unexpected and out-of-place remark that kindled the spark of my curiosity. When that happens something inside of me knows that there is a story worth pursuing and my insatiable "desire to know" is unleashed. Beth displayed the qualities of a somnambulist and I knew I wanted to continue to work with her. But this particular story would have been dropped, had it not been for that chance remark. Without that, this glimpse of our long-forgotten history would have remained buried for all time.

It was obvious Tuin was ignorant of the real meaning his statement held for me. He was merely quoting from his knowledge of a legend. He thought it referred to a ship that sailed down rivers, and he didn't understand how it could have happened. I would have to tailor my questions to the level of his mentality and understanding.

D: *Is the ship still there?*
B: No, it was a long time ago. All we have now are the knives and the pots. We take care of them because we cannot get any more. The shaman, the wise man, he still has some pieces of metal in his house that he uses for secret things. He shapes them for how it is needed for charms, amulets or for holy things.

D: *Have you ever seen these pieces?*

B: Once. He did not know that I had seen them. I have not told anybody. I was not supposed to see them. One was large, like an animal, like a wolverine. (He had difficulty finding the words to describe it, and used terminology he was familiar with.) What is the shape? I cannot describe the shape. It sat flat on the floor, and the sides came up straight like a tall tree. But on the front part, it came up and then it would slant back and then it was flat on top like a flat rock. It was made out of metal, kind of a dull silver-gray color. On the slanted part there were things sticking out that were darker colored. I did not know the purpose of them.

D: *Were there many of those strange things sticking out?*

B: Yes. Some were long and skinny. About this long (hand motions showed about an inch) and some were round.

D: *And these were on the slanted part. Did these things move or do you know?*

B: I do not know. I just got a glimpse.

In the locale he had been describing of a simple isolated village, I cannot imagine anything more out of place. Apparently he did not know what it could be. He barely had the language requirements to describe it, so it was definitely something foreign to him. But it sounded similar to some type of control panel, or perhaps some type of machine.

D: *Were there any more of these big slanted things?*

B: No. There was just the one. But nearby there were pieces of metal piled up. They were all jumbled together so I could not tell the shapes.

D: *Maybe he uses those for the amulets.*

B: I think so.

D: *Do you think he would use that strange-looking object for anything?*

B: I really do not know. It is said that there were such things on the ship that crashed. But it would be too heavy for a ship. It would make it sink in the river. I do not understand it.

Since it was obvious Tuin was speaking from his perspective and not Beth's more modern one, I would have to communicate with him in terms he would understand. I would especially have to keep my questions within a simple framework and deliberately not be suggestive until I found out more about this legend.

D: *What about the legend? Did it say what the old ones looked like?*

B: They looked like us but they were taller. They could do wondrous things.

D: *Then some of them lived? They didn't all die when the ship crashed?*

B: That is how we are here. We come from the old ones. We are the only ones.

D: *Then they stayed there and made the village?*

B: Yes. Their ship could not go anymore. They were traveling to somewhere else. I do not know where.

D: *Do the legends say if they were dressed differently?*

B: (Thinking) The legends say that at first they wore white clothing, silvery-white, and it did not wear out and it did not tear. But then as time went on some of their descendants had the custom of burying them in their clothing, so that we do not have any now, *if* it ever existed. Maybe being out in the woods makes me question too much.

D: *It could be. But you're supposed to be descended from these people. Is this why your people don't leave this area?*

B: Partially. There are so few of us. Not many. There is no one else. If some of us were to leave the area there would not be enough for them to survive, or for us. It would hurt us, too.

D: *Then you are all needed. Everyone helps each other.*

B: Yes, there are not many. We be careful. The legends say if you are not careful the Mother Earth, the Mother, she will be displeased and not let the crops grow.

D: *That makes sense. Do you know of any other villages or groups of people?*

B: There *are* none others. We are the only ones.

D: *Have you ever traveled to see if there are others somewhere else?*

B: I have. I am a hunter. Sometimes I go further than what is needed for hunting.

D: *Have you ever seen any other groups of people?*

B: No. As far as I go there is woods and more woods and mountains.

The mountains are high with the tops that stay in snow all the time. The beasts of the forest, they know this, too; they are shaggy. I have not seen anybody else.

I knew my time was running out for this session. Normally in the hour I allot for the first time, I can go completely through the important events of a life, since most follow the pattern and are very mundane. I now knew that I was on the trail of something and there would have to be more sessions to clarify these legends Tuin spoke of. When I want to continue to work on a story I always ask the entity's permission to return. I believe if I do not show them this courtesy as a separate personality they will not answer my future questions. This also helps establish the trust and rapport that is so important in gaining information. Normally the entity is only too glad to talk with me. Tuin was no exception.

B: Yes, I enjoy telling you about my people. We are proud. We are good people. It is interesting to talk to someone who does not know. It is like explaining things to a child, and children like me.

D: *You explain things very well and I like to learn. Then with your permission I will come back sometime and we can talk again. And I won't disturb your work and your hunting?*

B: No, you are not disturbing. I will be looking for you.

Since it was obvious that Beth was an excellent somnambulistic subject and I wished to work with her again, I conditioned her with keyword suggestions before bringing her back to full consciousness. I like to work with keywords (which can be anything) because it saves me a lot of induction time and I can concentrate on the story I am exploring.

Upon awakening I asked Beth what she remembered about the session. Her only conscious memories were glimpses of lots of trees.

When I told her about the regression she said she could make only a few conscious connections with that sort of life. She loves cold weather—the colder the better. She likes to go barefoot, and even in winter she wears much less clothing than the average person. She has to have a window open in her room, especially in the winter. She loves the woods and goes spelunking (exploring caves) with a group of people as a hobby.

Many times once the subconscious has been stirred into exploring a past life, it will start revealing little bits of information through dreams or intuitions or impressions. I asked her to be alert for this to happen.

During the next week she had a very vivid dream of walking through a pine forest. The ground was covered with thick pine needles and she could hear the wind singing through the trees. It seemed to be trying to tell her something. The dream left her with a very happy and comfortable feeling.

Chapter 2

Calling the Spirits

Naïvely and innocently Tuin had begun to relate the story of his ancestors. He had mentioned it in an unassuming manner, as though he had been speaking to a child. But what seemed to him to be merely an old story had an entirely different meaning to me. It sounded as though a spaceship had crashed near where his village now stood. It had been traveling across the "void" to some unknown destination when it was disabled. Apparently the occupants were then unable to leave the Earth, and Tuin and the villagers were their descendants. An incredible story, yet because of the way it was presented to me it had the indelible ring of truth. I wanted to know more about this legend since I believe that most legends have some basis, no matter how remote, in fact. I was now faced with two mysteries that I wanted to track down and somehow verify. First, I wanted to find out everything I could about the "old ones." Secondly, I wanted to try to discover where and possibly when the crash had occurred. I would indeed have to probe like a detective if I were to put these things together and find my answers. But I love a mystery and a challenge, and I had just been handed a wonderful one.

I had not yet been given enough clues. The locale of Tuin's village was sketchy and could apply to many places on the Earth. He lived in an isolated spot in a river valley surrounded by mountains topped with perpetual snow. This suggested a northern climate, but on which continent? The clothing and housing did not sound like Native Americans. I thought the time period could not be very remote since they were not primitive. They knew the art of weaving since some of their clothes were made of cloth. They used metallurgy which is a complicated process. People who are isolated and who believe they are the only people in the world would have no sense of time, such as years, that we could relate to and identify. Through questioning I would have to find out what type of culture they had and when it could have existed. In order to find these answers it would eventually require a lot of research, but that has never bothered me. I love to delve in libraries for that elusive bit of information once I have a story that is worth pursuing.

Tuin had mentioned a drink made by the farmers that was mainly consumed during celebrations. One way to identify a culture is through its belief structure. So when Beth and I met the following week to continue with this story, I intended to explore this line of questioning. The keyword worked beautifully and she immediately entered a deep somnambulistic trance state, and I began.

D: *What kind of celebrations would you have?*

B: We have several ceremonies. There are main ones and there are smaller ones. And these ceremonies, they keep the times of the year in the proper places, and help the years to pass, one year to the other, in the flowing cycle of life: the harvest, the spring. And in the winter, midwinter festival when the sun starts coming back.

I asked for a description of the celebrations.

B: For the harvest we move the kettles from where we usually cook and build a large bonfire. And we start out dancing to help get relaxed. You try not to worry about your child that is sick or about the bugs eating your grain or what have you. You dance, you relax. And then the wise man, he starts singing the special songs. The ones that call down the spirits.

I asked if they used any type of musical instruments at these festivals. He said they had a few, but they were used for private use and group entertainment at the inn. He said, "We like fun. When what must be done is done, why keep working when you do not have to?" He described a small hand-held drum that was covered with a delicate piece of skin. It was not struck; it was brushed with the fingertips to make soft sounds. There was a set of sticks that were shaken or rubbed to make a clacking noise. Tuin mentioned a carpenter in the village who was experimenting with different wooden shapes and gut and trying to produce a stringed instrument. Tuin thought the man's attempts were humorous because the strings kept slipping off, and the sounds produced were not melodious. Tuin much preferred listening to the singing of the birds.

While we were on the subject of music, I asked about the songs that were sung. In other regressions I have been able to get the subject to sing in the native language. This is rare but it does happen occasionally. Sometimes you can learn a great deal from the melodies without hearing the words.

B: It depends on the purpose of the songs. The songs are powerful. They hold the spirits. You have to be careful about singing. You may call the wrong spirit. The spirits speak, but not like you and I. They sing. That is why sometimes they speak to you in the wind. The wind is a powerful spirit. You must be careful with music. You must be respectful.

D: *Then you only sing these songs as a group with the wise man leading you?*

B: It depends. Sometimes just the wise man sings. When he starts singing you sit quietly. We either watch the flames or we look at the stars.

D: *You don't have any dancing?*

B: Not when he is singing. The dancing is to get your mind relaxed for the proper attitude of singing. You cannot be concerned with regular things when you are singing. Just about every song calls some sort of spirit. The lullabies that the women sing to their children for them to go to sleep? Even though they sing them fairly often, their songs are protection. And they call up little spirits to protect their children from harm while they sleep.

D: *I was wondering if I could hear what your music sounded like. Could you sing something for me?*

B: I do not sing well. Most of the young women, regardless of how charming they are, say they would rather hear me tell stories than sing the songs. I have become uncomfortable singing around people. I mostly sing to animals. There are some songs that I sing to the trees. They do not really have words, but the sound is what counts because of the purpose of the song. I call upon the trees to help me to hide and be in harmony. And so, since the wind sings through the trees, the wind does not necessarily always use words. So I sing to the trees without words. That way if I have to sing quietly, I can. And if it is one that I particularly like, I remember it. But usually I go ahead and make up another one the next time.

D: *Then no one else hears them.*

B: The tree, do not forget the tree I am singing to.

She demonstrated by crooning several bars that sounded like wind blowing: an *ooooo* sound.

B: I cannot make it very long.

D: *That sounds like the wind. It really does. But when the women are singing the lullabies to the babies, do you remember what that sounds like?*

B: I remember the tune, but cannot sing the words for you because it will call up the spirits.

D: *But that's a good spirit.*

B: True, but if you call them up for no reason, they do not like being trifled with. It is said that the women are best at calling the spirits. I am not sure how they do it. I think it is similar to how I apologize to animals. Everybody has something they do better. There are some old women who are said to be able to see things in the fire. Sometimes they are right.

D: *When they do this calling of the spirits, is it only during the celebrations?*

B: No. Everyone has personal spirits they can call upon. Some of the women who can see the fire, the spirits show them what they need to know in the fire. My spirits talk to me in the wind. The spirits sing, you know. I can hear the wind, they sing to me. It sounds like the wind but it seems to be a higher whistling above the wind, and the whistling makes sense somehow. It is like they are saying the words while they are singing real high. And it is soft and only someone who can hear the wind can hear the words and understand them. To others it just sounds like the wind blowing. It is said that some people, their spirits talk to them from the water. Some can hear the river telling them things. Some can look into the water and see their spirits showing them things. The spirits speak more than one way to some people. But usually everyone finds the way that is best for them.

D: *Do you have what I would call a "religion"? Do you know what that is?*

B: No. What is a religion?

D: *It means a belief ... well, a belief in these things you're talking about, the things you can't see. And some people believe in one power over every-thing that they call "God." Do you have a belief like that?*

B: Not like that, if I understand you right. The spirits are there to help us. It is said that the ability to hear the spirits or to communicate with them like we do, comes from the life force. Everyone has this ability, somehow or another. Sometimes there will be a child who cannot communicate with the spirits and we feel very sorry for it. Its mind, it has a very closed experience.

D: *Yes. Even though everyone has this ability, some people just don't recog-nize it and they don't use it.*

B: Oh? In our people everyone has this, except with some of the children some of the time. If they are slow sometimes it is more difficult for them to realize when the spirits are speaking to them. Everyone feels sorry for them until they learn.

D: *Do you have a name for the language that you speak?*

B: It is the language we speak.

D: *It has no name that you call it?*

B: Well ... it is the language of *here*. What would we call it?

D: *I've heard in some places far beyond the mountains, people speak different words and other people can't understand them.*

B: But we are the only people. There is only one language. There are none other. We are the people, this is the land.

I returned to questions about the festivals.

D: *Do you like the festivals, the celebrations?*

B: Yes. When I must be with people it is nice to be with people during the festival. I prefer being with the animals. They are harmonious. Men have to work at being harmonious.

D: *Do you have a favorite festival or celebration?*

B: It is hard to say. They are each special. They have their own meaning. You call down the spirits, things happen. Sometimes when the wise man is singing, his voice will travel around the fire but he is still sitting where he is. That is a sign that a spirit has come. Sometimes the fire will change colors or will change shapes. Certain ways mean certain spirits. It is very real. No one doubts what is happening.

D: *Are these good signs when the spirits come?*

B: It depends on which festival it is at. If the wrong spirit comes, that means someone is not harmonious. And you must help them to become harmonious so that the right spirit will come. There are winter spirits, there are summer spirits. If you get a winter spirit in the summer, it does not do you much good. If you get advice from the winter spirit in the summer, it will not work too good. But the summer spirit will give you advice for how to work your crops so they do good.

D: *How to plant and everything?*

B: *When* to plant. They tell the wise man. You can hear them singing, but sometimes you cannot understand them. The wise man tells whoever needs to know or tells the whole group. There is another ceremony when the day and the night are perfectly balanced.

D: *(I was thinking of spring.) Is this the beginning of the growing season?*

B: No. The growing season has already started by then. Everything is coming up good, and the trees are coming out, and the animals have come out. You see, when this ceremony comes along, first it has been winter and then the growing season has started and everyone who knows growing lore has been working hard getting their crops planted and such as that. And I have been busy hunting and we all need a break, so we celebrate and have a lot of fun. It is a time of celebration, because we have shaken off the sleep of winter. I have been really busy hunting to get a variety of things for the feast that will go along with the festival. And different ones have been out in the woods gathering the things that have sprouted, greens and mush-rooms and such. So as to have plenty to eat at this festival, and every-one is really happy. They are decorating things, like putting new trimming on their clothes and such, to make everything new looking and special.

D: *How do you celebrate at that time?*

B: It depends on how old you are. If you are *very* old, you talk about how this past winter was not as bad as ones you remember when you were 12 summers old. If you are slightly younger, you talk about what new things all of us can try to help increase the production of grain. And if you are slightly younger, say my age, you make plans on what you are going to be doing for the summer. And the ones that are slightly younger, well (smiling), they tend to sneak off into the woods and have fun of their own. There is a ceremony that starts the celebration. It is a growing ceremony to make sure that we are in harmony with the spirits so that the crops will grow. And the appropriate songs are sung. Then afterwards, all celebrate at the big feast.

D: *Are there any legends that are told at that time?*

B: Yes, mostly legends dealing with growing or how the old ones' crops, when they did start to grow, yielded very well. Legends about how they grew their crops and how they learned to be in harmony with the Earth, and such as that. And legends about why things are done with the crops the way they are done, and how to do it and when. When to plant, how to plow it, where it would be good. When to get ready to harvest it. Things like that. The farmers know what they need to know to do it. I am a hunter, I really do not know how they do it. To be in harmony you must go with the seasons. That is the only balanced way to do it. The next major festival is when the day is longest, and the night really is not there at all. You know how after the sun sets, but before it gets dark, when it is kind of dusky? Well, the longest day of the year is like that all night long. And on the nights before and after it does not really get dark either.

D: *Like three days in a row?*

B: Longer than that actually, because for the central part of summer it really does not get dark. But on that particular night the sun rises the earliest and sets the latest. You can see all night long; it is no problem.

D: *During that time of the year, does it get very hot?*

B: Ahh ... what do you call hot? It is summertime.

D: *I've heard there are some places where it gets very hot and you don't even like to wear clothes. It's not like that?*

B: No, it is not like that. There is still snow on the mountains. And the wind blows down from the mountains and is always cool.

D: *On the longest day of the year, do they have special legends at that time?*

B: Yes. The legends recounted on the longest day of the year are about life. Why things are the way they are, and how they came to be that way. Also, it is the time of year that if anyone has learned or discovered a new way of singing to the spirits that seems to be effective, they show how it works to the other people. We determine whether that should just be a personal song or perhaps a song that more can adopt for particular purposes. And if anything new has been discovered about the growing of crops or anything like that, the farmers tell of it then to make sure it is not forgotten.

I have had regressions where natives used drug-induced states during ceremonies to heighten their spiritual awareness. So I asked if they drank or ate anything special at that time.

B: No, just whatever is appropriate for that time of the year. However, the wise man does have certain types of herbs and powders that he puts in the fire. All the smoke changes color and odor. He puts in a lot to make sure we can all inhale some of the smoke, because it helps us to relax and get ready for the legend telling. Some of the herbs open up the mind so we can remember back further, and also so we can remember more of what is said that night. We may not necessarily be able to remember it the next day but we know it will be there.

So it appeared that they did use a form of a hallucinogenic.

D: *Does the wise man wear anything different during the ceremonies?*

B: He has different headdresses that he wears for the different festivals. In the summer he gets some of the wheat stalks without the wheat, and weaves them until they stick together, and stiffens them up with clay of different colors. He puts leaves and such on it, and uses different kinds of clay to make designs.

D: *I can see the symbolism of what it's supposed to represent. It's made out of the things of the fields.*

B: And the wise man paints designs on it with different colors of clay. It means certain things to the spirits, to help us have a good harvest later on at the harvest festival.

D: *What kind of designs does he put on it?*

B: Different shapes. Some are like a three-sided figure, but with kind of squiggly shapes as though attached to the three-sided figure. (She made hand motions of a triangle, *etc.*) Like having an arrow with a squiggly shaft, not that any such thing exists.

D: *Coming out of the bottom of this three-sided figure?*

B: Yes. Sometimes he makes a round circle with lines coming out of it—like the sun shining. They mean special things, and since they do not seem to mean anything to me, it is hard to remember what they are. It means something to the spirits. He does it in red and dark reddish-brown on white. All of our pottery is made out of red clay. White clay is special, it is sacred. All the women know where the clay is found. Whenever they find white clay they bring it to him.

D: *You said there are some ceremonies where they just repeat the legends?*

B: That is not all the ceremony, but ... how shall I explain? Everyone knows how it goes.

D: *Except me.*

B: Except you. You are very strange. We have the rituals? (He was not sure of that word.) The ceremony starting out. At certain times of the year, the way the balance is between the darkness of night and the lightness of day, they help determine when certain ceremonies will be. And at that time certain sets of the legends will be recounted for certain reasons. Like in the winter, there is one point when the sun is very shy, it seems like. The sun is not there much at all and the night seems very, very powerful. That is the way the spirits are balanced at that time. On the night that is the longest we have the winter ceremony, and that is when certain legends must be told and passed down. That is when the night part of the harmony is at its most powerful, because the next night will not be quite as long. The wise man is the one that keeps track of this. In the wintertime the night is much longer than the day. The daytime gets very short. It seems like you have been up for a long time before the sun finally rises. And you eat your midday meal, you start doing daytime activities, and the sun has not been up long when it sets again.

D: *I suppose you must work fast on days like that.*

B: The light of the fire helps. There is not that much to do in the winter. You were asking about the many celebrations. There is one you have missed.

D: *What one was that?*

B: The one after the summer festival. In the fall when the day and night are balanced again we have another celebration. It happens near the end of harvest when we are celebrating a good harvest, or if it has not been a good harvest we sing songs to the spirits to help us make it through the winter. At this time, since the nights are getting longer and the work of the summer is about done, we start teaching the children of the village the things they need to know. We pass on the knowledge. Then at the celebration the wise man reveals what abilities the children who have reached the right age seem to have, so they can start learning during the winter. The winter when it is quiet is good to be taught and to develop, like for listening to the wind or seeing the fire or what-have-you.

D: *That would be a good time to learn because of the long nights. And he knows which of the children will be able to do different things.*

B: Yes, he has been observing them and he is the wise man. He knows how to make the decisions. For the winter festival the wise man's headdress is made out of the skin of a creature I caught once. I have not seen the like before or since.

D: *Oh? It's not a real creature?*

B: It was real when I killed it. I apologized to it. I was very careful with *that* one. I did not know how the spirit of the creature would feel with my killing it. But the village was very hungry then. It was in winter and we needed food.

D: *You mean it was an animal you had never seen?*

B: Yes. The color was not so unusual. It had long shaggy brown fur, but its head was different. The ears were pointed and somewhat shaggy. And from the center of its muzzle it had a horn coming and curling up slightly. The horn was about this long (about a foot), about this big around (about two inches across) and it curved up. And it was ridged like a ram's horn. It had long fangs, and a kind of a beard. I did not know what to call it.

D: *It was not like a bear?*

B: No, not at all. A bear is peaceful; this animal was a meat-eater.

D: *(I was thinking of various possible animals.) It was not like a ram or something similar?*

B: No, a ram has two horns coming out of the top of the head. This one, between the eyes and the nostrils, midways down, this horn came out. And I do not know the purpose of this horn. It could be used to push something out of the way, but it could not wound because it was not long enough. If it were a little longer, perhaps. I killed the animal. I brought it to the village. And the wise man, the shaman, he said it was a sign.

D: *Had he ever seen an animal like it?*

B: No. The butcher and the skinner were told to take a special care, which they did. And so they preserved the head. They cleaned it out but they left the bones in place and now the wise man wears this for the winter festival.

This certainly did sound like a strange animal. I felt compelled to ask more questions.

D: *Did it walk upright or on four legs?*

B: On four legs. It came up to the mid-thigh.

D: *Then it was not a large animal.*

B: Hmm, kind of wide and long, but it was powerful. I would not want to tangle with it.

D: *What about a tail?*

B: (Pause) Yes. It hung close to the body. It was shaggy, too, like a long bear's tail.

D: *I am trying to picture what it looked like. Have you ever seen a horse? (I was thinking of the possibility of a unicorn, or maybe where the legend originated from.) Do you know that word?*

B: Ah. The word, I know the word. Ah. I have not ... I do not recall seeing the animal.

D: *Even though this doesn't sound like a horse, I thought maybe it might be similar.*

B: No. A horse—it eats grass, doesn't it?

D: *Yes it does, like the oxen.*

B: No, this was not a grass-eater.

D: *It ate meat, and it had long fangs. What were its feet like?*

B: Ah, yes. The claws would be out and one would not want to tangle with them if the animal was angry. But when I came across the animal it was not angry.

D: *It had claws like a bear?*

B: Ah. More like a cat, but they did not go into the fingers like a cat's claws do. (He meant they didn't retract.)

D: *Hmm. It does sound like something strange. I don't think I've ever seen an animal like that either.*

B: It is the funniest one I have ever seen.

D: *No wonder the wise man was impressed.*

B: He asked me to tell him all the details of the hunt, which way the wind was blowing, if there were any snow, for he thought it was a message from the spirits. He needed to know everything, so as to be able to know what the spirits were trying to tell us. The wise man may be the only one who understands the mystery. I do not. I only know that it saved the village from hunger. It must have been sent by the spirits. That is the only answer.

Upon awakening I asked Beth what she remembered about the session.

Text continues, page 30.

B: I remember this man with a headdress on. It was white, kind of triangular shaped.

She was making motions and I repeated them for the tape recorder.

D: *The headdress was like a triangle across the forehead, sloping down on the sides slightly?*

B: Kind of like a triangle with a curve part of it.

D: *And it comes to a point on the top.*

B: Yes, say about a foot or so above the head. Let's see, there should be some designs on it. Kind of like a stylized picture of their sperm.

D: *You described something that looked like that. Like an arrowhead that had a squiggly stem. But it was more round than an arrowhead?*

B: No. It was kind of like the curved triangle shape but flat on one side.

She said she could draw the designs, so I got out the tablet and marker, and she proceeded to sketch what she could remember.

B: And I see him with another headdress on—some kind of a shaggy brown animal.

D: *Like an animal's head or what?*

B: Yeah, and it looks like some of the skin too, because I can see a couple of paws on his shoulders. And the head is horned and it has fangs. Ferocious-looking animal; I'd hate to tangle with that thing.

D: *You talked a lot about it. Does it look like anything you've ever seen?*

B: Really no. It looks kind of strange. I think I could draw some of it too.

D: *I got a good description but it would help if you would draw it. (She drew a sketch of it.) What else comes to mind?*

B: A large fire, but that's about it. And a field in the sunshine.

Those were all of her conscious memories of the session. It often happens that the most vivid memories are those scenes that occurred just before coming out of trance, similar to the remnants of the last dreams before awakening.

While I was directing some of my questions in an attempt to establish the locale I had not forgotten the possibility of the Nordic countries of the European continent. I remembered hearing about the Basque people who claim they have lived in the Pyrenees Mountains thousands of years before the arrival of Europeans. Their origin has long been a mystery, even to themselves, primarily because their language is unlike any other verbal communication on Earth. Their legends claim it was spoken by Adam and Eve, and that one of the sons of Noah settled in the mountains before the confusion of tongues at the Tower of Babel. The clothing also seemed to indicate a race of this type rather than Native Americans or Eskimos. I soon had to eliminate the Basques because Tuin's climate seemed to indicate he was living within the Arctic Circle. His description of the length of the days at different times of the year definitely placed him in the far north. But we still had no idea of the time period he was living in. If the climate of the world had changed dramatically over several centuries the location could be somewhere else. I had to continue directing my questions by finding out about animal life and anything that might help to narrow the possibilities.

Chapter 3

The Village

*I*N ORDER FOR ME TO TRACK DOWN the location of Tuin's village I would have to try and get as much information about it and the living habits of the people as I could. Just as a detective puts together all the various clues to help him derive at a suitable solution, I would have to put together all the bits and pieces of Tuin's life that I could find. This was the only way I could trace the locale of the crashing of the old one's ship.

The village seemed to be operating on a socialistic type of principle. By this I mean that all the people seemed to have a job to perform that would benefit the whole. Each seemed to depend on the other, they were indispensable to each other's welfare. This was the main reason no one had ever ventured very far away. They knew that the village needed each person. Their individual skills were essential for the livelihood of the group as a whole. If even one of them were to leave or were to allow their knowledge or skill to die, the village would suffer. This gave each one a unique responsibility. They were a very close knit group. Each had their place and their role in the community, such that they operated as a cohesive unit. This may also explain their abilities to read each other's thoughts and to sense each other's emotions. It may also explain their lack of violence and negativity. They functioned in complete harmony with each other. They had apparently been living this way for many generations. The total isolation of being cut off from any outside contact with the world probably accounted for much of their benevolent harmony. They had no disruptive influences from other ways of life or thought patterns. They simply lived in a honest, respectful way and in close contact with nature. They had no choice because they knew of no other way to live. This also explains why some of my questions did not make any sense to Tuin. He simply could not conceive of any other living conditions.

D: *Are there a lot of people in your village?*

B: What do you call a lot? There are enough. Sometimes the winters are hard and some die. Then it is difficult until some of the younger ones grow up to take their place.

D: *I was thinking that if it's been a long time since the coming of the old ones, that there would be many, many people there.*

B: No, there ... well, I do not know the numbers for it, but we have, oh, 20, 30 houses. That is enough for all of us to sleep in. There are several people in each house. And each person sleeps in whichever house he is comfortable in.

D: *That might be between 40 and 60 people, if you know numbers like that. (She frowned.) Not that many numbers?*

B: Perhaps a little more. I am not sure.

D: *Then it has grown since the old ones came.*

B: That is hard to say. They say there were many old ones, but many died and only a few lived.

D: *I think you told me everyone has a job, in order to help the community. What about the old people?*

B: The old people, their tasks are lighter. They are honored. They helped the village all their lives. And now when they get too old to do what they did all their lives, we let them live in peace. Usually they make things with their hands, baskets, things like that. Even though they are old and cannot work they want to stay busy.

D: *They are taken care of by the village?*

B: Of course, for they have the legends and the knowledge in them, too. They have heard them all their lives and so they help pass down the legends. That is important. We cannot lose the knowledge. I make sure they get meat. Rabbit, deer, but they do not need a whole deer.

D: *Can you describe what the smaller dwellings look like?*

B: They are different according to who lives there, according to how they want it on the inside. If the woman who lives there is particularly skilled at weaving she would have the tools of that on hand, whereas another house may not necessarily have it.

An unusual incident happened at this point in the regression. The session was being held at my friend Kay's home. Her dog was in another part of the house and it suddenly let out sharp barking. Normally the subject will not hear anything in the immediate vicinity. When they are in trance they are usually so absorbed with what they are observing that noises in our time do not seem to bother them. I have had telephones ring that startled me, but the subject will display no reaction. I have also had loud noises such as outside traffic or lawn mowers that are so noisy they almost obscure the sound on the tape recorder, and the subject will say later that they did not hear anything. In this case with the barking dog Beth reacted strangely. I suppose Tuin's hunter's ears were so attuned to animals that he picked up the sound and did not realize it was coming from another time period. Beth seemed confused. She stopped talking and listened acutely, the hunter's instincts sharpened. "I hear an animal!" she remarked. Kay went to see what the dog was barking at. Beth's manner was one of readiness and preparedness as well as confusion. I wish now I had asked him what kind of animal he thought it was, because I do not believe dogs existed in Tuin's area. Instead I gave suggestions that she would not be disturbed. After a brief pause, she dismissed the sound and continued.

B: Usually our houses are of trees that have been cut down. Of course the branches are cut off. And then they lace the ends together with green skin. When it dries it is very tight. And they put the clay to seal it. One would have to repair it each spring, but that is normal. The clay holds during the winter. In the winter when it snows, the winds blow and they could cause something to become loose. It is hard to see where you want to go. You stay inside.

D: *Is there any furniture?*

B: Usually not that much, for we prefer sitting on the floor. But one can make a seat by making a frame and stretching a skin on it. The old people tend to do that; they say the ground is too hard to sit on.

The floors are usually just the ground. Someone will either build a house on top of a flat rock, or if it is just the ground, there is a way of packing the dirt down to where it is very hard. You do not get dirt on you like you do outside. Sometimes the women, if they are good at weaving, will weave things to put on the floor so it would not be all dirt. The houses are the size they should be for the family living there. There is the main room. And for summertime sleeping there is a little side room that is open so that the little ones can sleep in the fresh air without having to worry about animals. It has to have a little bit of wall to keep out the animals, and then it is open. It is under the eaves of the roof so that if it were to rain they will not get wet.

D: *What do they sleep on?*

B: A frame with a skin stretched across. This frame is usually about this tall off the ground. (Hand motions of about a foot high.) And it is made wide enough for one or two people. If the women are good with weaving, they weave blankets to sleep on. And then many times they use skins from the animals I bring.

D: *Do they eat on the ground?*

B: No. There is a low ... (trying to find the word) table. You can sit on the ground and eat at this table, if you wish. Or sit on the ground and eat on the ground, whichever you prefer.

D: *I was wondering how they cook inside in the winter. Is there a fire in the house?*

B: Yes, the heat so that you will not get cold. Usually at one end of the house there will be a place in the floor built out of rocks and clay for the fire, so that the children will not fall in it. There is an opening in the roof to let out the smoke without letting in the rain.

D: *I wondered how the smoke would get out if the fire was inside the house.*

B: The wise man showed us how. At the end of the house, at the wall—well, a little way from the wall so that you will not catch your house on fire—you build a fire here (hand motions) and you put many layers of clay on the wall there to protect the wood from the fire. The fire causes the clay to get very hard. After this happens— like in a new house, it takes a while to break in a new house. After this is dried, then one can make a tube out of clay and weeds, something like a hollow log, going up to the opening. It is above the fire and the smoke heads toward it. It helps the smoke to go up to and out the opening without getting into the house too much.

It sounded like he was trying to describe a rough version of a chimney.

I asked if he would be able to draw the houses so I could see the shape. He said he would try but would make no guarantees. I had Beth open her eyes and handed her the tablet and marker. Her eyes had a glazed look typical of others I have asked to open their eyes while in trance. She marveled at the mysterious substance which I called "paper," and tried to understand how to hold the market and make it work. I have gone through this same procedure with every subject I have asked to do this while in trance. They view these objects as unfamiliar and strange. I have to divert their attention back to what they are doing or they will continue to be distracted.

B: (She marked on the paper.) It is blue like the sky.

D: *Yes, and it's able to make designs. Can you show me the shape of your houses you live in?*

B: I will try to make them look like houses, instead of just stick figures. You know what I mean?

She drew a house somewhat resembling a log cabin. She pointed to the drawing, referring to what appeared to be bindings holding the logs together.

D: *What are those made from?*

B: Leather. It would be passed back and forth until everything was wrapped.

D: *Are the bindings only on the ends like that or are they all the way across?*

B: They are basically on the ends. If the logs are cut right where they balance, that is the only place you need them. But if one side is particularly long, sometimes in the center there will be extra bindings. And in between here it would be stuffed with clay and leaves to fill in the gaps. The roof is more round than it is square. More like a dome than a point.

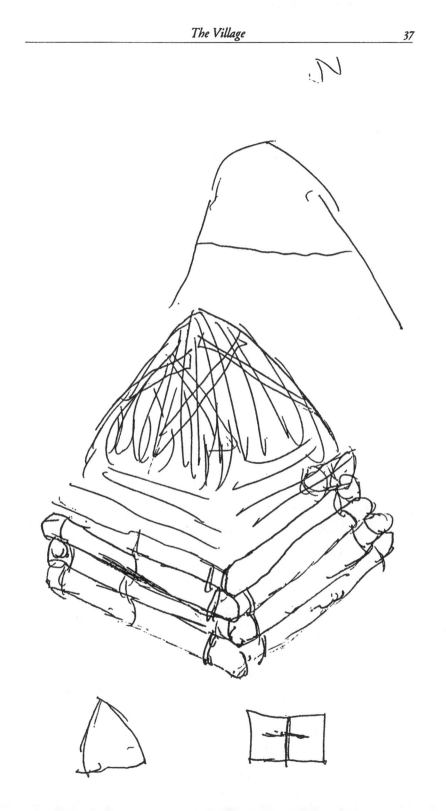

D: *What are the supports made out of that hold the roof up?*

B: Poles, usually. They are not bent. They just meet together at the top and when you put the grass over it, it rounds it off, to where the snow would slide off. And some people like to try to put clay on the inside to help keep out rain. Some do and some do not. It depends on how you like things. We would put the long grasses on the roof. And then on top of that we would put poles around to help hold the grasses down. And usually at the side would be the opening built of clay for the smoke to come out. The doors would be usually covered either with skin or bark, usually skin because you can tack it up tight. There are openings in the walls (windows), so you can open it up and let light and fresh air in, and then close it to keep the cold out. These would be covered either with slabs of wood and/or skin.

I next asked if the construction of the larger two-story building was the same as the smaller houses.

B: Yes. For the two-story house, it is wider on the bottom and it goes narrower up on the top, to where the second story is smaller than the first story. (She drew it.) It is slanted to help the walls to hold together.

She had finished the drawings. I took the tablet and marker away and told her to close her eyes once more.

D: *What is that larger building used for?*

B: Different things. When it is bad weather, like in winter and people want to meet—tell stories—they meet in the large building. The winter evenings get long. Staying in your own house all the time— it is not good. There is a fireplace there. In the cold weather it is needed. Sometimes the farmers meet and decide about crops for the next spring, where to plant what. Sometimes people meet just to have fun.

D: *Do they have any trouble with food in the winter?*

B: They store food. The meat that I hunt is dried and it is used. Some of the vegetables are stored, the ones that can store. In the winter we eat a lot of stew.

D: *One time you told me that sometimes they cook in one big pot outside, and everyone eats one meal together—unless there was a lady who wanted you to eat especially with her. (Laugh) But what do you do in the winter? You do not eat outside, do you?*

B: Oh no, no. Many people each prepare the meals in their own dwellings. Or, if they want and the weather is not too bad, a few families will gather in the large building and they have a meal together. Sometimes I have to eat outside if I am hunting.

D: *You said the larger building had two floors. What is on the upstairs floor?*

B: Sleeping rooms mostly. ... A meditation room. There is a pallet to sit or lie on. And there are shutters that you can open to where you can look out across the mountains. And there is a metal bowl in which you can make a small fire in case you want to meditate upon the flame. People go there to be by themselves. They think things out.

D: *Do you do that sometimes?*

B: Sometimes. I do most of mine in the woods.

D: *Have the people always believed in meditation?*

B: I think so. It is known to be beneficial.

D: *You said downstairs was the fireplace and a meeting room, and that you sometimes use the sleeping room in the back. Are the other sleeping rooms for people that do not have a regular home?*

B: Yes, or for young people who want to get together.

During another session I came across Tuin when he was away from the village. He was watching the river from high on a mountainside. Since the river was an essential part of the village's life—I wanted to know more about it.

B: I am up on the mountainside, leaning on a boulder. The river is quite a ways below. I was listening to the song of the river. It is in harmony with the song of the Earth, and it helps me to be in harmony.

D: *What's your favorite time of the year?*

B: I like all the times of the year. They follow each other in harmony in the way they should go. Each time is beautiful to itself. Spring is special because you can leave the houses again. You can go outside and be close to the Earth Mother again. It gets cold in the winter so you stay inside.

D: *Can I ask you some questions?*

B: You are the one who asks questions.

D: *Yes. Is that river always flowing all the year?*

B: No. You can tell the fall is coming because it starts freezing over. First skim ice and then it thickens. In the winter it flows fairly swiftly but it is under the ice. And in spring it makes a lot of noise when the ice breaks up. Some places it is a stone's throw wide, and other places it is more narrow and swift. In the spring it rushes faster from the rains and the melting snow. At one point it is partially blocked by rocks and some trees. There is some water pooled up there. It has been that way a long time. I do not remember how that happened.

D: *What is your source of water when the river freezes over in the winter?*

B: Oh, there is plenty of snow. You bring the snow inside; it melts and you drink. You have to bring in a lot, for the snow melts down to very little.

D: *Do you have boats?*

B: Uhh, we have a few that we use in the summer: sometimes for fun, sometimes for fishing. Some of the farmers like to fish when they want to rest from farming.

D: *How do they catch the fish?*

B: It depends. Usually they lure it with a flower or a bug or something. Or if they do not have time to sit and wait, they make something like a net to be weighted under water and it traps the fish.

D: *What do the boats look like?*

B: Uhh, they look like boats.

D: *I mean, are they large? How many people could sit in them?*

B: Ahh, two or three. They are made out of wood because wood floats. They are flat, like a raft but with sides. You cannot make them go where you want to go. They are hard to handle. They get a long sapling and they push it at the bottom of the river, and they go out into the current. Sometimes the young boys will get the sapling and a raft and in the spring when the current's going fast they go out into the center and just let the raft go where it will.

D: *That sounds like it would be fun.*

B: Yes, you get wet.

D: *Do you like to fish?*

B: I could, but I am always in the woods. I like seeing them.

D: *Has anyone ever thought of following the river to see where it goes?*

B: Not far. Where it comes from, it comes from the mountains. There is nothing there but snow. And where it goes, there is a waterfall. It is very beautiful. It is ... oh, slightly taller than a tall tree. And is crashes, booms and bangs. You cannot go over the falls. But when you stand there the river goes on and there is nothing else there. I do not know where it goes.

D: *Does the waterfall ever freeze and stop?*

B: Sometimes in the depths of a winter that is particularly cold, it will freeze. But usually there is some water still seeping. It is very beautiful when it is frozen. But it could do all kinds of things in the winter and I not know it, because I normally do not go that far. It is about three days' journey.

D: *Oh, I thought it was close. And you said you had never gone much further away than that?*

B: No, not in that direction.

D: *I wondered if anyone ever got curious and wanted to follow the river and see where it went.*

B: Oh, yes. The young boys—there is always a time when they are wanting to follow the river to its end. So they go and they follow a ways. But then they see that hunting is not as easy as what it seems when they see me do it. And there are no plants along the way that they can eat. So they get hungry and they come back. They say that it went on, that they did not find the end.

D: *Then no one has really left the village to find out.*

B: No, not within memory.

Thus far my questioning had revealed few clues. The people were positive there were no other people on the Earth but them, mainly because of their isolation. I thought someone might have attempted a journey down the river and located others, because throughout history groups of people have always settled near water. But the waterfall made this impossible unless you were traveling on foot, and Tuin was the only one capable of making such a trip. Since all of the people had their duties and were an essential part of the survival of the village, it was not advisable to travel away from the group. The clues still gave the indications of being located somewhere in the northern hemisphere. The houses also did not offer any clues. The drawings did not resemble any type of Native American dwellings, or houses used by Eskimos. They appeared to be unique in their own way. I was beginning to wonder whether any of my questions would yield the location of Tuin's village.

Another method is questioning about food—the types of things eaten and their methods of preparation. Some are unique to certain parts of the world.

D: *You don't have what we would call months, do you?*
B: The cycles of the moon.
D: *Do you have names for the cycles of the moon?*
B: No. Each person uses the description they like best; everyone knows when they are speaking of. The farmers usually use some names, and those of us who do other things use different descriptions. There is the moon the farmers call the harvest moon. In that time of the year I am not harvesting. I am busy—well, I suppose you could say I am harvesting animals for the winter, but I do not describe it that way. There is the planting moon. There is the fishing moon when the fish come back. That is in the spring.
D: *Didn't you say that you eat fruit that grew on the trees? What does it look like?*
B: Oh, some is purple; some is brown or golden.
D: *I think you told me they were very juicy too. Sweet?*
B: Umm. Sometimes. Sometimes your jaw locks.
D: *Do you have any way of keeping those for use in the winter?*
B: The farmers know of ways. Sometimes I dry some to mix with dried meat to carry with me when I go hunting. The people would get sick if we had just meat in the winter. We would not be in harmony with the Earth.
D: *Do you know what salt is?*

B: (She thought and then answered.) No.

D: *It is ... oh, I guess it's something like an herb, only it comes from the ground. It is white and is used to flavor food.*

B: There is a plant we have. It is found in the fields. We burn the plant and what is left with the ashes is white and we add that to food.

D: *No, this would be something that would be dug out of the ground. Sometimes it's on top of the ground.*

B: I have found that in the woods sometimes. The deer like it. What we get from this plant is the same.

D: *Do you have any trees in the woods that produce anything to eat?*

B: Yes. There is the oak tree. We gather acorns in the fall. I gather a few to eat for myself, but the major gathering is done by the young boys and girls. The oak trees are near the village, only a pleasant walk away. It helps supplement the grain we raise. We roast them. We use the meats in soup and grind them into acorn flour to mix with the grain to make cakes and breads.

D: *Is there any other kind of seed or nut that you eat?*

B: Some of the pine trees produce edible nuts. They are very sweet.

D: *Oh? I'm used to seeing pine cones.*

B: Yes. The pine nuts come from pine cones. Some trees produce small pine cones and some produce larger pine cones. At a certain time of year, usually in spring, you can gather the pine nuts from the larger pine cones. (Pause) Let me think. Usually it is the pine trees and the oak trees that we eat from. Sometimes when I am hunting I will find another tree that has nuts. The shell is so thick and the meat is so small, it is not really worth the effort. I am wanting to call it hickory—hickory nut? It tastes good, but there is not very much there.

D: *I've heard there is one type of tree; you may not have it where you live. But you can cut through the bark and it has something sweet there. (I was thinking of maple syrup.)*

B: Some trees, you can use the sap for different things. And the sap has different flavors, if you wish the taste of the sap. Pine trees and other evergreen trees, spruce, cedar, you can get the gum from the bark and you can chew it. When you first chew it, it cracks up in your mouth. Then when it warms up, it softens up and sticks back together, and it turns pink and you can chew it. And it tastes like the tree smells, so it tastes good if you like the smell of pine trees. It is very popular. The old people cannot do it because it pulls their teeth out. We mostly use the sap of the evergreen trees. There is a tree that has a sweet sap but it is runny and if you want to get any of it you have to get a skin to catch it and it is a lot of trouble. It is so runny and it is slow. You have to specially treat the skins to make sure it does not soak through when you get it. It is so difficult to get. We hardly ever get very much of it at all. If you want something sweet, it is easier to get honey. You can find the honey in the woods in hollow trees and such.

D: *What about the bees?*

B: There are ways of taking care of the bees. If you build a fire around the tree the smoke and heat drives the bees away or makes them go to sleep, to where you can get the honey. Another thing you can do whenever it is a warm day, you get the leaf of this herb, and the smell is very crisp and clean, and the taste likewise. You chew on one of the leaves and let this taste in your mouth. When you go to the stream and drink water, the water feels extremely cold because of this particular taste. The leaf is generally about this long (about 2 inches), pointed with little jags around the edge. Usually at the end of the stalk it will have a group of flowers, kind of a spike, like a spear-point. It is wide at the bottom and narrow at the top with little flowers all over.

D: *What color are they?*

B: Sometimes white, sometimes light purple.

My research indicated that he was probably referring to a variety of the mint plant.

D: *Do you ever have anything else to drink besides water?*

B: Well, you can get water and soak leaves in it, or heat water up on the fire and put leaves in it and make a drink that way.

D: *Is that good?*

B: Depends. Sometimes. If it is for medicine, no. (I laughed.) But usually if you use herbs that smell good it is going to taste good. You can also put some flowers in it. Some people use it as a treat and others like to do it often.

D: *You told me once about a drink that the farmers make.*

B: Oh, that one. (He was smiling broadly.) Some of the growers of grain like to crack the grain, and let it soak in water. After a while it ferments, although I don't really know what causes this. The others think it is a really good drink, and they have it sometimes at the spring festival, but it makes my head feel funny. I do not like that.

My friend, Kay, had written down a list of questions about these people and passed it to me. Some of them I knew would be impossible for Tuin to answer, since the villagers were the only people he had ever seen he would have nothing to compare with. But since they were questions most people who are not familiar with this phenomenon would think of, I will include them here.

D: *Does everyone in the village have the same color of skin?*

B: The skin is generally the same. There are shades. Some are slightly lighter; some are slightly darker. And usually most people's hair is black like mine. Sometimes a child is born with hair the color of sunset. But this does not happen very often.

D: *What about the eyes. Are there different colors among your people?*

B: Usually they are either brown or ... well, there is a small flower that is violet-colored. Darken that to the darkness of midnight.

Kay was wondering if they had slanted eyes. I knew if they were the only people, they wouldn't have anything to compare with. But I asked anyway.

D: *Are your eyelids different shapes?*

B: They are shaped the way they are shaped.

I chuckled inwardly because this was the type of answer I had expected.

D: *I just wondered. Does anyone have eyes the color of the sky, blue?*

B: No. That would look very strange.

D: *I've heard of things like that. That's why I wondered.*

B: Well, if you ask questions, you must ask questions everywhere, I suppose.

D: *(Laugh) I find lots of knowledge everywhere. But you said the women wear their hair long or tied up in the back. And they had some kind of a pronged thing they put in their hair to hold it together. What is that made of?*

B: Sometimes out of bone, sometimes out of wood.

D: *It holds their hair into a knot in the back?*

B: Yes, twisted somehow. Sometimes certain families will use the same way of doing it, and sometimes different women will do it different ways according to how they feel.

D: *Is all the hair straight?*

B: Well, it hangs.

D: *Do you know what curly means?*

B: No.

D: *It's twisted. You've seen animals sometimes that have hair that looks different.*

B: The sheep has shaggy hair that is not straight.

D: *Okay. Do the people have hair like that?*

B: No, that is sheep hair.

D: *(Kay passed me another note.) Your people are so much in harmony with each other. But do you ever have cases when one person would hurt another in your village?*

B: Sometimes accidentally. Like when a child is being careless when they are playing and they accidentally run into someone else.

This was definitely not what Key was looking for. She was trying to find a flaw in these people. It was hard for her to believe a group of people could be so easy-going and compatible.

D: *Do you ever have a case when someone would deliberately hurt someone?*

B: Sometimes when someone's companion dies and they drink too much of the juice that the farmer makes. They are sad and they are numb and they do not feel the harmony of the Earth. They wish to strike out because they miss their companion. But we understand because they are not in harmony just then. The time passes and they are in harmony again.

D: *Do you have anything that is called punishment in your community?*

B: Is it like correcting a child?

D: *Something like that, yes.*

B: When a child does something that he or she should not, something that would endanger them or be a danger to the village, we correct them.

D: *How do you do that?*

B: Different ways, depending on which family.

D: *Do you ever have to correct an adult?*

B: (Surprised) Why, no! Why should we? They know how to live.

I was laughing inwardly because I suspected these would be the answers Tuin would give to Kay's questions.

B: If you are in harmony with the Earth, when your song is in harmony with the Earth's song, you know what to do. And if you know what to do, it is correct.

D: *That's very good, but some places are not that lucky. Some people are not in harmony and they get into all kinds of trouble.*

B: They were not taught well when they were children.

D: *That's very possible. Yours is a much better way to live, a happier way.*

B: It is the way it should be.

D: *What do you do in your village when someone gets sick? Do you have any sickness?*

B: Not many. This is true when you are in harmony with the Earth. Sickness is when you are not in harmony. (The word "sickness" was separated: "sick–ness.") And everyone is in harmony. When it happens it is usually in the winter, either one of the old people or someone very young. Sometimes there are injuries, like if you harm your arm or your leg or what-have-you, sometimes the bone has to be pulled back into place and bound up until it heals. The arm will be stiff afterwards, perhaps crooked, but you can use it. You just learn how to work around it. Any of the old people can treat these things. They, particularly the women, know about herbs and such. I help them sometimes. If some of the women know I will be going in a particular direction for hunting, they will ask me to look out for a particular herb that does not grow near the village. I am always happy to help out with that. The wise man, he is sometimes

consulted if it is a mysterious illness with fever. That happens sometimes in the late winter.

D: *Does the wise man know how to treat that?*

B: Usually. Sometimes if the child is too young or if the person is too
old, they die. But that is part of the natural order of things.

D: *Oh, yes. But it is good that you do not have much sickness. You are
healthy people.*

B: We try. We stay in harmony with the spirits, and the spirits help us
to stay well. If we stay in harmony with their singing, if our lives sing
in harmony with the spirits' singing, we stay healthy.

D: *When someone does die, would you bury them?*

B: Yes. We build a fire and reminisce of the person and things they did.
The good things, the funny things. How the things happened in
their life. About their family. The wise man tells us about some of
their ancestors. Then we call upon the spirits to welcome them to
that part of life. And we tell them they will be happy there.

D: *Many people think it is a very sad occasion when someone dies.*

B: It is sad for children if their mother dies. And yes, we will miss their
daily company. They will start singing with the spirits. But perhaps
they will speak to us with their spirit.

D: *When someone dies in your community, is the wise man or the people
able to speak with them after they have died?*

B: Certainly. Their spirits have rejoined the Earth Mother's spirit. And
sometimes they want to tell their family something that they feel they
should know, but forgot to tell them before they went.

D: *I remember you said your people were very much in tune with the spirits.*

B: Yes. That is the way it is.

D: *It's very natural. You're very lucky that your people are so open to these
things. Many people have closed all these things off.*

B: I do not wish to speak about those—too sad.

Chapter 4

The Legend of the Old Ones

D: *When I first spoke to you, you told me some of your legends. I found them very interesting.*

B: You did? Everyone knows the legends.

D: *But to me they're new. I would like to hear some more of them.*

B: What about?

D: *Can you tell me more of the things that have been handed down?*

B: If you like, I can. Would you like to know why I apologize when I hunt? There is a legend that says at one time the animals could speak like men. And it was very distressing to the hunter to try to hunt because the animal would be crying for pity. So the hunter would apologize, saying, "I am sorry, I need your spirit; I need your flesh for my people or we will die. You have lived a full life; you have children. Your children will live. It is time for you to go to the other side. May I kill you for your flesh?" The animals would cry for mercy and it would be very difficult for the hunter. The hunter must kill some animals for the people, but not too many, for the animals must also live. And so finally an agreement was reached with the help of the spirits that to make it easier for the hunter—the animals would no longer speak. But to show the animal that the hunter remembers, we apologize to the animals just as if they could still speak.

D: *Some people think there's no harm in just killing. I think it's good to consider the animal as having feelings. This shows that you are a very compassionate person. That is good. Then you only kill just enough to eat, never too much?*

B: Well, some to store for the winter. But ... (deliberately and seriously) I cannot conceive of killing an animal and just leaving it for the vermin. It is not done.

D: *Some people do. In other parts of the world.*

B: Their spirits must be displeased with them. That is why the spirits are with us.

D: *Yes, because they know you are doing it the right way. Do you have any other legends?*

B: Yes, we have a legend about everything. You keep asking like a child would. That is interesting.

D: *I have a great curiosity. This way you can help me to learn. Do they have any people in your village that are known as teachers?*

B: Well, the old people who cannot work any more; they know the legends. They tell them to the young children. The young children like the old people and it helps for their mothers to be able to get some weaving done, or whatever, without the children in the way. That is how we learn our legends. The wise man knows them all. He makes sure they are handed down correctly. Some of the old people, they like to make it sound better than what it was, and things could get changed very easily that way. The wise man sees that this does not happen, for it was said that the legends must remain true so we will know who we are. One of the functions of the wise man is to make sure that it stays accurate.

D: *But that is difficult when much times goes by. Do your people have any system of writing? Do you know what that is?*

B: Yes, I know what that is. Some do, some do not. I do not. I feel that if I can read the signs of animals, why should I worry about the signs of men. Some of the farmers use writing to keep track of their crops and how much they have so they will know how to distribute it during the winter.

D: *This means they would know numbers and counting?*

B: I suppose. They have marks to represent how much of things.

D: *Would the wise man have a way of writing the legends?*

B: Probably. That is part of his life. He, perhaps, has things written down. I do not know. I find it best not to be too nosy.

D: *Tell me another legend that is popular with the people.*

B: They are all popular with different ones. Ahh ... I remember, you were interested about the boat crashing.

D: *Yes I was. I found that very interesting.*

B: That is a long legend. At some of our festivals the wise man takes all night long to retell it.

D: *Could you tell me some parts of it?*

B: Yes I can. The part that interests me is how the people got started after the boat crashed—according to the legend. For we descended from them. That is what the wise man says.

D: *It's part of your history.*

B: Yes. They found the world to be different from what they were used to. They did not know the plants. They did not know the animals. Sometimes the wise man would give examples of what they called things. It is very amusing, but I think these were made up for the children. For example, they said, "There is a thing that flies, the color of sky, that makes the noise like a babbling brook." Everybody knows that is a bluebird. They had these lengthy descriptions of things. "There is the animal with a tree on its head." (I laughed.) That would be a buck. Some of the descriptions are very funny. "There is the animal that cannot stand still," because according to legend—and this part is for children—"it is afraid of ants. And it is always jumping to get away from the ants." That would be the rabbit. (I laughed.) The legends say that at first the people lived in their ship. That is strange; our boats are open. But apparently according to legend this one was not open. And they got tired of living in the ship as the ship was dead. So they cut down trees and built houses. Used to, they would use wood for the roof as well. But for some reason they stopped doing that, and now we use grass for our roof, which is better. I think they wanted to not use too many trees. For some reason they thought this was bad.

D: *Maybe they thought they would use them all up.*

B: There are so many of them, so many trees.

D: *These people, did they have tools for cutting the trees and building the houses?*

B: Supposedly these were in the ship. It must have been a big ship. Too big for our river.

D: *Have those tools been handed down?*

B: I do not know. Some of the tools we have are handed down, some are made. If those tools were real, I imagine the wise man would have them or would know what happened to them. I remember that some of the smaller ones were buried with the people.

D: *Are these the same houses that you use?*

B: No. When they first built the houses, so the legends say, sometimes they would use things from the ship. The ship was made to be taken apart. I suppose they would have to with it being so large, to be able to carry it. And they took it apart and used things from their ship. This is what legends say.

D: *What other things from the ship did they use in the house?*

B: I do not know. I have heard the women tell the children that they had things for cooking that could do things that anyone knows regular things cannot do. It is just things you tell children to keep them amused. There is a legend about a wondrous pot that could cook without a fire.

D: *That would be interesting if it were true.*

B: It is not true. You have to start a fire to cook, everyone knows that. There is a legend of a wondrous box. You open the box, you put something in this container. You close the container, and before you can repeat your name, the thing is cooked.

D: *Oh! Wouldn't that be wonderful?*

B: It is made up. And according to legends we still have some things. I imagine the things in the wise man's house are part of it. Some of the knives that we have do not go dull; that is very wondrous. The farmers have this tool that they have the oxen drag through the earth to loosen it up for planting. I think they call it a "plow." They have other tools that they use for reaping the grains and such. The way you can tell if something is from the old ones—it will not wear out like our tools do. Perhaps it will in time, but it takes many lifetimes or much longer.

D: *You said the wise man had a pot, too.*

B: Yes. It is hard to describe it. I do not know what he uses it for. It changes appearance. I do not know how that happens.

D: *It changes color or shape or what?*

B: The shape stays the same, but it starts out looking like it is made from one type of metal, and it changes appearance and it looks like it is made from another type of metal, not related.

D: *How big is this pot?*

B: Well, it is fairly large. (She made hand motions showing something roughly three feet by three feet.) It curves, almost round, but not quite.

D: *That is large. Does it have a lid on it?*

B: No. It has a handle. The handle changes shapes. It changes position, but you can carry the pot with the handle.

D: *Where is the handle located?*

She made two hand motions that gave me the impression of a bail handle either sticking up or laying down. But the next hand motion was confusing because it didn't seem like a bail.

B: Or sometimes it just sticks out the side, but then that is very awkward, it would seem.

Her motions indicated some kind of a straight handle that she could grasp with her hand.

D: *Umm. Does it change by itself or do you have to move it?*

B: It appears to do it by itself, like the color changing.

This was another object that I had no idea of what it could be.

D: *That is a strange pot. Is there anything inside of it?*

B: I do not know. The wise man uses it for something. Some of the farmers say sometimes they dig up rocks that are too hard to be used—perhaps they have metal in them—and they give them to the wise man. I think he puts them in the pot and something happens to them.

D: *Then* he *knows how to use it.*

B: I think so. We do not have much metal. It is said that the metal we have came from the old ones. It is very precious.

D: *You have no way of finding any other metal?*

B: I do not know. Sometimes in the stream some metal is found in amongst the rocks that is the color of sunshine. It is nice to use to make playthings for the children. It is too soft to make tools from, but it is pretty. Sometimes they make amulets out of it. Also it is said that in the old ones' boat they had things to plant, and some grew, but some would not. The first few winters here were very difficult for them. It is said that many died and only a few lived.

D: *They didn't have much food with them on the boat?*

B: They did, but they ran out. And it is said that what they planted would not grow or would grow in strange and wondrous ways.

D: *Do you know what those plants were? Do you have any names that they might have passed down in legend?*

B: No, I do not know. Perhaps some of the farmers might know. The wise man would know. I just know what we have now. There are plants that we eat the roots from. The tops we also eat but they can be bitter. They changed, it is said. They used to be different, but they grew and you could still eat them.

D: *How were they different?*

B: I do not know. The wise man would know.

D: *Were there any other things they planted?*

B: They planted grains. According to legend they used to yield wondrous amounts. The farmers dream of making the grains yield that way once again, but they do not. Perhaps some of the old people got hold of the legend before the accuracy was established. Perhaps the grains just yielded the same the whole time, and they just said it yielded better because they were homesick.

D: *Did the old ones bring any certain type of trees with them?*

B: I do not know of any trees that they brought. The trees we have, they are all over. I just live here and as far as I go when I am hunting they are always there.

D: *Did the old ones bring any animals with them, or do you know anything about that?*

B: I do not know. The oxen do not resemble anything that I find in the woods. I suppose the old ones brought them, perhaps that is why we never eat oxen. There are not that many. The farmers have been talking of trying to increase the number of oxen to make their work easier. Perhaps they will.

D: *You said many of these people died because it was very difficult at the beginning.*

B: Yes. Maybe their clothes were not warm enough for winter. And for some reason, the crashing—perhaps because it was a bad thing—threw off the reproductive cycles of the women, so no children were born. Or if they were born they did not live. The legends say some of the children were not right. It is said that some of the bad spirits infected the children and caused them to grow in ways that is not right for us. (This was all said with sadness.)

D: *What happened to those children?*

B: They died.

D: *Then how were they able to have normal children?*

B: I do not know. That is why I think it was made up. I mean, to have children, it is obvious. It is the normal cycle of things.

D: *Do you think those people looked different from your people now?*

B: Ahh, I am not sure. It is said they were taller, more slender. They are described as being fair. I do not know how; I cannot picture it. Some were said to have hair the color of wheat, which is very strange.

D: *Are there any people in your village that have hair that color now?*

B: No. There are people with hair the color of mine, and there are people with hair the color of the sunset. (Did he mean red?) Sometimes when babies are first born their hair is the color of wheat, but usually it turns to the color of sunset.

D: *But then somehow over the many years or whatever it was, the people's skin and hair changed in color.*

This problem of genetics was bothering me. If the old ones were fair, where did the darker colors come from?

D: *Do they have any legends about why your people look different today than they did in those days?*

B: I am not sure. There are just rumors of legends. It is said that the people from the boat felt heavy here. I do not understand that. And it is said that they felt very ... pained. They could not figure out the moon for some reason. They made a lot of significance about the moon. They talked like it was something very unique. To me, the moon, she is the most beautiful one. But the old ones said things about the moon being so big. And earlier legends say they were amazed to see the moon. It also affected the women. They said that the moon was "different." Some of the stories we tell children—you will notice they have no doubt been embroidered. But they say that where the old ones came from they did not have a moon. Then when they landed here they thought the moon was another Earth, until they looked at it and realized that she is very beautiful. They saw that the Earth is the mother and the moon is special. And so they were glad that they had come to Earth and not to the moon. It is said in the legends—particularly the ones we tell children—that the old ones were amazed at the strength of the sun. They thought that the sun was like a strong warrior, very bold. They said that the sun was so bright, there was so much light here. They felt that the Earth was a fair place.

D: *Maybe this was why the plants grew differently.*

B: Why would that be? The light is light.

D: *Some people think that the sun and light affect the growing of the plants.*

B: It makes them green; it makes them grow. I do not know why it would change things. I think that is just a legend. You have legends too, I see.

D: *Oh yes, everyone has legends and stories.*

B: You have to be careful. Sometimes if you believe them too much you can be misled.

D: *Oh yes. That's why I like to hear other people's stories and see how we are alike or different. But it is true, you have to be careful not to believe too much. Treat it as a story. Did they have any legends about lights?*

B: I am not sure. They said that the Earth was a fair place, much light.

D: *What do your people use whenever it gets dark? Do you have any way of making light?*

B: Yes, we have lamps. Sometimes we use fat from animals that I have hunted. Sometimes we use some plants that, when you press them a clear liquid comes out, like melted fat. And it burns somewhat. But usually we go to sleep when it gets dark.

D: *And you also have the fires that make light. Are there any legends of the old ones using something different to make a light?*

B: They did not need the light like we do. It is said that the old ones could see very well in the dark. When they did need light they would have a lamp, but it did not use what we use. It is said that the lamp was like the pot that cooks without a fire, but that is just legend. If that were true, life would be very easy. It was said that some of the old ones could kill an animal from beyond bowshot distance.

D: *How did they do that?*

B: This will sound funny but this is what the legend says. They felt that since the sun was such a strong warrior, they would have the sun help them to hunt and use the sun spear to kill the animal. So they made a wondrous device that would borrow the sun spear. And they would throw the sun's spear toward an animal. If there was nothing standing in the way, the animal would be killed and there would be a small hole where the spear had entered. (She made motions with her hands, showing a hole about the size of the tip of her finger.) Apparently the sun spear was very hot like the sun, and the meat would be partially cooked around that hole. And they would alter the sun spear or they would use the sun's rays to cook the meat or dry it. They were very amazed at how strong the sun is.

D: *Wouldn't it be wonderful if you could hunt that way?*

B: Perhaps, but then I might be too far away to apologize properly.

D: *They had many wonderful things. But you said the wise man tells these legends all night sometimes?*

B: And more, yes.

D: *Do you mind telling them to me?*

B: I do not mind. Sometimes it is difficult for me to remember them. I do not usually tell them; I just listen. The ones who tell them, they remember them better.

D: *But you've heard them so many times they are in your memory.*

B: I am skipping a lot though, I feel. We do not know all the story ourselves. Sometimes there seems to be gaps. Perhaps a wise man died before he passed it on. We remember what we can, but that is why the wise man tries to keep it accurate so there will not be more gaps. (Proudly) We survived. We are the people.

Chapter 5

The First People

$\mathcal{A}$ STRANGE PHENOMENA OCCURS when I am time traveling and conversing with people living in the past. The personality of the person the information is coming through totally disappears. They have no memories other than those of the revived entity who lived hundreds, and in this case, thousands of years ago. I have observed this switching occur many times.

Thus I had to speak to Tuin in a way he would understand so I could gain his confidence. This was the only way I could obtain information about the legends. He did not seem to be suspicious, but I always feel that having the trust of the entity is essential in these regressions.

D: *Do you remember talking to me about your legends?*
B: Yes, I do. You are like a child; you do not know them.
D: *I have a lot of curiosity, and one of the jobs I have been given is to record the history of your people.*
B: To record? How do you mean?
D: *Well, do you know what writing is?*
B: The wise man does it.
D: *It is a job I have been given: to write down the story and the legends.*
B: Will you be able to remember all this and write it down?
D: *That's why I was given the job, because I can remember. Everyone has their job. That's why I ask you so many questions. They don't want the history to be lost.*

B: No, this history, the legends must not be lost. The knowledge must be passed down.

D: *That's what I was told.*

Since he told me that legends were recited during the festivals, I thought that would be a good place to start. I could have him relive the actual ceremony, but he said they were very long, often going on all night. It could be done, but he would have to repeat verbatim everything he was hearing. I chose to rely on his memories of the stories. They should be fairly accurate if he had heard them all his life.

D: *When the night is the longest and you have the ceremony, what part of the legends does the wise man tell you at that time?*

B: On the night that is the longest we gather together and he tells us the legends of the journey of the people.

D: *Can you tell me parts of it?*

B: There are two or three different reasons given as to why the old ones had to leave their earth and cross the void. Some say that their people had been out of harmony with the earth for so long that their earth was dying and they had to leave. Some say that their sun was out of harmony and was dying. And there is another set of legends that say they were part of a large people and the old ones made them angry and had to leave. Either way they left in their ship.

D: *Maybe they were all part of the reason.*

B: Perhaps. They built their ship out of metal. Most extravagant—and it does not float well.

D: *No, it doesn't. They must have had secrets.*

B: Of course. The old ones are synonymous with secrets. They left in their ship and traveled across the void. I have gotten the feeling from listening to the legends that they were not planning on coming here.

D: *It was by accident?*

B: Yes. Their ship was damaged. I guess it was going to sink. And they landed here in the valley, though the legends say they crashed.

D: *You don't know where they were going when they happened to come here?*

B: No, I do not know. And they could not travel further. After traveling across the void they were very travel-weary. They wanted to stop and rest; perhaps fix their ship and then continue their journey. They stopped for a space of time. I do not know how many seasons. That part has been lost. But after that space of time some legends say that they were so tired and so many were ill they did not want to travel on. They wanted to stay here on the Earth. And the legends say they had forgotten how to travel.

D: *Maybe so much time had gone by.*

B: Perhaps. And so they stayed and gradually ... see, when they first came here they were out of harmony with the Earth, and it took a long time.

D: *What do you mean?*

B: Well, they were out of harmony. It seemed like the song of their lives, the song of their bodies, was not fitting in with the song of the Earth. Consequently, very few babies were born. Their crops did not grow well for they did not know how to sing in harmony with the Earth. But the Earth, she was patient and she kept working with them. And she gradually shaped the songs of their lives and the songs of their crops to where it was in harmony with the song of the Earth.

D: *That's beautiful. Did those people live a long time in those days or did many die during this?*

B: They felt very ill for a long time because they were not in harmony with the Earth. They did things out of harmony. They did things at night and stayed inside in the day, for they said the sun was too bright. Apparently they would feel ill whenever they were in the sun. They said it was too strong. It was beating them down to the Earth. Apparently they could see well at night. And besides, they said the moon was so very bright. They were so amazed at the moon. They had not seen the like before. They were always exclaiming on her beauty. She is very beautiful. She will be shining tonight.

D: *Oh? There will be a full moon tonight?*

B: No, it is not full moon. Three-quarter. The full moon was about four nights ago, but she is very beautiful. The old ones used to study her like I would study animals. It is said that they had magic eyes. They could look at her face and see it very closely. It is said that some old ones saw that other old ones had—well, this is what the legend says. It does not make sense. But it is said that sometimes when the old ones looked at the moon with their magic eyes they could see that another group of old ones, who were not of them, had visited her; had camped there in the moon. I do not know how they did this. This is what the legends say. But then, most legends do not make sense anyhow.

D: *But they're interesting. Did they have any way of talking to them?*

B: I do not know. I think that the other old ones were not there at the time, but had left behind signs that they had been there. Some of the legends say—now I do not know where they could have come from for this to be true—but some of the legends say that where they came from when they started their journey, there was no moon. Now, the moon is there for all to see. She is very beautiful. She has helped me many times.

D: *Maybe where they came from, they couldn't see it.*

B: Well, some of the things passed down in the legends say that when they started their journey there was no moon, and they kept the seasons of the year by the position of the sun and stars. When they came here, according to the legends, they were very worshipful towards the moon because she makes it so much easier to keep the seasons in their proper places. The legend says they lived a lot longer than what we do now. But that is all right. We have a full span of years. They gradually came in harmony with the Earth and learned to grow the crops and learned the habits of their little brothers and sisters, the plants and the animals. They learned to be in harmony with them so that they could live. And they had children, and their children had children and so on and so forth, and we are descended from them.

D: *And that's how is all began. Is there anything in your legends of anyone else ever coming into the valley?*

B: No. The legends say that when the old ones first came here there were another people here in the valley. Not very numerous, but a few.

I was wondering about this problem of genetics. Maybe this was the answer.

D: *What type of people were those?*

B: From what the legends say they looked pretty much the way I look.

D: *Oh, I thought you meant that when the old ones came to this valley, there was no one there. They were all alone.*

B: They were very few but they were the only people. We are the only ones: there are no other people.

D: *The people who were there when the old ones crashed, what type of houses did they live in? Do the legends say?*

B: No, the legends do not say. But they do say that they were in perfect harmony with the Earth. And at first they were scared of the old ones. Since the old ones were not in harmony it was painful for the first people to be close to the old ones. As the old ones came to be in better harmony they started being able to mix more, to where finally they were living together as one people.

D: *I kept wondering about that. You told me that the old ones were very light, very fair and had hair the color of wheat, and that your people now were not that color. I could not understand that. It would be like the animals when they breed, they have the different colors. This could be the explanation. The original people were dark-haired like you are. Is that right?*

B: These people that were here, yes. And they were also shorter than we are.

D: *But you don't have anything in the legend about how they lived?*

B: No, because our legends come from the old ones and the first people avoided the old ones.

D: *Do you think the old ones are the ones who discovered how to make the cloth?*

B: They knew how to make cloth, but the first ones knew how to make cloth too. So our cloth-making comes from both groups.

D: *I guess between the two, the old ones and the first ones, they could have figured out how to make the material. Do you think the first ones taught them how to make clothes?*

B: No, they had clothes when they came. But the first ones did teach them about skins and leather. When the old one's clothes were buried with them, the people started dressing like the first people. The way we dress is the way they dressed.

D: *Then the first people shared with the old ones.*

B: Not at first, for it was too painful.

D: *They were afraid?*

B: They were not afraid; it was just painful. The old ones were not in harmony with the Earth. And the first people were in perfect harmony with the Earth, and the difference between was painful to the harmony.

D: *I suppose there must have been some types of food growing there.*

B: Some grains, a few vegetables. The old ones brought some food with them. Some of it would grow and some of it would not. And so, I imagine we have both types now.

D: *Do you know if any of the plants you have* are *the ones that the old ones brought?*

B: The old ones brought the plant that we weave cloth from. The legends say the old ones would design plants. They would make them grow like you would make a set of clothing. And this plant was made, not to eat, but to produce fibers for clothing. (Incredulously) Now, the plants grow as they grow. I do not understand it, but that is what the legend says.

D: *How could you* make *a plant the way you wanted?*

B: Perhaps the old ones had the power to alter the song of life.

D: *That would be an interesting idea. What about any other plants that they might have brought with them?*

B: Some of our grains, it is said, they brought with them. Some of the grains the first ones had. And so, it is hard to say which is which.

D: *They might have mixed together.*

B: True. They may have.

D: *You said there was some kind of vegetables that were grown. I mean, roots and things like that.*

B: Yes. Most of those were brought by the old ones.

D: *What do they look like?*

B: I could tell you what they look like now. They may have changed like the animals did. One plant makes roots that can fit in the hand comfortably, and these roots are the color of the setting sun. They are good to eat. Another root is yellow and it has different flavors according to how ripe it is when you pick it. It is more of a round shape. The other one is pointed at the ends and kind of roundish in the middle.

D: *Is there anything else like that?*

B: None that I can remember. There are other things that we eat, but the legends do not say where in particular they come from. Some of the fruit trees, the seeds were said to have been brought. One in particular has a juicy, kind of yellowish fruit. It is sweet and has a large seed in the center. The farmers have to be very careful growing it, because it can be damaged by the cold very easily. They pamper those trees. Somehow the farmers do not let them grow very big, because they are able to stand the cold only if they are kept wrapped up. That is one of the farming secrets. I do not know. I am a hunter. One kind of fruit grows on a vine. It is long, a little bit pointed at the ends, and it has yellowish flesh with lots of seeds scattered throughout. It fits into the hand well. You just grab them when you are picking them. Another one is from a tree. It is a red-brown color and also has seeds scattered throughout the flesh. It is very good in late fall.

D: *Did either of those come from the old ones?*

B: We are not sure. Some of them grow out in the woods but most of them are planted.

D: *Some of them may have spread to the woods in the olden days.*

B: Yes. Sometimes they mark an old homesite.

D: *I thought maybe all of your food came from the old ones.*

B: Oh no. Legends say most of it did. The people who were here mostly hunted. That is where I learned my hunting, for with them being in harmony with the Earth they could hear the animals. The old ones could hear the animals as well, but it was too painful for the hunter. The animals would beg and plead and say, "Don't kill me." But I have told you this.

D: *Yes, you told me about that. You said that after a while the spirits changed it so they couldn't hear the animals any more.*

B: Right. You do remember.

D: *Which was more merciful.*

B: For the hunter anyhow.

D: *In your legends, are there any important events that happened to the old ones after they came here?*

B: It was very important when they made contact with the people who were here already. If they had not made contact with the first people, they would have died. The first people helped the old ones to become in harmony with the Earth.

D: *But they didn't try to hurt them, did they?*

B: No, no. It was just that the old ones' songs were so out of harmony because their minds worked so differently, that it was painful for the first ones to be around them. Then they were able to alter their thinking to be in harmony with the Earth so that they could work together, and learn how to live in harmony with the Earth so that they could survive.

D: *You said that some of the first children that were born to the old ones didn't live or they had things wrong with them. Was it a long time before they finally had children that could survive?*

B: They kept trying to have children, and most of them would die or could not have children themselves. But a few of them were able to live and were normal and could have children. There were so few of them for so long, that it took many generations, three or four generations, for everything to work out for them.

D: *Do you think many of the old ones died before they had children?*

B: I do not know. I think that they tried to have children and the children were having problems living. Since most of their children had died there were not many people. The few that were still alive tried to have children, and many of them died, but a few of them lived. By then the first ones were helping. So gradually they became strong again and they were in harmony with the Earth.

D: *Did the legends say what was wrong with the children?*

B: Their bodies were not in harmony with themselves or with the Earth. Sometimes things would be misplaced or missing. Parts of the body would either be drastically different from what it should be or not there at all.

D: *Then there was much strangeness and that was why they couldn't live. Do your legends tell of any other important events that happened during their time?*

B: During the old ones' time? That was the main thing. The old ones seemed to think that being here on the Mother Earth was important. I do not know where else they would be.

D: *Did the old ones ever try to leave?*

B: Where would they go?

D: *I don't know. That's why I thought that would be important if they did try.*

B: They liked it where they were. It is beautiful here. Why would they leave? It is home.

D: *Can you think of anything else important that is mentioned in the stories?*

B: Well, another thing that was important is that they managed to get the crops in harmony with the Earth so that the food would start growing again. This took much work. It is said it took many years. It was very hard beforehand. It is said they had a big celebration when their first successful crop was harvested. This was very important, because now they knew that they would have plenty of food to live on. It was a matter of being in harmony with the Earth. When the crops started living and their children started living, they were very happy because they knew they would survive.

D: *Then they lived there and grew old and died, and the blood is passed on to your people. Did the first ones help them with the growing?*

B: I think so. I am not sure. The first ones told the old ones about acorns and pine nuts, and taught them about being in harmony for hunting. They taught them about planting and harvesting—everything you need to do to live.

D: *They told them which things were safe to eat in the woods?*

B: Yes, and which things were good for medicine. It is said that the old ones had their own medicine, but they did not have much of it and did not know how to make more. Which is strange. Medicine is medicine. You go out in the woods and there it grows.

D: *Maybe the herbs that they used didn't grow here.*

B: Well, perhaps. They would have had to have been from very far away.

D: *Do you know what they used their medicines for?*

B: The same things we use our medicine for: fevers, cough and things like that.

D: *If the first ones hadn't been there to show them these different things, the old ones probably would have died right away. The first ones could have been afraid of them and not wanted to help them at all.*

B: That is true.

D: *Can you think of anything else that was important from the legends?*

B: One of the legends say that the old ones used to communicate with other old ones. There was a magic rock. They would speak to this rock and the rock would speak back. It is said that they were speaking to other old ones in the void. But that is just a legend. I do not think there is anyone else. I do not know of any legends of anyone else. The legends say this rock was very wondrous to behold. It was similar to clear quartz when you see the veins of gold running through. This rock was clear like that. It is said you could see veins of different color running through. And these different colors would pulsate when the rock was being used for talking. They said it was large. If you were looking down on it, from one edge to the other it would be two hand-spans. It was angled, but the legends do not mention it having a regular shape, although some legends say it was kind of lumpy.

D: *Lumpy? (I could understand angled, but not lumpy.) When they spoke to these other old ones through the void, did any of them ever come to find them?*

B: They tried but they could not find them, and so they did not come.

D: *Do you know what happened to that rock?*

B: No, I do not know. I have never seen it. The wise man might have it. He has other things of the old ones.

D: *Of course he wouldn't know how to use it.*

B: He might. A wise man has knowledge that has been passed down from wise man to wise man.

D: *Did they ever say anything about where their power source came from that they used in these wondrous things?*

B: It is said that since the old ones considered the sun to be so powerful, that they used the light of the sun. That the spear of the sun would pierce the rock and cause the rock to be alive. (This sounded like he was reciting something from memory.)

D: *Is this the same as the sun spear they used to kill the animals?*

B: They had a different … tool for that.

D: *Then each one was used for a different purpose.*

B: There is another legend that says that sometimes the old ones would talk to a wall, and the wall would answer.

D: *A wall?*

B: Like a wall of a room. And the wall would answer, as if there were an old one standing on the other side of the wall talking. Some legends mention that there would be a particular part of that wall that they would touch and it would light up. I do not know of any details. It could be at one time there were details and that part has been lost. Sometimes in the past some of the knowledge has been lost, although we have tried not to lose any of it.

D: *Well, if it's just handed down by word of mouth, things do get lost. But when the wall would light up, did they see anything or did they just talk to the wall?*

B: I am not sure. It has been said that they would see scenes of places far away. Some people who study the legends say that some of these scenes were from across the void. I do not know.

D: *Was the wall in their house or on the ship?*

B: On the ship. There may have been more than one wall like this because the legend just says they would go into a room and speak to a wall. I do not know if it was one room and one wall, or if there was a wall like that in every room. I do not know. I am a hunter.

D: *That's why I like to hear your legends, because it's interesting to try to figure out what these things were.*

(I had to pause while I turned the tape over.)

D: *That gave me a moment to write it down. I write very fast.*

B: You must. Will you be able to read it?

D: *I can because I have the knowledge. That's why I ask so many questions. I'm trying to understand it too and figure out where they came from and who they were.*

B: Yes. But if you are able to figure it out, you are doing better than I.

D: *But it is important that you have kept the stories alive. Do you think it was many generations from their time to yours?*

B: Yes, it is. The legends say it is many, many generations.

Chapter 6

When the Moon Walked
a Different Path

*D*URING ONE SESSION Tuin was on a hunting trip when I asked him to tell me more about the legends.

B: It has been said that sometimes in the past the moon walked a different path than she does now. That is one of the legends. In the old ones' time, it is said that ... (trying to remember) the path that the moon walked and the path that the sun walked were more harmonious than they are now, and the path of the stars, too. For at one time a certain number of the moon's cycles *always* coincided with a certain number of the sun's cycles. I was trying to remember the numbers that were told me. I am not good with numbers. Give me a moment. (Pause) Okay. It is said that there were 12 moon cycles for one year, exactly, *all* the time, *every* year. And the art of keeping track of the paths of the stars and sun and moon was not as intricate as it is now. For *every* year when certain stars would arise, it would *always* be a certain portion of a particular number of moon cycles, from the solstice or the equinox, depending on how far you wanted to count it. And then one time something happened. There were bright lights in the sky and the Earth shook. It was a very terrible time. The crops did not grow that year. Many people were killed and it was during that time when most of our knowledge was lost. The ones that survived knew they had to keep alive the knowledge that they still had, even though it was not nearly what our people once had. And it took many generations for the paths of the moon and stars and sun to settle down again. After two or three generations, the wise men observed the paths and tried to figure out what had happened. They realized that they were much more complex now. The path of the moon and the path of the sun no longer coincided.

D: *It was no longer exactly 12 moon cycles?*

B: It was more like 13 and ¼ or something like that. I do not know, I am a hunter. Before the change occurred anyone could keep track of it. It was easy. The wise man and the elders knew the reasons behind it. Then when the change occurred so many were killed that very few knew the reasons behind it. They ended up dying, to where the wise man was left with very little knowledge to work with. And he tried to figure out what happened to the paths of the sun and moon.

D: *Something definitely must have happened at that time. You said there were bright lights in the sky and the Earth shook. Do the legends say what else happened?*

B: It is said that at one point the paths of the stars and the sun reversed temporarily, to where the sun was rising where it should set, and setting where it should rise. The legends do not say how long the sun was rising where it should set. But after the first time when the Earth shook and there were lights in the sky, the wise man thought the sun was rising where it should set and setting where it should rise. No one could keep track of time then, for all the movements of the stars and the path of the moon were backwards. How can you keep track of what time is passing? And then—it does not say how long—but after a period of time something else happened. The Earth shook some more and the sun once more began rising where it should and setting where it should, even today. But now the paths of the moon and the stars are no longer with the path of the sun. And it was very complex to keep track of it now.

D: *I bet that was a frightening thing to see.*

B: Yes. It is said it was very, very wondrous and terrible.

D: *How did the people die during that time?*

B: With the Earth shaking and such, it was very stormy. They said the winds protested and were crying to the Mother Earth. And they were blowing so hard that they made trees fall down, so people were killed from things falling down and flying in the wind.

D: *Before this happened, were the seasons different? The hot and the cold, were they different than they are now?*

B: (Thinking) The length … they were slightly shorter than they are now and they always coincided with the cycles of the moon. The year seems to have lengthened after that happened, but not by much. To where as now the growing seasons still coincide with the cycles of the moon, but the exact seasons according to the solstices and the equinoxes do not coincide with the cycles of the moon. It is said that the weather was different. That the winter winds came from a different direction and summer was then a bit longer, but not too much different from now. The main difference was the direction of the winter winds that they had to adjust for.

D: *Do you know what direction that was?*

B: No. The legends say that it was warmer. It was not as cold. Life was easier, for the summers were warmer and the winters were not as harsh. There was not as much snow or rain. It was very difficult when the Earth walked a different path and the year became longer.

D: *The days were different lengths?*

B: The days were a little bit shorter but not by much. It was mainly the years that were shorter.

D: *But, you said in mid-summer the days are very long.*

B: That is the way it is now.

D: *It wasn't like that in those times?*

B: Not as much. The days were still very long in the mid-summer but there would still be some darkness. And in the middle of the winter the nights would be very long, but there would still be some light during the day. It is more extreme now. It was not as cold and there was more rain than they have now; less snow than they have now.

D: *I wonder what that light in the sky looked like?*

B: Well, there are several descriptions and they seem contradictory. Some of the light was like the winter light, but very fantastic. In the colors that they come in: red, blue, green and white. And there was many of these to where you could even see them in the daytime. Normally they are there in the winter and you just see them at night.

I thought he was probably talking about the northern lights or aurora borealis.

D: *But during that time there were more?*

B: Yes. And they were seen in the daytime as well, and now they are never seen in the daytime. It is usually at night. Also, there seemed to be a comet in the sky at the time, and it seemed to fly down to the Earth. But it is said that the wise man that translated this thinks they did not actually see it fly down to the Earth, but it seemed to be heading *toward* the Earth Mother. Then when the Earth started shaking and things went bad, the comet was no longer seen.

D: *Do you think it might have hit the Earth?*

B: The legends say it may have. But they look so small in the sky though. You know, you could cover all the parts with your hand and fingers depending on how far away they are.

D: *Do you see many comets?*

B: Not many. One or two. When you first see them they are very small, and you could cover them up with the joint of your little finger. Later on they seem to grow and get larger and cover more of the sky until they pass and get smaller. Then one night the sun sets and you do not see them anymore.

D: *Do these happen in the winter or the summer?*

B: The comets? Either, it does not matter. These comets appear when they appear.

D: *Do your legends say what a comet might be?*

B: No. It is just a star that walks a swifter path.

D: *That would be a good description. You told me there was one group of stars that the old ones were very interested in. Did that also change position in the sky during that time? (See Chapter 9. The old ones were interested in the Pleiades.)*

B: Well, all the stars shifted positions, not just those. The stars themselves stayed in the same position. It seemed like *we* had moved, or they had all moved together. Will you remember these things I have told you about?

D:　*Yes. I want to help so they won't be lost. Have you caught very many animals?*

B:　While I have been talking to you? No, not really. I was enjoying telling you about the winter night-time lights. They are very beautiful. I have been following some deer though. I ought to be able to get some when we are through talking.

D:　*I've never seen those lights. They must be very beautiful.*

B:　They are. Sometimes the women will weave a patch of cloth that hangs on the wall. The lights look like this when the wind is blowing. (He was making waving motions with his hand.) But you can see the sky through them and you can see that there are different colors.

D:　*(I was not sure what he was talking about.) Oh, you mean the cloth is very thin?*

B:　No. The lights in the sky.

D:　*But you said they weave a cloth?*

B:　I was using it to compare with how the lights look in the sky. But you will be able to see them in the sky this winter at night time. Just go look.

D:　*I probably just didn't look at the right time; or didn't go outside when they were there.*

B:　Well, it is cold in winter.

D:　*Yes, that's probably why I didn't see them. Do you ever see those lights any other time of the year?*

B:　Well, sometimes in the dark of night we see them. But in the summertime it stays light most of the night, so you do not see them very much. The sunlight overpowers them. So we mainly associate them with winter because you see them so much in the winter because it is dark.

D:　*What about the fall and spring?*

B:　Well, it is proportional to how much darkness there is.

It occurred to me to try to find out if the legends mentioned dinosaurs or extinct animals. This would help me to date the time of the old ones.

D: *Do you have any legends about animals that might have existed that were different than they are now?*

B: There are many legends about animals. Most of them we tell the children.

D: *Yes. But was there ever a time when the animals were different?*

B: Yes. I am not clear about the details. It seems, if we are listening to the legends, that all the animals were somewhat different. They have changed. There are not big differences, just small ones here and there. So that if one were to go out into the woods with the animals like they were then, it would look subtly different. You would not notice it right away. Some animals would be slightly larger or slightly smaller. Their coats would be slightly different, or some would have a different number of toes on their paws. As I said, subtle differences. And some legends say there were some animals that looked like they were in between animals that we have today. One legend talked about an animal that when it had children, some of its children were very large and some were very small. The large children grew up to be bears and the small children grew up to be raccoons.

This sounded like one of Tuin's stories for the children.

B: That is one of the legends. It is true that the raccoon is little brother to the bear and they look very similar. But it would have been a strange set of parents indeed to come up with such different children.

D: *But isn't the raccoon a different color?*

B: Not that much different. Besides, the colors do not mean that much because the coat color can change with the seasons. It is the build, the way the bones do that count.

D: *Well, doesn't the raccoon have different markings than a bear?*

B: Somewhat. The facial markings are different. But who knows, when the bear had a long tail maybe its tail was striped, too. (I laughed.) We do not know, now that its tail is too short to have any stripes on it.

D: *Are there animals that change their coats?*

B: Yes, there are some. The animal that hops and the animal that pulls its claws back change their coats. I am not sure about the bear. Sometimes it seems that they do, and sometimes I wonder if it is two different bears. Usually bears are black or brown, and sometimes, usually in the winter when it is snowing, I see white bears. It could be that the black or brown ones change their coat colors like the other animals do, or it could be a different bear. It seems like it looks a little different. I have not really figured it out. We only see them in the depths of winter when there is a lot of snow. It is always by accident, so I do not really know where they stay.

D: *Do you have any other legends of animals that were different in the time before?*

B: Let me think. ... Some of the birds used to be different. Their colors have changed, it seems like. If you follow the legends, the changes have been gradual. According to the legends some of the crest of feathers on their heads used to be shaped a little bit differently. Not drastic, just slightly, and it has altered a little bit. Most of the legends about birds are for children, like the one about how the blackbirds came to be.

D: *Yes, you told me that one. (See Chapter 9.)*

B: I really cannot think of any other animals that have changed.

D: *I wonder if there were some kind of animals that are not there any more. Do you have legends about some that have disappeared?*

B: There is a legend about a strange creature; I do not know what it could be. This creature was supposed to be very small and could fly like a bird, but it would sting like a nettle. It is said that this creature liked to sing and it was always humming real high. We have nothing like that. I do not know what it could be.

I thought at first he was talking about a bat, but the singing wouldn't go along with that unless Tuin had the ability to hear sounds that are out of our normal range.

D: *How could it sting?*

B: It was said that it would bite you and suck your blood, and leave a welt behind. They were considered to be very irritating. There were other flying creatures that were small. They would either hum or buzz or they would do some sort of singing. But we do not have them now.

I was trying to figure out what this strange-sounding creature was.

D: This would have been a strange creature because a bird can't bite.

B: It was said that it was as small as the tip of your finger. That is really small for something to have wings.

He made hand motions to show the size. Now I was really confused. It couldn't be a bird or a bat such as I was imagining. Only insects would be that small.

D: Do you have insects where you live? (He seemed confused by the word.) Bugs? (He still seemed confused.) I know you have bees because you talked about honey.

B: Well, we have bees but not many others. ... There are some creatures in the woods that seem to be related to bees. ... What is the word? ... Wasps? ... Is that a word?

D: Yes. That's another kind. It doesn't make honey but it's like bees.

B: Yes. And there are small creatures that live in the ground and the bears like to eat them. But I pay no mind to them. (Possibly grubs.)

D: This one you were talking about that was as small as the tip of your little finger, could it be something like that?

B: Ahh ... not a bee, not a wasp. It is said that the legends also describe bees, and the description for bees are different. Apparently these others were smaller. I do not know how; I have never seen any like that.

D: I was thinking it might have been something like that, rather than an animal.

B: Well, the bees are animals, too.

D: In a way. Yes, I suppose they would be. It depends on which class you want to put it in, which category.

B: They do not have roots and leaves like plants. They do not sit still in the sun. They move around like animals.

D: Well, I always think of an animal having fur.

B: That is one type of animal. Some animals have fins, too, you know.

D: You mean fish? We always put the ones that live in the water and have fins all by themselves.

B: Oh, but that is stupid. They all dance the dance of life and they all sing the Earth's song.

D: *We put the birds by themselves, too.*

B: You are strange.

D: *When I think of animals I think of the larger ones that have fur. Now I can understand your terminology and the way you think about them.*

It was useless to argue against his beliefs and terminology. His logic often seemed to make more sense than ours. When I asked the question about extinct animals I was thinking of dinosaurs and such. I was not expecting him to answer with the description of something as minute as a mosquito, which is probably what it was. His answers were often amusing and always enlightening.

D: *Are there any legends of large animals that may have disappeared?*

B: There is one. I am not sure what it is called. I can describe it. It was said to be as big as a house. It had horns like oxen and large ears. And its nose could not be told apart from a tail. Long fur, lots of fur. I do not know what it could be. It sounded like something ferocious to hunt. I would not want to; it would be difficult. It would supply a lot of meat though. It was said to be very good to eat.

D: *Where were its horns located on the body?*

B: In front. The legends are not clear if they were horns or long teeth. They describe it both ways.

D: *Maybe it was two different animals?*

B: I do not think so. I think it is just something that has crept into the legends.

D: *Were the horns shaped any certain way?*

B: They were curled. They would go out straight and then curl up and around.

She made hand motions. It was obvious he was describing a mastodon or mammoth.

B: In the legends they were said to be very dangerous.

D: *When did these disappear?*

B: When the Earth changed its path.

D: *Were there any legends of anything else large like that?*

B: Not that I can recall. It is said that the cats used to be larger. They are large enough as it is; I do not worry about it.

D: *Do the legends say anything about snakes?*

B: The legends mention snakes. We occasionally see a couple, but we really do not have that many. It is said that when the Earth changed its path the snakes did not like the upheaval from it and so left. The fishes changed. Apparently the waters used to be warmer, and the fishes that liked cool waters better stayed. That is all.

Since the old ones had no legends of dinosaurs they must have crashed after their time, but before the time of some great cataclysm.

I found that there were four major advances of ice during the Ice Age, between which there were periods when it melted back. The last ice sheet disappeared from North America between 10,000 and 15,000 years ago. With the retreat of the ice, many forms of animals became extinct, to be replaced with modern animals. Among those to disappear was the mammoth. In 1989 the nearly complete skeleton of a mammoth was found at 9,000 feet in central Utah, setting a high-altitude record for the extinct mammals. The mammoth was believed to have become mired in a bog at the edge of a glacier 10,000 to 15,000 years ago. This historical information gives us an approximate date for the crash of the Old Ones. Could the catastrophe the legends spoke of have been intense enough to cause part of the Ice Age?

*A*FTER BETH AWAKENED from the deep trance she had a few memories of a scene she had seen. This often happens even with somnambulists. They may not remember much about the session and the story they have been relating, but they will remember bits and pieces, and maybe a certain scene. This is very similar to the way we remember snatches of dreams when we awaken in the morning. She described it to me.

B: I remember a feeling of deep, crisp cold like in the depths of winter and I remember seeing the northern lights, aurora borealis. The curious thing is that I've never seen these in real life.

D: *Neither have I. He said they're most noticeable in the winter.*

B: That's true, but you have to go further north than here [in Arkansas] to see them.

D: *And they were common where Tuin is.*

B: I've heard tell that in our part of the country in the depths of winter, at certain times you'll see traces of them when you're looking north, sometimes during the meteor showers or solar flares. But it doesn't happen very often. Yet I remember seeing them very clearly during the session. They are out at night. They look ... (she had difficulty finding the words) almost like fireworks. They look like ripples of energy. (She made a whirring sound: *rrrrr.*)

D: *Whirling?*

B: This is hard to describe. The major line of it, like the base of it, for example, would be like in a squiggly line. But it would be a series of bright-lit points, with energy running upward from it, like a curtain of energy.

Tuin was trying to describe it and he mentioned something about a curtain, and I couldn't see the connection. I didn't know what he meant, a curtain of streaks or what?

Red, blue, green, violet, white

She then drew a picture of the aurora borealis as she remembered seeing them. She thought this would be easier than trying to describe the phenomenon.

B: It's in different colors. There were deep reds or blues or violets or greens usually.

D: *I've heard of them but I've never seen them.*

B: That's the way with me. And this sight of seeing them, in my mind, seems to be associated with cold weather.

I consulted the Collier's Encyclopedia for information about the aurora borealis. Tuin was correct in describing it as resembling a curtain. They are called "curtains of light," and often appear as draperies.

> *The display usually starts as a homogeneous arc (identical or uniform parts), which is one of the most common forms and has no ray structure. The brightness may be more or less constant in time, or show pronounced pulsations for periods of less than a minute. If the display increases in brightness, the homogeneous forms often break up into rays, rayed arcs, draperies, or a corona in which the rays appear to converge overhead. The "flames" are strong waves of light moving rapidly upward and are often followed by the formation of a corona.*

Although the cause of the auroras has alluded the scientists, it is believed that it is linked with solar flare activity occurring on the sun.

The maximum zone of frequent occurrences of auroras seem to extend around the globe from Alaska, Great Bear Lake, across Hudson Bay, south of Greenland and Iceland, and north of Norway and Siberia. The main land masses where the phenomenon can be seen are Alaska, Canada and Norway. This information helped to pinpoint the location of Tuin's group.

In our present time the maximum seasonal activity is at its peak in equinoctial months, spring and autumn (March-April and September-October). Tuin said it occurred during the winter. Could this be an indication that Tuin was located so far back in time that the seasons were different? Or that the auroras occurred at a different seasonal period than they do now?

Auroras of low intensity appear as white. The colors in our time have been observed as yellowish green, and occasionally violet and red. The colors are caused by nitrogen and oxygen in the upper atmosphere. The atomic oxygens are responsible for both the yellow-green and the red auroras in ray forms. The strong emission of molecular nitrogen are seen in red or violet auroras at the bottom of arc or drapery forms. Tuin saw deep reds, blues, violets, greens and whites when he looked at the auroras. The slight difference in colors (blue for instance) could indicate that the molecular composition of the upper atmosphere in his day contained a heavier concentration of certain elements. It could also mean that Tuin's eyes saw the color spectrum differently.

Tuin's comments about the length of the day and the night during the longest and shortest days of the year again points to his location being in the far Northern Hemisphere. North of 66½ degrees North (the Arctic Circle) there are 24 hours of darkness on December 21, and 24 hours of daylight on June 21. Since his length of days and nights were not total darkness or sunlight, I would suspect that his region was slightly south of the Arctic Circle. This information combined with his mention of the aurora borealis points once again to the Alaska-Canada region. There are parts of Siberia that fall within this area, but I believe because of Tuin's reference to various animals and other identifying factors that he was living in the far northern part of the North American continent.

Chapter 7

The Blanket Design

*A*NOTHER METHOD OF LEARNING about Tuin's people was to ask about clothing. Certain types and materials are distinctive with certain time periods or countries.

D: *Where do they get the material that your clothes are made from?*
B: I am not sure. I am usually hunting. A lot of skins are used. There is a plant that the women use. They get the stalk of this plant, and I think they soak it in water somehow and sometimes beat it between stones. But I am not really sure what the order is. After they soak it and beat it to separate the fibers, they spread it in the sun.
D: *Wouldn't the fibers be very short?*
B: Well, they twist them together to make them longer. (Hand motions) They also get the hair from the goats. It is soft and makes good cloth, but goat hair is short, so I imagine it would take a lot of it. The women have things they weave them on. I do not know how it works though. It is very mysterious to me.
D: *But then your hunting would probably be mysterious to them.*
B: I think you are right. I suggested once—when the women were low on fiber—I pointed out to them that the bark of trees have fiber in them. Why not try that? They agreed that the fiber was there but, they did not know how to prepare it to where it would be fiber and not bark. They said it would be too much work. I am just a hunter, why should they listen to me? But I told them, why not keep it in mind.

Tuin described the plant that was mainly used for the fiber. It was about mid-thigh high, consisting of a central stalk with broad, flat, pointed leaves. These leaves were about an inch-and-a-half wide, coming out of the stalk on four sides in a spiral. The bloom, at the top or crown of the plant, was a small bluish-purple flower with a yellow center, enclosed in a cluster of leaves. The best fibers for clothing were in the stalk. This description fits the flax plant, which has been cultivated since prehistoric times for the use of producing linen.

He said there were various kinds of looms. A large frame was used for the blankets. He used hand motions to demonstrate that they wrapped the fiber around shaped sticks that were passed back and forth. His explanation showed that he had apparently watched the procedure, but did not understand it. Some of the women could weave quite rapidly. There was also a smaller frame that was used to make strips of cloth, such as that used for a shirt or belt or something similar. This would hook to the wall, with the other end hooked to their clothing. They would lean back to keep tension on the material.

D: *Do you make your own clothes?*

B: Usually, except when there is a girl or a lady of the village who wants to become on better terms (smirking).

D: *(Laugh) How do you sew the skins together?*

B: There are fibers in an animal's body that you can use. Fibers that join the muscles, the meat together. You can use this or you can use small strips of skin. And I punch holes in the skin and lace it together. These are skins that have been cured. First I use my knife to cut it into the shape that it needs to be. And lace them together with the small strips of skin or the fiber from the animal's body.

D: *What do you use to punch the holes?*

B: Oh, usually I have a small bone. There are small bones that are sharp. And if I do not have a small bone handy, then perhaps the tip of my knife.

D: *Very clever.*

I was surprised to hear that Tuin also enjoyed doing a type of weaving.

B: Those are the things that I like to do in the winter. The days, or rather the nights I should say, they get long. You must do something. If you just sit there the walls close in. And you know I do not like being under the roof anyway. So one of the things I do is get cords and thongs and tie knots in them different ways and work designs with the knots. I know it keeps me from underfoot, it keeps me out of trouble. Sometimes I keep what I make, sometimes I give it away. It depends on what shape it takes. One lady took one of them and hung it up on some hooks and she uses it in place of a cradle. And someone else took one and hung it from the ceiling. She uses it to divide one of her rooms.

During another session I was able to get information about the plants used for dying cloth.

B: I have been in the woods hunting, but not for animals this time. I was being lazy today. I was hunting for certain herbs and roots for the women.

D: *What kind of herbs did they ask you to find?*

B: Different ones. I find them according to how they smell and how they look. Certain flowers. There is a flower that is light lilac color with a yellow center that they use for something. I do not know what they use them for. And a small white flower with four petals. And different plants like that.

D: *Do they only use the flower?*

B: No, they use the entire plant. I only bring back a few roots. I leave the roots so the plant can grow back. But they like for me to bring the whole plant. There is another one that is a darker purple that they use to stain their yarn to change the color of it.

D: *That one's not used for medicine then.*

B: Umm, yes. It could be, but it is also used for coloring.

D: *How do they do that?*

B: They mix the flowers, and sometimes they use any berries on hand, with a certain kind of bark, usually like oak bark. And they boil it in water and it makes this dark mixture. They put their fibers in it that they are trying to stain this color. When they first pull the fibers out, the color is very dark. But as it dries in the sun the color softens up.

D: *Are there any other colors?*

B: Brown and a light yellowish-green that fades to yellow.

D: *What about white? Do they wear white?*

B: Oh, sometimes, but the colors look prettier. But it is not like the clouds are white. It is more like straw is white.

There are many avenues to explore when trying to establish the locale and identity of an unknown people. A friend, who is an expert on Native Americans, advised me to look for any designs that were used for decoration by the people. Since this type of thing is often passed down from generation to generation, this can sometimes establish a particular tribe. Many designs are common and generically used by several groups of people, but there are also those which are unique in certain areas. I tried to pursue this area of investigation.

Tuin had already described the strange designs that were used on the white headdress that the wise man wore for the summer festival. I asked if there were other types of designs that were used on their clothing or household utensils. He said that the women were quite adept at weaving baskets and blankets and they often worked designs into them.

D: *You said they make things out of some kind of clay? Do they put any kind of designs on them?*

B: Oh yes, always. Usually it is designs that look like lightning, around (hand motions).

D: *Up and down? Kind of jagged?*

B: Yes. And some make vine tendrils and open leaves, and do that around. And some put animals on there. You can use whatever strikes your fancy. It helps you identify it as being your pot because that is your design. You pass down to your children the designs the way they are traditionally, and then you show them that they can change them and do anything with them they like. You show them some of the things you have done. And the person who is learning the craft from you learns the traditional designs and then starts making up designs of their own. And they pass down both ways.

D: *What do the traditional designs look like?*

B: Some designs look like clusters of rocks and some look like the branching patterns of different kinds of trees—sometimes the shape of leaves or just something made up.

D: *Something from nature then.*

B: Or from your mind. Maybe one of the weavers will see the shape
    of a particular mountain she likes and she will make a design based
    on that shape. There is a design that the women have for their blan-
    kets that is called "the old one's ship." It is very ornate, and I sus-
    pect they add a little bit to it each generation. But they pass it down
    as a traditional design even if they have added to it.

Now he had attracted my interest. If they had a design called "the
old one's ship," it just might give me some information on what the
spacecraft looked like. He couldn't find the words to describe it but he
agreed to draw it for me. Normally I am prepared for the possibility of
having the subject draw or write while under hypnosis. But this time I
was caught off guard, so I tried to make conversation with Tuin while I
rummaged through my case for a tablet and a marker.

B: It is the most ornate design that the women weave. I might not be
    able to draw it the way it really looks. I mentioned it because you
    seemed interested in the legends of the old ones. Most of the design
    is made of different colors according to how the light affects. Cer-
    tain parts of the design are always made the same color.

I finally had all the materials. I had Beth open her eyes and handed
her the tablet and pen. She reacted the same as many other subjects who
speak from so far back in time. Although the paper and marker are common objects in Beth's modern-day world, they were completely foreign
to the mind of Tuin. She felt the paper as though trying to understand
what type of a substance it was. Then she examined the pen as though
trying to figure out which end to use. She remarked about how strange
the objects were. I had to show her how to hold it. It was obvious that
Tuin was dealing with an object he had never seen before. He cautiously
made a few marks on the top of the page and remarked, "It is black. I
will not be able to make it the right colors." I encouraged him to go
ahead anyway and see if he could reproduce the design for me. After he
began to draw he soon became accustomed to using the marker. He
worried about drawing it in the correct way, because he said the women

Text continues, Page 88.

made it balanced when they were weaving the blanket. He began at the bottom of the picture and made commenting remarks as he proceeded through the design. It took several minutes to finish because it did turn out to be complicated.

B: This part down here is always made orange or yellow. It is probably a fire. And it is like this on this side too. This is the one part of the design that is always made the traditional color. And out here sometimes they go into curlicues. And sometimes they make these curlicues silver, and this part up here gold. (This was the lower part that resembled fire and smoke coming out of the bottom of the ship.) This is where their imagination does strange things. Sometimes they put little lines up here. Like I said, they get pretty ornate. (This was on the body of the ship, the part that resembled rocket boosters.) Now sometimes they put a door in it, but not like any door should be. (He may have meant that the door was too far above the ground level. It was also a strange shape.) And in the door sometimes they depict fanciful things, just a whim of how the weaver wants to do it. You can really use your imagination. Sometimes they will make pictures of furniture with curlicues added. And sometimes they will make fanciful pictures of the old ones. Usually they will make them very tall and thin, and generally silver-colored. Sometimes they will make a chair of the old ones. It is said it moved and you could lean your head back. And always up here usually some silver star is put. (He drew a star over the doorway.) Except it is balanced. My star is not balanced. I am a hunter.

D: *Is this design repeated over and over again?*

B: Usually it is done as the central part of the blanket or what-have-you. The ornate part around it is repeated over and over, but there is only one boat of the old ones. It is only made once. And then on one type of blanket, this part (the fire and smoke) is extended into increasingly ornate designs. Going into different colors according to different patterns. Then in the rest, (the sky) a sun, but sometimes they will do part of it with stars and moon.

D: *That part (the sky) is dark colored?*

B: Well, it depends on what color they want to use. Stars, they do like that (he made little round circles), but different colors. And sometimes they do them in the designs that the stars are. (Did he mean in the shape of the constellations?) There are a few with more ornate designs according to how the weaver wants to do it.

He had finished. I took the tablet and marker out of her hands, and she closed her eyes and relaxed once more. This is always an interesting phenomenon to observe. It seems so artificial, not natural as it would be if the subject was awake. As though the person was a robot obeying a command in a glassy-eyed manner. In this case, the command to draw, which was an unnatural function for Tuin. When it is over and I remove the materials, it is as though a switch had been triggered and they immediately return to the former trance state. I have often wondered what the other personality would think if it were to notice me or something else in the room. Would it surprise or frighten them to find themselves in strange surroundings when they open their eyes? But this has never happened. For some unexplained reason when they open their eyes to draw or write or look at books or pictures for me, they never notice anything except what their attention is drawn to—the task at hand. This is a good thing because I have enough trouble explaining the writing materials to them, without having to worry about explaining the surroundings. Once they relax again the other personality continues to function within its own environment with no indication that anything out-of-the-ordinary has occurred.

The drawing definitely seemed to suggest a spaceship with fire and smoke coming out of the bottom of its rocket boosters. I complimented Tuin on the drawing. He was not impressed.

B: It is not good. Do not tell any of the women I drew that. They will not speak to me for a season.

D: *(Laugh) No, I won't. Anything that we do is only between us. No one else need know. That ship, is that the shape it is supposed to be? Pointed like that?*

B: Well, that is what they say. I do not know. It has probably been changed through the years.

D: *Because it looks a lot like the shape of a mountain, doesn't it?*

B: Yes it does. According to the legends it might have been more slender, but that is the way it goes.

D: *Then as the women make the designs, they change them?*

B: Yes. Perhaps they do not mean to.

D: *But it's natural to do that. I have heard of some ships being completely round.*

B: How would you guide it?

D: *I don't know. I haven't figured that out yet. Of course, you don't know how that one was guided either, do you?*

B: No.

D: *You have given me a great deal of information, and I am recording and writing it down. No one will know but us. The women don't need to know.*

B: They know it. I have just been telling you what everybody knows. Just do not let them know I drew you some of their designs. I do not want the friendly ones to get mad.

D: *What you tell me isn't any of their business. It's just interesting to me. I like to come and visit with you.*

B: You have been here a few times already. We have done a lot of talking.

D: *But you don't mind it, do you?*

B: No, or I would not be here. I would be out hunting.

D: *I think it's very good that we preserve this history. Then many people will always know what happened to your people. Can I come again at different times and speak with you like this?*

B: If you wish. Just do not tell anybody about the drawing.

D: *No, no. I promise, I won't. It's just between you and me. And it will go into the history. I can show it in that.*

B: Will the women see it?

D: *No, they won't see it at all. I'd like to come again when I think of some more questions.*

B: *You* cannot think of questions?

D: *Well, right now I can't think of any more.*

This seemed to be the only point that bothered Tuin. He was afraid the women would find out about him drawing their designs. During the weeks we worked on this regression he brought up this point several times, that I was not to tell the women what he had done.

An interesting point was brought up later about the shape of the star that he drew on the spacecraft. It is six-pointed, but it is not shaped like the Star of David. It seems to be standing on two legs. I made a mental note to ask more about that later.

Chapter 8

The Hunter's Tools and the ⟨*Animals*

CERTAIN TRIBES can be identified by their arrowheads and implements. So I questioned Tuin about his hunting tools.

D: *You told me once that you use a bow and arrow to hunt. What do you use on the tip of the arrow?*

B: There is a certain kind of rock that you can hit with another rock and shape it to a very fine edge. This rock is usually white on the outside, and you knock off the white layer and it is gray or black or dark green on the inside. Kind of shiny. And it is very easy to be shaped. You have to be careful; it could shatter. But once you get it shaped right, it is not apt to shatter. Depending on what the arrow is used for is how it will be shaped.

A Native American expert asked me to try to get a drawing of the arrowheads. This would help to identify these people. I got the marker and tablet again and had Beth open her eyes. When I handed them to her she again marveled at the materials and tried to figure out which end of the marker to use. I waited as she began to draw. She drew the pictures of several different shapes of arrowheads. The first had what appeared to be two hooks, one on each side. He explained that this was so it could be bound to the shaft. It didn't appear to be very pointed.

B: It does not need to be pointed. The edges are sharp like a knife, to where it will pierce the flesh. (He drew one that seemed to be pointed on both ends.) One binds one part of it to the shaft like this. (He drew the binding over the pointed end.) These are small, they are for smaller animals and the shaft is very small and light. It is made to slip into the body of the animal and usually kills them immediately. And some of the farmers use this in a game of skill against fish.

D: *With it having points on both ends, does that make it easier to tie it on?*

B: Well, when you are chipping the stone for it, it happens that is the way it chips. When you are coming with this kind of point, it is easiest just to go ahead and point it at this end, too. (He drew the one with a hook on only one side.) The stonemaker tells me this is the most difficult one to make, because it is apt to try to shatter if you are not real careful and do it just right. He shapes it with a fine edge with the hook at the back side of it. I use it for larger game that is apt to run off after I have shot it. As they run, the point will keep working its way into the body, and this will keep it from falling out. The one with the two points is just for regular hunting. It has sharp edges and so it just goes in. And this is to make sure it goes directly in and does not fall out, until I am ready for it to come out.

D: *I see. Do you shape the arrows yourself?*

B: Only in emergencies. There is an old man in the village who does it very well. That old man has an apprentice. He is teaching him how to shape these rocks. Everyone in the village has their job, so that all things may be done.

D: *I thought maybe you might make the points out of pieces of metal.*

B: Sometimes. But the metal is too valuable and it is often that arrows are lost. So if you are needing a sharp edge for something that will end up being lost, you use something that is easy to be gotten, like a rock, and save the metal for knives.

D: *Yes. If you miss the animal, you can't find the arrow.*

B: (Proudly) I do not miss. I am a hunter. But the animals sometimes run off.

D: *You know your job.*

B: Well, everyone should.

D: *Do you ever use any larger arrowheads? (I was thinking of spears.) Or are these the only kind you use?*

B: Ahh, they are sufficient. One thing that I do to help with the bears. I need an additional, larger one. Sometimes it is hooked or not hooked, but it is larger. I will go ahead and draw the hooked one for you. (He drew the one that looked like a spear.) Usually it is not really an arrow, it is more like a throwing stick.

D: *Is it sharp on the sides?*

B: It is best if it is. It is not as sharp as this one. (The one with two hooks.) This one has the finished edges, it is very sharp.

D: *Do you have something that you put your arrows in?*

B: Usually I have sort of a bag for them. (He made motions as if it was around his waist.) I hang it from my belt.

D: *What about your knife? How is that shaped?*

B: I will have to draw it smaller than what it is. (He drew the knife.) The handle is long enough for the hand, and the blade is about this long (roughly a foot long). Some of them are longer, like this (only a little longer), and heavier. Different sizes for different jobs. The people who prepare the meat use the knives. The ones who prepare the skins also use them, but they can also use stones. Some of the knives just have an edge on one side and some have an edge on both sides. The ones that just have an edge on one side, we usually have a special piece of leather that we can put here, like this, to pad the hand so it can be used for scraping the skins. (He drew the piece of leather on the side of the knife.) You just wrap that on there when you need it.

D: *And this knife was made from the metal from the old one's ship?*

B: Yes.

D: *These are the only kind of weapons that you use?*

B: Yes. And sometimes there is a way of throwing stones when you do not have an arrow in hand. You have a strip of skin that makes it easier, so that you can throw the stone.

I took away the tablet and marker and she closed her eyes again.

D: *It looks like these are quite sufficient. You can do all kinds of things with them.*

B: Yes. They get everything done that needs to be done.

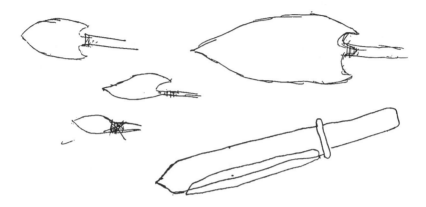

Tuin's hunting arrows and spearheads seemed large compared to normal Indian finds. Then I came across an article in the October 1988 issue of *National Geographic*. This was the story of the discovery of the famous Clovis Points. These spearpoints were made from chert (a flint-type rock) and chalcedony (a translucent quartz), and were found in a farmer's orchard in central Washington state. They are believed to be the oldest artifacts ever found in the New World. The archaeologists think they are the work of the Clovis people, a group of hunters who pursued Ice Age mammoths and other animals into the area nearly 12,000 years ago. The largest of the spearheads was nine inches long, so it would seem that Tuin's hunting equipment were of a similar nature.

I thought one method of discovering where Tuin and the village were located would be to identify the animals and plants native to the area. At least it would help zero in on the correct part of the world.

D: *You said you have oxen there? Do you have any other tame animals?*
B: Ah yes. There is another animal one person keeps to provide milk

for the infants when their mothers dry up. It looks like the goats that are up in the mountains but it is smaller, has little horns. We would like to try to keep some of the mountain goats in the village, but they keep wandering off. All the women say that the hair would make good blankets. It is thick and matted. But they are hard to catch; they are never amiable. The males have horns that are very thick and hard, and they are ridged. They curl like that. (He made hand motions. The horns curled backwards like the big-horn sheep.) When a goat is killed, when any animal is killed, everything is used—the hoof, the bones, any horns, the skin.

D: *Nothing is wasted then.*

B: The mountain goats are very agile and they are well developed for climbing the mountains. This smaller goat this person has—it does not climb mountains. It is always getting into trouble.

D: *(Laugh) Is there just one or does he have several?*

B: I am not sure how many.

D: *Then he milks these?*

B: Is that what you call it? I had wondered. I knew that he got the milk from the females. But I am usually hunting when he is taking care of his goats.

D: *Do they get milk from any other animal?*

B: The female oxen, but it is not really used, except maybe for cheese for the winters.

D: *Are the oxen ever eaten for food?*

B: (He interrupted with an emphatic...) No! That would be stupid. There's not enough of them to kill. The farmers could not farm without the oxen. If we run out of meat then *I* go out into the snow and try to find an animal, or we just eat vegetables for awhile.

D: *What are the oxen used for?*

B: The farmers use the oxen to pull things. Whenever they need to get a rock or a stump or something out of the way they use oxen to help pull it up if need be, and to drag it out of the field. The oxen are stronger than men.

D: *Do they have horns?*

B: Yes. They are almost straight. (Used hand motions.) Pretend that

I am an oxen. Two horns on each side and they go out like this.

He held his arms out to the sides as far as they would go. I got the impression of big horns going straight outward.

D: *Do the male and female both have these long horns?*
B: Yes.

I was thinking of a yak since the horns did not sound like a water buffalo.

D: *Do they have long fur, too?*
B: In the winter.
D: *You told me you thought the oxen might have been brought by the old ones.*
B: The legends say they were.
D: *It must have been a large ship to carry so many things.*
B: It was said to be large.
D: *Do you think the small goats might have come from somewhere else?*
B: I am not sure. I do not know. He might have brought some goats from the mountains to start with. But they do not look like the ones from the mountains. You can tell they are both goats but they do not look like the same kind. They are smaller and not quite as shaggy.
D: *Maybe a long time ago they might have taken some and tamed them.*
B: Perhaps. I do not know.
D: *Have the people in your village ever thought about taming any of the wild animals so they might help them?*
B: Help them? How do you mean?
D: *Well, you use the oxen for different things. Have they ever tried to tame any other animals to help like that?*
B: It has been talked about. It has not really been done. The one with the goats said he would suggest they try to use the goats, but they were kind of stupid and stubborn. Anyhow, there has been some talk but we have not really seriously considered it.
D: *Have you ever thought of taming a wild animal?*
B: Probably a bear would be good; they are strong. But that would be difficult to do.
D: *Sometimes it makes your work easier if you use an animal to help you.*
B: Yes. ... How would that affect hunting though?

D: *What do you mean?*

B: Well, if one tames the animals and uses them to help you work, then what would you hunt? What would you eat?

D: *You wouldn't tame them all, just a few.*

B: Oh.

D: *The oxen are already tame, aren't they?*

B: Well, you have to train them when they are young. But yes, they are not like the wild beasts.

D: *They're not that hard to tame?*

B: Not if you know how, but then I do not know how. I am a hunter.

I was trying to think of other tame animals that they might have.

D: *Do you know what chickens are? (He shook his head.) It is a type of tame bird that is raised for meat, and some people eat the eggs.*

B: The eggs of the birds are so small. Why eat them?

D: *Do you eat birds?*

B: Not often. They are so small, not much meat.

D: *Some places in the world there are larger birds and they have larger eggs. That's why I wondered if you had them where you live.*

B: No, just the birds that are in the trees. There are slightly larger birds—hawks and such—but one does not eat them. They live up in the rocks. They are hard to get to. Deer is easier to get when you need meat.

D: *What about wolverine? (He had mentioned this animal earlier.)*

B: The wolverine does not ... the fur is good, the meat, ah, not as good as deer. But when one needs the meat, one needs the meat.

D: *It doesn't matter what it comes from.*

B: Yes. Deer is better. Bear is good.

D: *Is there anything else that you would kill for meat?*

B: Ah, a small animal. I am not sure what it's called. It has long narrow ears and it is furry. It has strong hind quarters. It tends to leap or jump instead of walk. It has a short tail with a lot of fur on it. They are small but can be good meat.

It was obvious this was not coming from Beth's mind, because she could certainly identify a rabbit.

D: *Oh yes. I've seen those. They are good but it does take a lot to feed many people.*

B: Usually I am the one who eats them when I am out hunting. We eat whatever comes along, but deer and bear are the most common.

D: *Do any of the animals ever come down into the village and attack the people?*

B: Sometimes in the spring when the bears first wake up and they are hungry—they will wander in. But bears are not harmful. They like berries more than anything. If you stay in harmony with the Earth you are in harmony with the animals and the animals are in harmony with you. And they do not come, for they know if you are in harmony there is nothing there for them.

D: *But you said before that your people built little shelters on the houses for the children to sleep in and to keep the animals out.*

B: That is usually the bear. If there is a doorway that is open and the bear smells something that it likes, like berries or something, it will come in to find them. Bears are always hungry.

D: *Are the bears large?*

B: Oh, they are bear size.

D: *(Laugh) As tall as you?*

B: When they are standing on their hind quarters they are taller than me. When they are on all fours, they come up to about right here (to his waist). But the bears are gentle. If you know how to treat a bear you do not have to worry about it.

D: *Do you eat the bear?*

B: Yes. Particularly in winter. It has to be prepared carefully, of course, but basically the bear is a clean animal. And the bear skin does very well for making things.

D: *I've heard there are some animals that sleep during the winter.*

B: That is true. We see them occasionally but not often.

D: *Is this one reason why it is difficult to find meat in the winter?*

B: Yes. Another reason that makes it difficult is that one does not want to go outside anyhow. It is too cold.

D: *Do you have very many animals that crawl?*

B: Mostly down at the river, and you only see them in high summer. In the water, sometimes on the banks—eels, salamanders, such as that.

D: *Do you have what is called "snakes"?*

B: Yes, usually they are black.

D: *Are there any that will hurt people?*

B: When you are in harmony with the Earth, you do not have to worry about them.

All this talk of harmony was beginning to sound like a broken record.

D: *But I meant, are there some that would hurt you if they would bite you?*

B: There is a type that would, that rattles its tail. But usually there are not many. When the weather gets cold they cannot move very well.

D: *But you don't worry about them even though you run around out there barefoot?*

B: They are so small, and they never move very fast. They are usually harmless.

D: *Turtle. Do you know that word? They have a hard shell?*

B: Oh yes. He is the one who carries his house with him.

D: *(I laughed at this definition.) Do you ever eat the turtles?*

B: No.

D: *Do you have what I would call a wolf?*

B: Yes. They are large animals, generally about as high as your waist. They have powerful shoulders. I do not tangle with them. (Either they were large or the people were small.) They pull down the weaker deer and such as that in the winter.

D: *Have you ever had to eat wolves?*

B: No, not while I have been a hunter.

D: *What kind of markings do they have?*

B: They are generally brownish in color with darker markings along the fringe of their tail, across the shoulders and accenting their face and the tips of their ears. Except in winter, they are white in winter.

D: *One time you mentioned a boar.*

B: Yes. You find them in the woods. (Distastefully) It is mean and ugly, although it sings the Earth's song too. Usually it is just above knee high. It has bristly hair and a short tail. Sort of scooped-looking ears, and the eyes are small and red. And its two bottom teeth are usually up over its snout.

D: *Hmm. Are they dangerous?*

B: (Emphatically) Yes! They are short-tempered. But you can hear them and you can feel them, so you can avoid them. You can eat them, the meat is very tasty, but one has to cook it carefully. The legends say that if it is not cooked carefully, it could disrupt the song of your body and produce discord.

D: *I wonder why one animal's meat would be different than the others?*

B: Most animals eat either plants or other animals, and we eat the animals that eat plants. But this animal eats both without caring. It will eat anything. So it is said that its meat must be prepared carefully, such as with other animals who also eat meat. They must be prepared carefully as well. They do not taste as well. I am not sure why. The legends help us.

D: *Have you ever eaten the meat of the sheep?*

B: Oh yes. It is good meat. The animals that eat plants have the best meat. The meat of the flesh eaters is too strong. It can go bad easily.

D: *Oh, it spoils in other words?*

B: Spoils?

D: *That's a word I use. It means that it goes bad.*

B: Yes, some animals even if it is fresh killed, it tastes like it has gone bad.

D: *Which animals are these meat eaters?*

B: There are different ones. The animals with the claws that they can pull back. We do not like to eat them.

These remarks about their meat-eating habits sounded strange until I began to think about our own. We also only eat animals that are plant eaters. There are several types of meat that have to be prepared carefully in our time—pork, for instance. If it is not fully cooked it will cause dangerous illnesses. I had never thought about it before. Maybe there is a health reason for not eating flesh-eating animals. This also goes along with the dietary laws mentioned in the Bible. I have always thought this was the reason for forbidding the Jews to eat pork. These dangers have been known since the beginning of time, but the reasons would have been too complicated to explain to people before the discovery of germs and microbes. It was simpler to tell people the meat of certain animals were unclean, and to forbid their consumption.

D: *I remember the time you told me about the strange animal that you killed. But you said its meat was all right, wasn't it?*

B: It tasted peculiar. We cooked it very carefully. We did not know
    if it was a plant or an animal eater. We assumed that it was an animal
    eater, for safety's sake. We cooked it carefully and nobody died from
    eating it. It just tasted very peculiar. One could not define it if it was
    the meat of an animal that walked or an animal that crawled. Some
    animals that crawl instead of walk taste different. But animals that
    walk on four legs taste like the way they taste. And with this animal,
    you could not tell whether it was a walker or a crawler or a swimmer.

D: *When you found that animal, were you guided to him by that same feel-
    ing in your head that you described in me?*

B: Yes I was. The feeling seemed different that time. Instead of being
    here like this (in the middle of her forehead), it seemed to be more
    like this (he pointed to both sides of his forehead instead of the
    middle). And I knew that it would be a different sort of animal, but
    I felt I would probably recognize it. I was surprised when I did not
    know what it was.

D: *Have you ever seen another animal like that since?*

B: Never.

D: *You were lucky that it wasn't angry. You said it had such claws and fangs.*

B: Well, I was quiet and in harmony. It did not know I was around.

D: *I have heard sometimes that there are animals that are deformed. They
    come from a strange mixture, and there would only be one of a kind. Do
    you know what I mean?*

B: Yes, like the farmer with the goats. One time a kid was born with
    a crooked leg. Sometimes I have seen strangeness in some of the
    animals, but you could still recognize the animal. Even if it had two
    different parents you could tell what the parents were. One time I
    saw one of the mountain creatures ... one of the meat-eating crea-
    tures with the claws that they can pull back if need be. They usually
    have yellow eyes, small ears, long tail.

D: *Yes, I think I know what you mean.*

    It was obvious he was referring to some kind of cat.

B: There are two different kinds and one time I saw one that was a
    combination of the two, so I knew that its parents was one of each.

D: *What do these two different kinds look like?*

B: One is kind of a golden mottled color—tawny-looking. How shall I describe it? It is golden-colored with a darker golden brown on its tail. It blends into it. And sometimes it has darker ears. It is about knee high but it is long and very graceful. The other one looks different. They are generally kind of a gray, bluish-gray color. They turn white in the winter. Sometimes you will see one that is almost black but usually they are gray-colored.

D: *Are they as large as the other one?*

B: More compact, bulkier. Maybe a slight bit taller and not quite as long, but they are just as graceful. They are more heavily muscled, it seems like. The golden ones have slender muscles that give them this particular gait. And the gray ones are chunkier built. They are graceful too, but in a more compact sort of way.

D: *They're not as big as a deer?*

B: No, they are not as tall as a deer, but they are more than strong enough to pull a deer down.

D: *How did you know that animal was a combination of these two?*

B: Because of how I saw him; he was only knee high and kind of long-bodied. He had a gray coat, but his coat was mottled with silvery designs. That and the tail went gradually to black. That told me it was a combination of the two, because it had the build of one and the basic color of the other, with the color characteristics of the first.

D: *I see. Do you ever kill these animals to eat?*

B: Only in winter when we need it. There are not as many of them as there are of deer. I am afraid that if I were to kill them the deer would become too numerous and they would starve.

D: *Yes, let nature take care of itself.*

B: Be in harmony.

D: *I was thinking that maybe the strange animal you saw with the horn in the center of its head might have been something like that. A strangeness, or a combination of something else.*

B: I disagree. Please forgive me. I considered that, but I could think of no combination in the animals that I knew that would come up with that one. And besides, with the feeling in my head being different, the animal was not in harmony with the Earth. I feel that perhaps the animal ... well, there is a legend that says this Earth is not the only one. There are several here and sometimes we might go from one to the other without knowing it. And I feel that on that winter day—it was dark—that I inadvertently went into the other Earth where these animals are, because everything felt different. The land was the same but the harmony was different. The wind even sang differently. But I needed the animal for the village. And then when I was going back to the village I felt things change again and everything felt right again.

D: *Maybe it was allowed to happen because you needed the meat.*

B: Perhaps so. One of the older men at the village believes that it happens quite often without our knowing about it, for some of the earths are closer to ours than others.

D: *You never know; anything is possible. Maybe these aren't just legends.*

B: Perhaps so. I tend to believe so. But if I go around saying to every-body that it is so, they might think that my wandering in the woods has affected me. They might say that anyway.

D: *(Laugh) That's true. But the wise man knew there was something different.*

B: Oh yes. I had never seen him react that way before to any of my kills.

D: *So it was something neither of you had seen. But your ideas seem to sound right. It could be.*

B: You are very diplomatic.

I was accumulating a great deal of information about Tuin's life and surroundings, so I thought it was time to present it to a professional. I asked my friend, Richard Quick, a retired zoologist, to read it and to give me his opinion. The following are his notes:

Notes on "The Starcrach Legend"

As I read the manuscript, I tried to make a compilation of all the stated characteristics of the environment and culture as they were reported by the subject. These characteristics could then be used to attempt to pinpoint the historical timing of the events and perhaps the physical location as well through the process of elimination.

I found the following items related to the culture of the people in question: agriculture or farming was utilized, including the use of grains, as well as vegetables, roots, wheat, beans and herb gardens. Peaches, apricots and acorns were taken from trees. Bread was baked from grains. Crops were planted before March 21, and fields were plowed.

The people made clay pots, did weaving and had written language. The only metal they used was that left from earlier times.

Their houses were wood with a grass roof, windows and shutters, and in the village was an inn with a sign over the door.

Regarding domestic animals, they had no dogs, but they knew of sheep, oxen (yoked together) and goats.

Environmentally, they knew of honeybees, mosquitoes, deer, wolverine, boar, bear (not grizzly), squirrel, flying squirrel, two types of cats, and a wolf that changed color with the seasons,[†] turtles, salamanders, eels and frogs. Crow, swans and bluebirds were also mentioned. The subject *correctly* characterized bees as "animals."

The trees in the area included oak, pine (two types), hickory, spruce and cedar.

Their clothes consisted of wool pants, a cloth waist wrap, leather vest, a leather cap with a brim, wrap-around skirt, and amulets. They were familiar with gold and gems.

They slept on beds with legs and stretched deerskin. They used tables and benches.

The mountains nearby had peaks with perpetual snow. During the longest day of the year, the night was only like dusk.

It seemed apparent that the geographical location of the group was the Northern Hemisphere. Many items that made the culture inconsistent with what we know of the natives from the northwestern part of North America could be explained by the influence of the star travellers in the distant past: domestic animals, written language, beds, cultivation of grains, and the use of metals.

The strange horned animal mentioned in the text has no known counterpart in the natural world we know today.

(Richard Quick, 1 November 1988)

[†]In present times, the only canine that changes color with the seasons that I am familiar with is the Arctic Fox, which changes from grey to white and back again. This also occurs with certain rabbits and certain members of the weasle family. I don't know of any feline that changes coat color seasonally. Because it is biologically possible, it may have been a characteristic in the past. Fossil and bone remains would not be able to determine such things as coat color.

Chapter 9

The Children's Stories

D: *I think you told me one time that the stars play a very important part in your culture, in your life. Is the wise man the only one who knows how to look at the stars?*

B: Well, everyone knows the stars' shape and what they are called. The wise man tells us things about the stars that seemingly do not make sense. But he says that the old ones knew these things because of their magic eyes. One thing that he says, is that the stars are all different colors like the flowers in the field. Well, it is true that some are red, but not many. Most of them are a kind of bluish-white color. But he says they are different colors and I suppose they are. He says that sometimes stars have clouds on them like the Earth has clouds, and the old ones said that is what caused it to lightning and storm. The sun would form clouds on it which would cause Mother Earth to form clouds in sympathy and it would storm. I have never seen clouds on the sun. It would be too hot to have clouds there.

D: *It would seem like it. Is that what he meant? That the sun would form clouds?*

B: Well, perhaps there used to be another word for it, but he likens it to clouds now. The legend says it darkens part of the sun.

D: *It's so hard to see the sun to tell these things. Then this is what makes the rain on Earth?*

B: Not always, just whenever it happens on the sun. It only happens very seldom. But when it does, yes, it causes rain on the Earth as well. That is what the wise man says the old ones said.

D: *What else did they say about the stars?*

B: Well, as you know, when you look at the sky the things move across the sky. When they go below the horizon they keep moving even when you cannot see them and so they move around the Earth Mother. That is what it looks like when you look at the sky. But the wise man says that it is not that way. He says that the Earth Mother really moves around the sun. And that there are mother earths moving around the other stars, too, but you cannot see them. But I disagree with the wise man there. I know what I see. And I can see the things going around the Earth Mother following the cycle of the seasons.

D: *Was there anything else they would see with their magic eyes?*

B: Well, there are the wandering stars: the sun, the moon and three or four others. Depending on how the weather is, depending on how many you can see. All the other stars stay the same and they move around with the seasons and to each other, but you can see these wandering ones move from day to day. A wandering one will go across and change its position with the stars. The wise man says that the old ones could see other wandering stars with their magic eyes that we cannot see.

D: *Did they have any explanation for why they wandered like that?*

B: I am not sure. I think I heard the wise man say once that there were other earth mothers, like our Mother Earth, going around the sun. I do not know. They are too far away to see if it is like us or not.

D: *Did the old ones leave any other legends or any information about the stars in the sky?*

B: Yes, there are different legends about the stars. The most common legend is that the stars are like the sun but they are far away. Like building a fire and then walking away from it, it gets smaller. It is said that when the universe started its song and the stars started their songs, part of the song was to have other earths, like this earth is with the sun. And so the wise man says that, to take it further, if there are earths singing their song there, there must be people on their earths in harmony with the earth, since the old ones came here. It is a legend. It makes sense in a way, but I do not understand how it could be.

D: *What don't you understand about it?*

B: Well, the people are here. The stars, they are in the sky. I do not understand how we could get from there to here or from here to there. I do not understand how it could be. But the stars are in harmony with the Earth and everything is in harmony.

D: *That would be hard to understand. Some kind of magic, maybe. But then the legends are just interesting stories, aren't they?*

B: The legends are the old knowledge.

D: *Does the wise man know how to look at those stars and tell things from them? (I was thinking of astrology.)*

B: Everyone knows how to look at the stars. How do you mean?

D: *Well, what information do you get from looking at them?*

B: The farmers can get, in addition to the moon, when to plant, and when to harvest. The stars tell many things. The stars help tell when the festivals will be. The sun, as it dances through the stars, one knows the passage of the seasons.

D: *But the other stars that stay the same are in different parts of the sky in different seasons. Are there any particular ones or groups of stars that you watch that tell the seasons?*

By checking the position of certain known stars it might be possible to determine where these people were.

B: Well, one thing you do; you go by how they are positioned against the mountains around the village. That is usually how we tell. Also, some appear in some seasons and go away, or go to sleep, depending on which legend you follow, during other seasons.

D: *Are there any kind of stars in the sky that stand out more than the others; that are more noticeable?*

B: The stars follow in a great circle and there is a point in the sky that they seem to center around.

D: *Is there any one star that is brighter than the others?*

B: (Hesitated as though thinking.) Different brightnesses. Different shapes. It is like looking at the clouds and you see shapes in the clouds. You can see shapes in how the stars are.

D: *Do you have any names for these groups of stars that you watch all the time?*

B: No. The wise man has some names but usually we just have descripπtions and everyone knows which one you are talking about.

D: *What are the descriptions?*

B: There is the seven jewels. That is where the old ones are said to come from. (Smirking. A disbelieving tone of voice.) Well, anyhow, it is said that the old ones felt that this particular group of stars were important for some reason. There are seven of them clustered together like in a small cup. Some refer to them as the seven jewels, but I think it looks more like a cup. There are three vessels in the sky. There is a large cup with a long handle, and a smaller one with a long handle. And there is this small cup. This is the one that the old ones felt was important.

D: *Seven little stars crowded together. (He was obviously referring to the Pleiades.) What direction is that if you were looking up at the sky?*

B: It depends on when you look. It travels in a great circle.

D: *All right. Say it's in the summer.*

B: (Pause) In the summer, it is … almost directly overhead.

D: *I wonder why that little bunch of stars was important to the old ones?*

B: I do not know. The wise man would know. And then there is … let me see, I do not ever call their names. I know them by looking at them and I am not accustomed to their names. I will have to think for a minute. There is one—well, a cluster of stars, I should say, but they are called the bird. And there is another cluster that is called the fish because it seems to be jumping out of the river of stars that run across the sky.

D: *Oh, is there something that looks like a river of stars?*

B: Yes. There is a band of them that goes across the sky. (Obviously the Milky Way.)

D: *Is this fish in the sky at a certain time of the year?*

B: In the fall. We see a hunter, he has wounded an animal and the animal is at his feet. And he is in the process of killing the animal. He also has a quiver of arrows hanging from his belt.

D: *Yes, I think I've seen that group of stars. (Apparently Orion.) I think we probably look at the same sky.*

B: It sounds like it to me.

D: *But you watch these stars and whenever they are in certain positions you know when it will be summer and winter. Is that right?*

B: Yes. But, of course, one knows by how many moons it has been, too. The farmers in particular have to know when the seasons are coming.

D: *You have already described the dippers.*

B: (She looked confused.) Dipper?

D: *Or did you call it that? Like a large spoon?*

B: Spoon? (Pause) There are the two shaped like cups with handles. These two groups of stars also remind one of an animal like a bear. Ahh … there is the big bear and the little bear.

D: *Yes, that might be what I'm thinking about. But they have long tails, don't they?*

B: Well, bears used to have long tails. That is what the legends say. Some will have partial tails now, but the legends say they used to have beautiful tails. And they were kind of "vain" of their tails. There are different legends, different stories according to what happened. One story says it was in the wintertime and the bear was hungry for fish. So he chopped a hole in the ice, or rather the fox chopped a hole in the ice. The fox has a beautiful tail, you know. He was tired of the bear having such a beautiful tail and being so vain. And so he got a large stick and he poked a hole in the ice, and he told the bear, "Well, gee, I know you are hungry for a fish. I know a way you can get a fish." The bear says, "How?" The fox says, "Go over there and stick your tail down in this hole in the ice, and when a fish comes along he will bite your tail and you can pull it out." And the bear said, "Well, all right, that sounds good to me." It was a dumb bear. And so he sat down on the ice, and while he waited the ice froze up. Meanwhile the fox had gone away and the bear got tired of waiting for a fish to come bite his tail. So he tried to get up and pulled his tail off.

D: *(Laugh) That sounds like a story you would tell the children.*

B: It is.

D: *Do you have any others like that?*

B: Oh yes. There is another one about a bear that liked honey so well that he would do anything for honey. *Anything* for honey. And one time he found a bee tree. But he reached and he reached and he could not get his arm in the hole to get the honey. But his tail could fit in the hole. So he stuck his tail in to get the honey, then pulled it out and was licking the honey off. And the bees got angry. They realized that someone was stealing their honey. So the next time he stuck his tail in the hole they started stinging his tail and made it swell. When he tried to run away his tail got left in the tree.

D: *(Laugh) Two different stories of how he lost his tail. I bet the children like those stories. Tell me another one. Not so much about the bear but about anything like that.*

B: (Pause) Do you know how frogs became to be?

D: *No. Tell me.*

B: One time there was this beautiful swan-type of bird. A bird who flew but could also swim on the water. And this bird saw this beautiful fish. Now ordinarily this bird *ate* fish. But this fish was so beautiful that the bird fell in love with the fish. And the fish saw how beautiful the bird was, and the fish fell in love with the bird. And the bird would go and swim on the water. Every day he was sitting there swimming and the fish would swim underneath and they would talk and spend time together. And they decided that they wanted to be together for the rest of their lives. And they said, "But we cannot make a home together. You, bird, fly in the air. And me, fish, I will swim in the water. We will just have to keep meeting like this. But we will try to have children." And so they had children. They laid the eggs and when their children hatched they were part of both. They could breath in the air or they could breath in the water, like both their parents. They could swim like their parent the fish could. At the same time they wanted to fly but they had no wings. So they kept jumping and jumping, trying to fly.

D: *(Laugh) That way they could live on the land, too. I never thought of things like that. These are interesting stories.*

B: Yes, they help pass the winter evenings.

D: *Are these stories that have come down through many generations?*

B: I suppose. I remember hearing them when I was a child.

D: *Are there any others like that?*

B: Let me think.

D: *They're mostly about animals, aren't they?*

B: Oh yes, oh yes. ... There is a particular black bird that is very noisy.

It is always scolding you and jabbering at you from the minute it sees you until you are out of sight. And then it keeps jabbering for a while. What happened was that many, many seasons ago there was this man who was a good man. But he had this companion that he lived with. And she was always nagging him, scolding him to do this and do that. He was a perfectly good man. He worked hard enough, yet she was never satisfied with anything he did. She had a pointed nose and she would wrinkle her nose and start saying, "You do not do this and you do not do that." The poor man was just in a bad fix. So finally one day he went out in the woods and he was singing to his guide spirits. He was singing so sincerely about the life that he had at home. He was not complaining; he was just saying it was difficult. The spirit said, "We need to do something about this. He is a good man." And so they said, "We will make his wife change." They meant it to be a good change and so they put the change on her. She was supposed to become a good wife and not bother him so much, and not talk so much. But she was so nagging and critical that the change did not take right. And she started nagging more and more, and more shrilly. She did this so much that she quit eating, because she was doing this all the time without stopping. So she began to grow smaller because she was not eating. And as she grew smaller the hair on her head was taking up more space on her body because there was so much hair. And it got to where it covered all her body and turned to feathers. And she flew away, nagging him the whole way.

D: *(Laugh) It turned her into a bird. I like the stories that you tell.*

B: Thank you. You are like a child. You ask questions.

D: *(Laugh) Can you think of any other legends about the animals?*

B: Many, many ... (I laughed.) Almost all the legends involve animals.

D: *Do you have one that's a favorite?*

B: Let me think. (Pause) Have you heard about the squirrel who wanted to be a bird? He loved watching birds fly and he was so jealous because all he wanted to do was fly. All he could do was climb trees like any other squirrel. He would run out to a tree limb and jump off, spreading his arms and legs, moving and tumbling and crashing to the ground. His mother, his father, his family, and his friends kept telling him how stupid he was and he would not listen. Finally, one night he went to sleep and the spirit of the tree came to him and said, "You want to fly, don't you?" And the squirrel said, "Yes, more than anything." Then the spirit of the tree said, "Well, do you mind looking different from the others?" And the squirrel said, "No, I do not care. I look different anyhow because I am always falling to the ground like no proper squirrel should." And the tree said, "Well, in the morning when you wake up you will be able to fly. Run out to the end of the branch and jump off as you usually do. Spread your arms and legs like you usually do, and see what happens." So the next morning the squirrel woke up and without waiting to look around and see what was going on, he immediately ran to the end of the branch and jumped off. He spread his arms and legs like he usually had been doing. But instead of falling straight to the ground, he started gliding and made it to the next tree. He was so astonished he crashed into the tree. And he looked down to see why he was suddenly able to fly. He had flaps of skin between his arms and legs now. And that is how the flying squirrel came to be.

D: *Oh, I like that story. (Laugh) I bet the children enjoy that one.*

B: Yes. We generally tell that story while we are gathering acorns.

D: *Do you have another that is a favorite?*

B: I cannot think of any right now. There are so many of them.

D: *I like those stories. There are many strange animals where you live.*

B: Oh, animals are animals. What are strange?

D: *They're not strange to you because you see them all the time.*

B: Yes. Strange only to children who ask a lot of questions.

D: *(I laughed. I realized he was teasing me.) You said that when the old ones came here some of the animals seemed strange to them, didn't they?*

B: That is what is said.

D: *Did the old ones have any legends of animals where they came from?*

B: It is said that they did, but those legends have not survived. The knowledge has been lost gradually, like when a wise man would be accidentally killed, or take sick or something like that before he had a chance to pass on everything he knew. It must have happened because there are many gaps in the legends. But that is life.

Chapter 10

The Creation Legends

B: It is through the legends that we are able to keep our identity as a people. We pass down to the children the wisdom of our forefathers, and the things that we have figured out. We put it in the form of legends to help make learning these things easier.

D: *Do you have any legends about how the Earth was formed, and how it all began in the very beginning?*

B: Yes. There are legends about the time of the beginning. And there are two or three different stories, I guess you could say. If you look just at them, they sometimes sound like they conflict with each other. But if one keeps in mind about the Old Ones and the miraculous things they could do, then they make sense.

D: *You told me how your people began. Can you tell me those stories about how everything began?*

B: One story that is told is called a "creation story." But I personally think it is closer to the stories of how the Old Ones came here. It is that kind of story, even though it speaks of the time in the beginning.

D: *Do you think they are speaking of the same thing?*

B: Yes, or perhaps in between the time when things were created and when the Old Ones came here. I will see if I can get things in order here. It has been a long time since I have thought of this story, and I want to tell it right. To find out the underlying truth about things, you have to look at what is around you and see how things work together. On a clear night when you look up at the sky you see how it is dark and scattered with stars. One legend says the stars really exist; they are really things. They are not just points of light to look at. And there is this great unimaginable void out there. It is said that the Old Ones could traverse this void the way you and I would walk through the woods. It would be most miraculous. They could travel wondrous distances through this void. They would go from one star habitation to another star habitation. They were not limited to just the village they came from. They could live anywhere they wanted to. And it is said that when they approached our sun, the place where we live appeared like a precious jewel suspended in the void. And that it was round and pretty, which is one of those things you just have to accept as part of the story. I mean, I walk through the woods, and the ground looks flat to me. But they said when you go far enough away from the Earth, it appears to be round. That is the story I was saying I thought was an in-between-type story. Back before there was anything that existed, everything was white. You know how just before the sun comes up and there is light all over but no shadows. That is the way everything was at the very beginning. Nothing existed yet. All there was was light. And the light was divided up into pieces, and these pieces of light became the sun and the moon and the stars. After the light was gathered up into pieces of light, it left dark between the places that were light. And this was where the Earth was formed, in the dark in-between out of dark materials, metal and dirt and such as this. And through the inter-action between the dark places and the light places an energy was caused. And this is how life was created.

D: *Do the legends say how this happened?*

B: They are unclear on this. Some of them just say "and it happened." And some of the others say that something happened to affect the light to cause it to divide up into pieces of light. That somehow a great sound was made and you could feel the vibration of it. You know how you can hum and you can feel the vibration in your chest. Well, this sound was so deep and so great, had you been there you could have felt it through the soles of your feet. You would have felt it throughout your body. You would have felt it everywhere. And the vibration of the sound is what caused the light to divide up into pieces of light.

D: And then this caused the material to form into the Earth?

B: (Sigh) I am not sure how that happened. The legends are not clear. Somehow after the light divided up into pieces of light, there was stuff left over in between that was dark. I guess the pieces of light soaked up all the light. I am not sure. And in the dark places in between there was still stuff that was dark. And so the dark stuff then collected together and formed the Earth and the trees and the plants and animals and everything. There is an order that they did it in, because first the stuff in the dark places collected together to form the Earth. You see, everything comes in balances. And some say that is the reason why the universe came into being, because there was just the light and it was not balanced. So it had to become balanced between light and dark. Then the material that was left over in the dark started dividing up and balancing out also, because the vibration of the sound caused things to keep changing and balancing out. For example, the dark part things collected to form the Earth, so you would have solid and void—a balance. And then on the solid part things again kept balancing out, to where you would have solid and water. Things kept doing this, and as a result that is how life and the variety of things came to be, the animals in the sea, the animals on the land, the plants and everything. Somehow it was to balance everything, and it is a very fine tuned balance. That is why it is important to live in harmony with the Earth, so as to not disrupt this balance. Now at the same time all this dividing and balancing was going on with the dark part of the universe that created the Earth and everything, we believe the light part was also still dividing and balancing out. As a result, there is the light we can see and light that you *cannot* see. It still divides up and balances into other forms of light and energy. And it is said that it has balanced out into as many different forms of light as there are plants and animals and such on the Earth, because everything has to be in balance. And since the dark part of the universe, representing the Earth or the material part, kept balancing out and dividing into many different things, the light part also did the same thing. So there are many different kinds of light, many different levels and such as this. You can only see just a little small part of it. And you either have to have special abilities to see the rest of it, or you have to be very spiritually advanced, to be able to comprehend these other kinds of light.

D: *You said there were two or three different versions of the story. Is that the main one?*

B: That is the most complicated one. It is the one with the most details. There is another version that we first tell the young children. It is the simpler version, so as to not get them confused. As you know, as children grow up and get older, they start asking more questions. And when they start wondering about more things, then we tell them the more complicated version. We tell them the simple version in the form of a story. We say that in the beginning all there was was just this light. No shadows or anything—just this light. But there were also spirits. And the spirits got together and said, "This light is very pretty, but nothing ever happens. We are bored. We want some changes. Let us see what will happen if we make some changes." And they said, "We will make this in the form of a game so that we can learn more about each other and develop and have fun." And as part of the game they said, "We have to set up a place to play our game." So they divided the light up into light and dark. And they made the Earth because they said, "We have to have a place to go to play our game." So they made the Earth to go with the sun. And they said, "We need a light for night time, too." So they made the moon. And then they said, "Everything is set up for the game. Now we need to set up the rules for the game. And the rules for the game are that each player can play as many rounds as they like. Or if they want to drop out for two or three rounds, that is all right, too." So each round in the game is when you are alive here on Earth. Your spirit is here playing the game. Then when you die that is the end of that particular round. If you decide you want to play another round, then you are born again. Or if you want to drop out for a round or two, then you do. And time passes, and later on if you decide you want to play another round of the game you are born again. But when we tell it to the children we add more special effects and make it really interesting for them. We talk about how the animals helped to decide how the Earth should be made.

D: *So the animals had a part, too?*

B: Yes, definitely, because the animals are part of life, too. All life is important. And we do it like we are telling spooky stories to children. (Exaggerated dramatic voice) The bears decided they wanted deep, dark woods, so they could growl in the darkness. And the birds said they wanted a lot of sunlight, so they were given the ability to fly so they could fly up to the top of the trees where the sun was. And the various animals said what kind of world they thought would be ideal, and so they were given the special abilities they needed to be able to enjoy that particular aspect of the Earth. And that way everything balances out.

D: *In that children's version, do they say how the animals came to be?*

B: In that version, when the spirits were deciding they were wanting to play the game, they realized that even though they had this place to go, the first spirits who came here to play the first round of the game found there was nothing but bare dirt. So they said, "This is not a very good game. We are not through setting this up yet. We need some changes." They called the other spirits down and said, "We are not through yet. What shall we do?" And they said, "First, this is nothing but dirt here. We need some water, too." And it was all agreed. "You are right, we need water." And so the rivers and the lakes were formed. And another spirit said, "How are we going to keep this water here? Every time the sun comes up these lakes start shrinking." And so another spirit said, "Why don't we do something really wild. Let's have extra water fall down from the sky." Well, all right, why not?

D: *Yeah, in a story you can have anything happen.*

B: Exactly. And they said, "We have water now, but it is still awfully quiet here." Then the spirits said, "When the wind blows, if it had something to blow through, it would make some sound. So let us make plants and trees, so you can hear the wind blow." And it was decided that would be good. And another spirit said, "The plants and trees are pretty, but something else is needed. What do we need?" They were thinking about it and thinking about it.

Something was definitely missing, but they could not quite figure out what it was they wanted to put in this game that we call life. And back then one of the things that the spirits could do was, if they were to pick up some dirt or clay and shape it into something, they could imbue it with energy, to where it could move by itself.

D: *Oh? To bring it to life?*

B: Most of the time they would do this to small things temporarily just to pass the time whenever they did not have anything to do. While they were trying to figure out what they needed to make this game more complete, one of the spirits got bored with trying to figure it out. So he picked up some clay and he shaped it into a small animal. He shaped it into a squirrel, actually, and imbued it with life. And the first thing the squirrel did was run up one of the trees. It ran out on the branch and started scolding everybody. And the squirrel was saying, "You idiots! Don't you realize what you can do? Make a lot of animals. Make a lot of little things like me that are moving around and having fun and keeping you guys straight, because you are too stupid to do it right all by yourselves. Make a bunch of us to keep you in line." And so everyone decided, "That is not a bad idea. Let us make all kinds of things like that." So they decided they would call that first animal a squirrel. And then they started making all the other animals. Usually at this point one of the children will ask, "But why did they make flies and bees and stuff like this?" And we have to explain to them that always before whenever they would imbue some of this clay with life, it would just be temporary life. And it would just run around doing things until it ran down. But the spirits decided that, to play this game for a long time, these little bits of life would have to keep going, without them having to re-create things all the time. So when they imbued them with energy, they did it in such a way that they would be like people. They could eat things and keep living. And usually someone asks, "What does that have to do with flies?" We point out to them that the birds had to eat something. So they had to create something small enough for them to eat because the bird's beaks are so small. So they created flies and such as this.

D: *I can see how this would satisfy a child and entertain them, too.*

B: Yes. We tell these stories when we are sitting around the campfire in the evenings.

D: *Then what is their explanation, in the children's version, of how humans were created?*

B: Well, the spirits are basically the same as we are; they look the way we do. When they decided to come to the Earth to play their game, somehow as they came closer to the Earth, they became more solid. If a child seems confused about that, we will tell them that we can explain it to them better when they get older. Then we can give them the more complicated version of the story. Then we can explain how the energy divided everything to where it would be balanced. The spirits live out there in the void where it is very light and mostly energy. But as it gets closer to the Earth and the more physical aspect of the universe, the light condenses down into solid physical form.

D: *Then in the children's version nobody had to create humans.*

B: No. The way we came into existence was the spirits coming here. And they simply became more solid as they got closer to the physical world. And because we are all spirits, we all really belong to the higher planes. We are just here temporarily playing this game.

D: *You said the spirits decided the animals had to eat things so they could keep existing. Did they figure that humans also had to eat?*

B: They discovered in the process of playing this game, that when they made rules to apply to the animals, these rules automatically applied to themselves, whether they planned on it or not. The way the universe is set up, things are balanced. Somehow whenever they decided on how things should be, for instance: that animals have to eat in order to keep living, that made it apply to all living things, not just animals. When the spirits realized this was what was going on, they started being a lot more careful about the rules they made. Because they did not want to limit themselves too much, and close themselves in with a bunch of rules.

D: *So any rules they made also applied to themselves. Is that what you mean?*

B: Right. They did not know it would happen that way. Because they were planning on the animals eating and living, and the spirits just flying back and forth playing this game and having a good time. And they discovered that as they made the rules for the place of playing the game here on the Earth, that when they came down here to play the game the rules applied to them, too. And they did not know it would work out that way.

D: *So they had to be more careful. Do the legends say this was before the coming of the Old Ones?*

B: Yes. That was before the coming of the Old Ones. And some of the wise ones, the elders, say that this story of the spirits deciding to come to Earth and play a game, may not have necessarily been *here*. They say there are some older legends that are hardly told any more that explain it. How can I explain this? To keep things balanced the lights had to be similar to each other. When the light was being divided up into pieces of light, each piece of light was similar to the other pieces of light.

D: *You mean it couldn't be very different, it had to be similar.*

B: Right. In order to balance out things had to be similar. So they say consequently it is only reasonable to think that the stars we see up in the sky are similar to the sun, because they are both pieces of light. And so, *if* the stars are similar to our sun, and some of the stories pointed out that the Old Ones could travel unimaginable distances, it would be reasonable to think that for these lights to be similar to our sun, they would have to be far away in order to appear to us the way they do.

D: *Yes, because they don't look as big as the sun.*

B: Exactly. In the evening when you build up the campfire and you start walking away from it into the woods, it gets smaller and smaller. The further away you get and the more trees and such are in between, it gets very small and flickery. Perhaps this is the reason why the sun looks so different from the stars. If this is true, then when the spirits started playing their game, it may not necessarily have been *here* with this Earth and *this* sun. It might have been somewhere else. Then the stories of the Old Ones tell about when they came here. It is really strange that you are taking this all in stride, because some of the more critical members of the tribe do not take the stories seriously. They say they ask you to believe too much that is not supported by what you can see around you.

D: *Do you mean the more complicated version?*

B: Yes. Because some of the people of the tribe are very literal. They say, "No way can the stars and the sun be similar. Anyone with two eyes in their head can tell that they are different just by looking at them." And they think that the elders of the tribe who try to pass on these other facts and other stories are trying to stretch it too far, in order to prove about how everything balances out.

D: *They only believe what they can see. Is that what you mean?*

B: Yes. I do not know which way it is myself. It is very complicated and I get confused trying to figure it out. Many times when I am out in the woods hunting I will go to a clear field at nighttime to camp. And in the summertime, particularly if I know I am in a safe place, I do not build a fire. I keep everything dark so I can look at the stars well. And it is very easy to think that maybe the Old Ones did travel out there. Because when I stare at the stars long enough I get very dizzy and I feel like I am flying. And so if I can have this feeling just by looking at the stars, who is to argue with what the Old Ones maybe could do. They could do many miraculous things.

D: *That sounds like it's possible.*

B: I like to think so, but not everyone goes by what I think either.

D: *You said it was interesting that I was understanding this. I don't know either, but I am always trying to find answers. And I think your stories may have a lot of truth in them.*

B: I do not know. They are very complicated. The elders, the wise ones, the few who study such things, say that the more you study it the more complicated it gets. That there is never any end to it. They like studying it. But whenever they try to explain it to people who do not study it, it is a lot more complicated. The reason why some of the things do not seem to make sense to them is because they do not know everything behind it.

D: *And they don't want to learn.*

B: Right. They do not want to put forth the effort to try to learn the additional complications.

D: *Do you think this is why it's easier to tell the children's version of these stories?*

B: Yes, because everyone knows it is a story and so no one really takes it too seriously. But the other version is just complicated enough that you have to take some of it seriously. It is just enough to make you uncomfortable if you do not want to believe it.

D: *They have to stop and think, and they don't like that.*

B: Yes. Right.

D: *This would make sense. Children's stories would be fun to listen to and you wouldn't have to take them seriously.*

B: Yes, this is true.

D: *Are those the main parts of the stories of the creation?*

B: Yes. I know there is more to it, but I am not knowledgeable about it. It is the elders that get into the more complicated versions of it. Because, as I say, the more they study it the more complicated it gets. And I have not studied it that deeply.

D: *It seems like only a few people would be able to really understand it.*

B: I do not mind explaining things to you. Being out in the woods and spending a lot of time alone, I have time to think about things and to figure out why things should be the way they are. Sometimes when I try to explain these things to some of the people in the village they do not always take me seriously, because they are busy with their own little lives surrounded by people all the time. I do not know you, but when strangers meet, if they are willing to talk about each other, where they come from and what they have learned, there is a better chance for them to get along.

Chapter 11

The Wise Man's House

I DISCOVERED that the information about the Old Ones was not contained only in the repetition of the legends of the Wise Man. There was tangible physical evidence as well. Tuin had mentioned that on one occasion he had been inside the Wise Man's house and had seen many strange things which he did not understand. He assumed they might have belonged to the old ones, but he also knew that the Wise Man had many secrets that the rest of the village did not have access to. He had much respect for the Wise Man and never asked about these things because he thought it best not to appear too inquisitive. They were objects that were definitely out-of-place in his primitive village. I thought if I could get more descriptions I might be able to figure out what they were. He spoke of these things in awe. He clearly did not understand what they could be.

B: I was not supposed to see some of them, I think. The Wise Man has more than one table in his house. He has tables of different heights to hold the things that he studies and uses for various things. It has to do with some of the knowledge he has that must not be forgotten. We do not know how to remember some of the things he knows.

D: *He must be very wise to know all these things.*

B: That is what a wise man is for. He has the knowledge that has been passed down. I do not know how he does it. I do not know if he knows *how* he does it either.

D: *Is there anyone in the village that the Wise Man is trying to pass the knowledge on to?*

B: Yes. He selects the ones who will be good to contain the knowledge and he trains them from early childhood up. He trains more than one to make sure the knowledge gets passed.

D: *Yes, because if anything happened to him, the knowledge would die.*

B: That would not be good. We would not be able to call the spirits then. We would die. Many times he has the women gather particular herbs for him. He has many herbs and medicines in his house, so that if someone falls ill and the usual remedies do not help, he can find another remedy. He has some things on the tables. I do not know what they call them or what they are made out of. It is smooth like water, it is hard like rock, but it is clear like air. And I am not sure what it is. (It sounded like a good description of glass by someone who had never seen any.) When there is a still pool of water on a summer day, you can feel it and it is smooth. This is smooth like that, but it is hard like rock and it is clear like air. He has things of different shapes made out of this. I do not know what they are or what they are for.

D: *But you can see through them?*

B: Unless something is in them.

D: *What kind of shapes are they?*

B: Some are various sizes, long and tall. Usually about this big around and about ... well, different heights. (About as big around as her thumb and finger touching.) And they sat on the table, and appeared to be closed at one end and open at the other. Like a closed fire-tube. (Apparently resembling the chimney he had mentioned earlier.)

D: *Are they attached to something?*

B: Well, he has them all together on a table.

D: *Do you know what he does with them?*

B: I do not know. I just got a glimpse of it. Some had liquid like colored water in them. Different colors, some were light green, and some were clear brown. I do not know what they were for.

D: *Did you see anything else?*

B: There was one thing that I saw—not with those, at another place— it was shaped like the sun. It was round all the way around. Wherever you looked at it, it was round. I do not remember if it was clear like air or not, but it looked like it was smooth and hard. It was too far away. I could not go over there. He would know that I was snooping, and I did not want him to be displeased.

D: *No. You must be careful even though you are curious. Was it very big?*

B: No, it was small. You could hold it in your hand easily.

D: *Was there anything else in different shapes? I am curious, too.*

B: I do not remember everything. There are so many things in his house that this one says that he cannot remember them all.

I wanted to know more about these special objects that were within the Wise Man's house, but it might be difficult to do if we only relied on Tuin's memory. The only way to truly obtain accurate information would be for him to report to me directly from the inside of the house. I decided to try an experiment.

D: *I know a way to help you, if you would like to try it.*

B: Describe to me how.

D: *I can count to three and you would be in his house and he wouldn't know you were there.*

B: (Surprised) He would not?

D: *No. And you could look around and describe these things.*

B: Would he not sense my song there?

D: *I don't believe so, not if we do it right. Would you want to try it? I promise I won't get you in trouble.*

B: We could try it.

D: *All right. I will count to three and on the count of three you will be in the Wise Man's house, and you can look around and tell me in detail what you see of these wondrous things. One, two, three. You are inside the Wise Man's house. He has no way of knowing you are there. What do you see as you look around?*

B: I see many things. There are many frames with herbs hanging from them. He has a ... oh, there is the cauldron I spoke of that changes color. He has it over the fire. He has something in it.

D: *Is he cooking something?*

B: Aw, it does not smell like food—it does not! Probably some medicine. (She was making faces as if it smelled awful.)

D: *Okay, you don't have to smell that. What else do you see as you look around?*

B: I see another room opening from this one where he has the odd-shaped thing, yes, the gray.

Her motions led me to believe he was talking about the thing that had sounded like an instrument panel.

D: *You mentioned that before. You said it was like a square but not quite.*

B: (Hand motions) Well, this way it is square, but this way it is not true square, it has a corner chopped off. (The top edge, *see drawing*.)

D: *This was the thing that was made of metal?*

B: Yes, some sort of metal. It is gray. There are little round things sticking out, and some slender things sticking out. They are all different colors. Bright colors that one sees in different flowers. Mostly red and yellow, a little bit of black.

D: *And you don't know what that's used for?*

B: No.

D: *I wonder if the Wise Man does.*

B: I do not know. He could, or it might be some of the knowledge that has been lost.

D: *Didn't you say there were some other metal things in that room?*

B: Yes. There is an odd-looking metal hat that is round. It has slender things sticking out of it. And it has some dust on it. He must not know what it is for.

D: *Like a hat that would fit on your head?*

B: A little large. It would fit loosely. It would cover up the hair and ears and block the eyes, too.

D: *Block the eyes? How would they see if they wore a hat like that?*

B: I do not know what it is for. (He had difficulty finding the words to describe it.) On the inside there are ... it looks to be small metal hairs, but they are thin and long (hand motions showed them to be about two inches long). They are firm but soft. If you were to put the hat on they would be against your head all over. But it does not look like it would be painful.

D: *Are they like the hairs on your head?*

B: Umm, maybe.

D: *Is there any way to hold it on your head?*

B: I do not know. I do not see. It just sits there. Maybe it is not a hat, but I do not see what else it could be. You place it on the head. Maybe it has something to do with the old ones.

D: *Could be, could be. What color is that?*

B: All colors. The inside is black and the hairs are silver. The outside is a sort of gold color and the slender things sticking out of it are mostly black and silver.

D: *Are there many slender things sticking out of the top?*

B: Well, they are about this long (a few inches). They start out like this big at the base (about as big around as her little finger) and they go up and they get real narrow and come up at the end. And there are … oh, I would say … well, the metal hairs on the inside are too many to count. On the outside, there looks to be … let me count them …

D: *Could you draw me a picture?*

B: It would be somewhat difficult, but I could try. There are about two or three twenties of protrusions. Two or three twenties.

I got the tablet and marker out. I had Beth open her eyes again as I gave them to her. He again marveled at the marker as he tried to figure out how to hold it and use it.

B: It is black.

D: *It is black, yes, it makes marks. Can you draw me a picture of what that hat looks like?*

B: I am a hunter.

D: *(Laugh) That's all right. You did very well the other time. I loved the other picture you drew for me.*

B: (He began to draw the hat.) If you liked that picture, your people must not have pictures.

D: *Well, it was very good for a hunter. Sometimes it's hard to describe things. It's easier to draw a picture; it makes it so much clearer.*

B: The protrusions, they are difficult to draw. They are about the length of the smallest finger. Two or three twenties. And they are all over the whole thing. I will draw some all around so that you may

Text continues, Page 130.

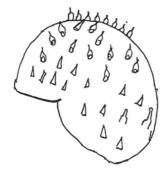

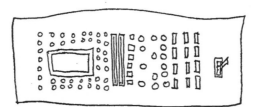

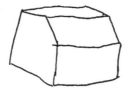

see it. They are close together like the ones I have drawn on top, but I am not a good drawer so I am not going to draw them all over.

D: *That's all right, just so I have an idea. … They're pointed?*

B: Some are and some are not. The pointed ones are easiest to draw. Some are flat and some are pointed. And they are all over.

He finished the drawing so I asked Beth to close her eyes again.

D: *I had the idea they were much larger. See, this way you helped me understand.*

B: They are the size of the smallest finger.

D: *And these cover the entire surface of the hat? And on the inside are all these little hairs sticking down. Is that right?*

B: Sticking in from all around.

D: *That's interesting. Could you draw me a picture of the way that square thing looks? You said it had all those little things on it.*

B: I could try.

D: *I would appreciate it if you could show me where the little things are located.*

B: I am a hunter.

I had Beth open her eyes once again to draw the larger object. I tried to keep her from drawing over the other picture which was on the same page. The sketching was tedious and took her quite a while to finish it. He made remarks such as: "First I will draw a picture of how it is shaped. The small things are round but they sit very straight. They are in straight rows like the farmers' crops."

When he finished the drawing of the instrument-panel-type thing, I asked her to close her eyes again.

D: *You've done a lot of detail in it. You may be a hunter, but I think you draw very good pictures.*

B: There are those who would do it better.

D: *Maybe so, but I can't talk to them.*

B: That is strange.

D: *On this picture, you drew one square that was larger than the others. What does that square look like?*

B: (He hesitated.) It is like a dark gray. It is smooth and hard.

D: *(It looked like a computer or television screen.) Is there any light or anything coming from these things?*

B: No, that one, it is just there. It just sits. I do not know the purpose of it.

D: *It looks complicated. Do you think these are things that belonged to the Old Ones?*

B: That is what is said. And there are other pieces of metal around that the Wise Man uses to make the knives and things. It is a metal that never grows dull. It is very important and precious. We do not know where to find any more of it.

D: *Do the other pieces of metal have any certain shapes?*

B: Not anything particular. Just like there are slabs of rock, these are slabs of metal. Some are large, some are small.

D: *Do you know how he shapes these and makes them into tools?*

B: No, it is said that the cauldron has something to do with it, but that is just a rumor.

D: *He has many secrets, doesn't he?*

B: Yes, he is the Wise Man.

D: *Is he the head of the village?*

B: The head? Oh, he guides us when we need it. But when one is in harmony with the Earth, one does not need guidance. When your song is in harmony with the Earth's song someone else does not need to tell you how to sing.

Chapter 12

The Life of Tuin, the Hunter

THROUGHOUT THE WEEKS that we worked on this regression, I was gaining much information about the Old Ones. But also interspersed throughout was the story of Tuin's life. We were able to follow this by taking him to important days in his life. Since his life was so ordinary and mundane, these times were few and far between. But they revealed a picture of a man completely contented to live a life close to nature among a gentle people.

D: *I'm going to count to three and I want you to go ahead to an important day in your life as you grow older. I will count to three and we will be there. One, two, three. It's an important day in your life. What are you doing?*

B: I have taken on a young apprentice hunter. Today is our first day to go hunting together. I have been showing this young boy how the animals speak to you. What signs they leave. It will be a long time before he learns it all, but he is quick; he is learning well.

D: *You must choose the right type of boy for these things.*

B: Yes, and finally there was one born and he is old enough to learn now.

D: *You don't want your knowledge to die.*

B: It cannot die. It must not die. The village needs meat. And each person must pass on their knowledge to someone who is most suitable to learn it, not necessarily your own children. Everything is important and we must keep all knowledge.

D: *This way he will have many years to learn these things.*

B: Yes, I want him to learn it while I am still strong enough to teach him well.

D: *And in time it just becomes a part of you—very natural.*

B: Yes. We are in the woods. I am showing him the signs animals make and what they mean. I think he may be able to hear the spirits singing on the wind. He seems to hear it best when we are in the trees. He is young still but the ability will develop. I am excited. I had become concerned. I was afraid that no one suitable would be born. But if one is patient all things happen. And I had been singing to the spirits about it.

D: *And you just knew when the right person came.*

B: Yes, the spirits helped me.

D: *Did the Wise Man have anything to do with picking the one to help you?*

B: Yes. It is generally agreed upon by the people. We know who is good for what task. The Wise Man merely confirms what we have observed. And I went to him and told him that I felt the one who is now my apprentice was in harmony with the Earth, and could hear the wind, and he said he would look into it. And he agreed with me after he observed him.

D: *That's very good that you have found this boy. Do you have a name that you call him?*

B: He has his child's name—Haork. [I had her repeat it. Ha–ork (phonetic). The sounds ran together.] When it is found out what the child will do, if the name does not fit or is not harmonious with the spirits, sometimes the name is altered.

Beth had reported a curious incident that happened at her home after our first session. She was outside and a bird was singing near her house. And for a short while she had the odd feeling that it was communicating with her. This went on for a while before the bird just became another bird again. For a brief while she felt in tune or harmony with the bird. The same effect as the wind communicating with her in the dream she had after that session. This could have been a carryover from Tuin's personality. She described it as a pleasant, although curious, experience.

During another session I found Tuin walking alongside the river on his way downstream.

B: I have not been in that direction for quite some time. The game should be good. I rotate where I go so I will not deplete the game in any one particular area, so there will be plenty. It is a clear day. It is early. The sun has just risen. Beautiful sunrise; it is reflecting off the snow, the peaks.

D: *How many days do you expect to be gone?*

B: Probably around three, maybe four. I have not really set a particular time, but I anticipate being gone about four days.

D: *Is that about how long you normally are gone on these hunting trips?*

B: Yes. Generally from four to ... seven or eight days, sometimes nine. Sometimes it is a short trip and I am just gone one day. Yet this time it will be about four days.

D: *If you found game before that, would you go back?*

B: It depends on how much game it was, and the time of year. If it is in high summer when it is warm, I try to get the meat back as soon as possible while it is still fresh. But if it is the way it is now, cool, I can stay out for several days and the meat will stay good. If it is in cool weather and the game is good I may go ahead and shoot more than I can carry back at once. But only the amount that the village needs. I will carry some back and get someone to come and help me carry the rest.

D: *I thought it would be hard to carry it back if you had a lot.*

B: You have to be strong. If I get a bear, I have to immediately cut the bear up in quarters and skin it. Put the quarters in the skin and hang it from a tree. This part is difficult. I get it into the tree where other animals cannot get it, and I will go back to the village to get some young boys to help me bring it back.

D: *I thought maybe you might try to carry the whole bear back.*

B: I am not stupid.

D: *(Laugh) I was thinking that the meat would be heavy. You are not that strong.*

B: No. I try not to kill more than I can handle at the time unless I am close enough to the village to get help easily. I do the best I can. I keep the village supplied.

D: *Are you alone today? One time you told me about an apprentice.*

B: Yes, the apprentice is studying today. I felt it would be good if the apprentice had an idea how the arrowheads are made. Sometimes when you are out on a hunting trip you have to make an emergency arrowhead. It is good to know what to do. So he is with the arrowhead maker today.

D: *How is he doing?*

B: He is doing well. He is learning patience.

D: *Is that the hardest thing to learn?*

B: When you are young. You see, the patience is what helps you be quiet and silent. And it helps you to learn to be in harmony. He is already in harmony. He has learned how to work with the harmony.

D: *What do you mean by being in harmony?*

B: Being able to know how the animals think, to be in harmony with the Earth, with her rhythms. If you are not in harmony you can damage the Earth. That would not be good. She is the mother of us all.

D: *You just have to feel it, and you know where the animals are?*

B: The animals will tell you where they are. You follow ... it is hard to describe. I feel in my head. (He pointed to the third eye chakra area in the middle of his forehead.) I feel *here* where the animal is and I follow that feeling. When I turn toward the animal it is stronger, and I follow the animal down. Plus there are the tracks and the signs. Some people can hunt using the tracks and the signs, and they do an adequate job. But the best way is to follow the feelings in your head and you find the one who is destined to help the village. My apprentice needs to learn to follow that feeling

D: *Does he also have the feeling?*

B: I think he does. He just has not learned to trust it yet.

D: *I have heard of people that follow the tracks and hunt that way.*

B: That is a very shallow way of hunting. I look for the tracks on the ground, whether any branches have been bent or broken, bits of fur. Those are the physical things you find. Then there is the feeling in my head that helps. And the wind, I listen to the wind. It tells me what I need to know.

D: *Where the animal is?*

B: Yes, or where I need to be when the animal comes by.

D: *But aren't there some animals that sleep in the winter and don't come out?*

B: Yes. The bear is one.

D: *Then you just look for the ones that don't sleep during the winter?*

B: That depends on what the village needs. If the food supply is good and we just want a little fresh meat for a celebration or to supplement what we have, I will find some small animals just to supply a bit of fresh meat, so you will not get tired of what you are eating. When you eat the same thing over and over, no matter how good the cook, you can get tired of it.

D: *Do you have one person that cooks for everyone?*

B: No, the women get together and cook things so there is a choice of variety.

D: *Then they don't each eat in their own home?*

B: Sometimes if the weather is bad, or if a woman has her eye on a particular young man. (She smirked and I laughed.) Women are sneaky, very sneaky. She will give him plausible reasons why he should come to that particular place to eat instead of with the group in general. And she will try to have some surprises up her sleeve. (She was smirking. It was obvious what he meant.)

D: *(Laugh) Why, is this what has happened to you?*

B: No. They have tried it. But I have seen it happen.

D: *It didn't ever work with you?*

B: Only if I wanted it to. Because I have these surprises up my sleeve as well.

D: *(Laugh) What kind?*

B: Oh, fun ones. The kind of fun it takes two people to experience.

Of course, they have that notion in mind, too. You usually surmise that.

D: *They wouldn't ask you to come to their house if they didn't have that in mind?*

B: No, they would not. However, sometimes there are one or two women who do that because they want something, and they use you. But that is not very often. They are not very popular so they do not succeed. Everybody knows who they are. They are kind of sour women.

D: *Unhappy, you mean?*

B: I would think so. They do not have as many friends as they could have. But they are not all that *un*happy; they are just not as happy as they could be.

D: *Do they have children?*

B: No, they are sour-pusses.

D: *Maybe that's why they are unhappy.*

B: Well, they brought it on themselves.

D: *Turned the men against them, is that right?*

B: Yes, for some reason they tend to be bitter.

D: *But you said you have no woman that is just yours?*

B: Well, there is one woman that I like to speak with. She and I have an understanding.

D: *But you don't live with her all the time.*

B: No, I just visit her. And sometimes when the weather is good, she will go into the woods with me. She says she is interested in some of the animal lore. But women are sneaky, so I question that.

D: *(Laugh) She's more interested in you than she is in the animals.*

B: I think so.

D: *Do you have any children?*

B: Umm, I think so. I think I have two ... by two different women. But I do not worry about them. All the children are taken care of. And everyone does what they need to do. Everyone is taken care of, and we do not worry about it.

D: *It's more of a group thing.*

B: Right. The children always know who their mother is, and they may have a pretty good idea who their father is. But there is no bind in the womb like there is with the mother. I mean, I could say anything. I could be your father, you would never know the difference. But I could not tell you who your mother was without you knowing the difference.

D: *Well, sometimes they can tell by the hair and skin coloring, can't they?*

B: Oh, sometimes, but when you are just ordinary looking it is more difficult. There are little differences that makes that person that person. Maybe their nose is shaped different, maybe their ears are bent a different way. There is one old man in the village, the children like him a lot, he can wiggle his ears. They think it is funny.

D: *He entertains them that way.*

I decided to move him ahead to an important day in his life as he was growing older. I counted him ahead to that time and asked what he was doing.

B: We are celebrating. We are all very happy. The Wise Man has found someone who will be good to remember the legends. It is noticed when you tell this boy something, he does not forget it ever. And so the Wise Man has decided to tell him everything about all the legends he knows, so that this boy will remember until *he* is old. And we are very happy because we know that the legends will be carried on for another generation.

D: *Is the boy very old?*

B: No, he is only about eight seasons.

D: *Is the wise man growing older?*

B: Yes. His hair is white.

D: *Then it would be very important that he tell someone before he dies.*

B: Yes. There is someone else who has been learning the lore to become Wise Man. And it is decided that the one who has been learning will be a temporary wise man and he agrees with this, for the boy is obviously the correct one. Together they are going to teach the boy to make sure everything is remembered. And so the boy will be a wise man when he is old enough to take responsibility.

D: *Has the other one already been told many things?*

B: Oh yes. The Wise Man has been teaching him everything, but his memory is not as good. He has an ordinary memory, while this boy's memory is extraordinary. But he can help the boy when the boy becomes a wise man, and that way it would be good.

D: *There are so many legends to tell him. It would take a long time to teach him all these things.*

B: Yes, but we are happy that this has happened.

D: *What kind of a celebration are you having?*

B: Ah ... singing, feasting. The songs we sing call the spirits down to protect the boy. And some of the farmers are drinking that drink.

D: *All right. I will count to three again and let's move ahead to another important day in your life as you're growing older. One, two, three. It's another important day in your life. What are you doing?*

B: The one who is my apprentice hunter is becoming a full hunter today so that I will not have to hunt so much. I am getting old.

D: *Is there a ceremony or some way you can observe this?*

B: Yes. In the evening the village gathers around the fire, and I and my apprentice stand on either side of the Wise Man. I tell the villagers that this man, meaning my apprentice, is now a hunter. He knows what I know. No knowledge has been lost. He has it all. And that he is in harmony. Then the Wise Man tells the villagers that he has observed that this man is in harmony because he has been isolated for the past three days and meditating. The Wise Man has been observing him and giving him advice. And he says this man is ready to become full hunter for the village. Now the village can have two full hunters until I have become too old. And then I can hunt part of the time or quit hunting. Whatever I wish. But this man will be full hunter from now on. And they may rely on him as they have relied on me. Then there are certain things he puts in the fire to make the fire jump up and the smoke turn colors, as part of the ceremony. And there is some singing. We see some of the spirits there and we tell the spirits of the nearby animals and of the trees around that this man will be communicating with them now for hunting. Then my apprentice tells the villagers that he accepts this responsibility and that he will uphold it. This makes him responsible, and so he does that. That is the solemn part, and after this part takes place then everyone gets happy. It is generally an excuse to feast all night long. Because the villagers say, "We will eat up all the food tonight so that you can get to work tomorrow and show us what a good hunter you are." (I laughed.) And that is it. That is what happens.

D: *Do you think he has learned everything you know?*

B: Yes. Anything that he does not know, it is merely because I have been hunting so much longer. I am more experienced.

D: *But you can still advise him.*

B: Yes, if he wants the advice. He does not have to ask me for advice now, but he can if he wants. He is in harmony with the Earth and he knows the songs of the animals. He will be able to hunt.

D: *Do you think he has learned well?*

B: Yes. Yes, he did.

I could sense from his voice that he was proud of the boy. He also felt that he had fulfilled his obligation of passing on his knowledge. He knew how important that was to the survival of the village.

D: *That's good. Then you won't have to work so hard now.*

B: That is true.

D: *What do you think you'll do now? Will you stay in the village?*

B: (Emphatic) *No!* Why should I? I do not like being under the roof. It is too crowded with people around. I will probably do some exploring to see what is beyond the hunting ranges.

D: *You've never been able to do that, have you?*

B: No. I go out further than most for hunting, but still I wonder what is beyond the next mountain. In every direction you want to go, there are mountains. So I will pick the furthest point I have ever been in any direction and go beyond.

D: *Have you ever had any desire to follow the river?*

B: Yes. I might do that, too.

D: *You can do that now because you won't have to come right back, is that what you mean?*

B: Yes. I will pack what I can carry. And I will do it in good weather, in the summer. I can hunt for my meat. I might even go a long way.

D: *Then will you come back and tell the other people what you found?*

B: If they want to know, I will tell. It will make a good story for wintertime around the fire. In early summer I could go and then I would get back by late summer to help supply meat for winter.

D: *Do you think you might get lost?*

B: (Indignant) No! *I* get lost? How can you get lost? You know where you are.

D: *Even if you went into strange areas you have never seen before?*

B: But that does not make any difference. You still know where you are. You are still in harmony with the Earth and you can still feel which direction is which. And you know which directions you have been, and how much trip you have behind you. And you know where you are on the Earth. When you are in harmony with the Earth, then everybody can feel the directions. That way you cannot get lost.

D: *Do you use the stars for your directions, or do you just* know *where you are?*

B: Oh, you know. They are right here. (He pointed to the center of his forehead.) The directions are here. The stars help. But this is more reliable because it can be cloudy at night.

D: *Yes, that is true. Or you could be in the thick woods and not see the sky. Then you always know how to find home again by using that part of your head. Some people don't know how to do that.*

B: Where?

D: *Well, didn't you say there were some children that were born that didn't know these things?*

B: Well, that is true, but that is so rare that one forgets.

I counted him ahead again to another important day in his life as he was growing older and asked what was happening.

B: The man who is hunter now, he has gotten married. And he has asked me to be a grandfather to his children. This is an honor since I never lived with one woman and raised children. I did not want to be under the roof. So what this man is saying is that he wants to be my son because he wants me to be grandfather to his children. And that way my line will be carried on. He can do this since he learned the hunting from me.

D: *I thought they didn't have marriage among your people.*

B: Generally, no, but occasionally when one is particularly attached to one person and they want to be with that one person, they will announce it to the village. And the Wise Man will say, "You two have chosen to stay together all your lives, where you feel that you are in harmony with each other, to where you must stay together. Therefore, we recognize this." Here the closest word I can find is "marriage," which is a word you once used.

D: *And it's not normal to be married, to stay with one person?*

B: No, it is not normal. It happens, but it is just every once in a great while. This is the first time this has happened in my lifetime.

D: *Then most of the time they just live with whoever they want to live with?*

B: Right. And that changes as you change in the path of your life.

D: *You told me once about a woman you liked. Is she still there?*

B: That was many years ago. She is still here. We are still friends. She is close to another man. We reminisce sometimes. There is another woman that I am close to.

D: *Do you still hunt?*

B: Not often. Never in the winter, no. I like to stay by the fire in the winter. The cold gets to my bones for now. In the summer I say I am going to go hunting, and I go out to hunt. But everybody knows I am really not. I just say that. I go out so that I may listen to what the wind has to sing to me. And I sing with the wind and I hear what the trees are telling me. And I listen to the harmony of the Earth. Because I do not like to be under the roof, and I cannot hear the harmony as well when I am in the village.

D: *But do you live under the roof most of the time now?*

B: No, in good weather I am outside, and I sleep outside. There is this one particular rock I like to sleep on. But in bad weather I reluctantly go inside. I still do not like to be under the roof, but my body says, "Go under the roof." My body does not cooperate too well. I suppose that is what they call "growing old."

D: *But your mind would still like to be out there. Did you ever travel to go see what was beyond the next ridges?*

B: Yes I did. There were more mountains and more mountains. I followed the river down. The people in the village say that I am getting old, and I am making up stories to entertain the children. I will show them "old." But I followed the river down and I found more people. (Spoken almost in awe.) But they were very different from what we are, and they did not feel to be in harmony. I did not try to contact them because it gave me a headache to be around them.

D: *Was it very far?*

B: Yes. It was several days' journey. I traveled for two moons.

D: *How did they seem different? Did they look different?*

B: Umm yes, they were darker. They all had black hair and dark, dark skin. But the main way they were different is that ... I cannot describe this well. In our village everybody can tell what everyone else is feeling without having to say what they are thinking or feeling, because we are in harmony with each other. But with these people, their harmony was different and I could not tell what they were thinking. And I did not want to go down in the village to see them, for I feared that if I did they may not be in harmony enough to know that I meant no harm. At the time the village still needed my help for winter, so I watched them for awhile. Then it was time for me to go back to the village so then I went.

D: *Did they see you?*

B: (Emphatic) *No!* I made sure that they did not.

D: *Did they dress differently than your people?*

B: Yes. Some. They seemed to have different customs, but I could not tell for sure since I did not speak with any of them. They used leather differently than we do, and their ornaments were different than ours. It was so many years ago, it is difficult to remember. Ahh … they did their hair differently than we do. We in our village, as you know, the men keep their hair clipped, cut off with a knife. And the women twist their hair up behind and stick ornaments in it according to tradition and how they want to do it. In this village the men let their hair grow long too, and they had it braided in different ways. Sometimes they would wrap the braids in strips of skin, sometimes they would not. And some of the men in the village would shave part of their head and let the other part grow long. It looked very strange. I could not figure out what the significance was.

D: *What part did they shave off?*

B: Well, usually the sides would be shaved off, and then there would be a strip down the center to grow long.

D: *And they still had braids too?*

B: Usually not. Then they just let it grow long. The women had made ornaments and such out of strips of leather and wore these different ways. And it seemed like the men in this village did not let the women do as many different things as we let our women do. They were not able to be as outspoken.

D: *Could you see what type of houses they lived in?*

B: They looked similar to ours, but there were differences. Nothing to remark on. They had different types of boats than we did. Since it was further down the river, the river is bigger at this point. They made flat-bottom boats that floated very well. And they had sweep sticks—I heard them called "paddles"—that they used to guide these boats across the water. And they did a lot of fishing. Most of their meat that they ate was fish. And the only meat they killed were the large animals for their skins. They would eat the meat too, but the fish was their prime source of meat.

D: *Were the boats large enough to stand on, like your boats?*

B: No. These boats would be long and narrow, curved up at each end, flat-bottomed. Usually two men would guide it, three at the most. And they would always be kneeling in the boats.

D: *Do you remember any other things that were different?*

B: Well, they did not have a wise man like we have. And they did not have any metal. Their knives were made from stone like the kind we make the arrowheads from.

D: *Did they have any kind of a leader?*

B: Yes. They had a leader that took care of the same functions as our wise man does, but I could tell that he did not have the knowledge he should have to be a wise man.

D: *I wonder if those people believe the same way your people do?*

B: I do not think so. I did not hear any of them call upon any of the spirits for anything. If they did, they had a different way of doing it. And they did not seem to be aware of things that they should be aware of. Like where the animals are and such as that.

D: *They hunted in a different way than you do?*

B: Yes. They depended more on the outward signs rather than the inward feelings.

D: *Did you hear them speaking?*

B: Yes. I could not understand what they were saying, so I paid no attention to it.

D: *They were like a different group of people altogether. But you stayed for a while and just watched?*

B: For a few days.

D: *Then when you came back and told the people they didn't believe you?*

B: They thought I was just making things up to entertain the children, telling about funny things other people did down the river. And the people would say, "We are the people. We are the only ones. What do you mean, 'other people'?" I know what I have seen. And the children think it is funny to hear the stories that Tuin makes up about people who do this and that. Everybody knows that nobody does that.

D: *But before you saw these people you also thought you were the only people, didn't you?*

B: Yes. I did not know there were any other people. I thought we were the only ones. I was just going down the river to see where the river went. And I went past three waterfalls and I was just following the river. I was surprised when I first saw another person. It was someone on the river in one of the flat-bottomed boats. It astonished me very much.

D: *I wonder how many more people are out there?*

B: I do not know. At the time that was the furthest I could go. That was half way through the amount of time that I could stay away from the village.

D: *Did you ever try again?*

B: No. There were so many other directions to go. I had seen it once and I knew I would not forget.

D: *Did you ever see any other people in the other directions?*

B: No. Just mountains and animals.

D: *Did you see any strange animals?*

B: No. I saw animals that looked like animals I knew, but maybe slightly different. Maybe a little bigger or a little smaller, or a slightly different color. But I could still tell that it was the same animal. There would be some trees that were different. Sometimes the pine trees would look different or there would be different kind of oak trees, but nothing drastic.

D: *You made a great discovery. You saw things that the other people would never see.*

I again moved him ahead in time to another important day in his life as he was growing older.

B: I am sitting on a boulder. I have been meditating with the spirits for quite some time. And I have just made an important discovery concerning the nature of the universe.

D: *Can you share it with me?*

B: It is hard to explain. But the fact that everything is *one* has just been strongly reinforced. The experience is very special.

D: *Do you meditate like this very often?*

B: Yes, now that I do not hunt. I come out into the woods a lot because I still do not like to be under the roof. I am too old to hunt so I *think* about things.

D: *Had you ever thought of this idea before?*

B: Well, of course, I took it for granted. I really did not think it out.

D: *You mean that everyone is one?*

B: That *everything:* people, plants, animals, Mother Earth, the sky, the air—everything is one.

D: *As though in total harmony? Is that what you mean?*

B: As though part of a large being which is working together.

D: *That would be a different idea, wouldn't it? Do other people in your village think the same way?*

B: Yes, for we believe that everything is one and in harmony. And I just realized that if everything was meeting together in harmony, it would have to be part of one body or being of some sort, because our bodies work together. Just close your hand and open it again. It tells you all you need to know about the unity of the universe.

D: *Do you think this one being would have a name or anything?*

B: (Emphatic) *Oh, no, no!* We are part of this being. This being is us. It is like a spirit. I do not know how to describe it. It is just an idea about how everything works together so well, because we are all part of a being. We may think we are apart, but that is an illusion.

D: *Of course, there are some things that are out of harmony though.*

B: Oh yes. When occasionally you forget yourself or something like that.

D: *But it's an interesting idea anyway; to think like that. I know you have different days that you celebrate and you talk to the spirits. You said you sing to the spirits and call them forth. But do the people in your village believe in one being or one spirit that is over all the rest?*

B: No! The spirits are all good and they all have their position of what they take care of and such, like the people in the village. Everybody is equally as important and everyone has to do what they must do. It is the same with the spirits, and the spirits are our friends.

D: *Then there is not one that would be like a chief over all the other spirits?*

B: No, the spirits are wise; they do not need a wise man.

D: *Some people believe things like that. That's why I wondered how you believed.*

B: That would be a childish belief.

D: *Then you believe in many spirits of different things in nature, or what?*

B: Everything, everybody, anything that exists has its spirit. A plant, you, an animal, a rock, the wind, the rain, the thunder, the lightning, the clouds, the sun, the stars, everything. Each star has a spirit. Some spirits are more powerful than others in certain ways, but they all have their abilities and powers. And they are there to help. All we need to do is communicate with them and present to them what we need, and they work it out to where it will be in harmony with everything else, but you still get what you want.

D: *Then do you sing to any certain spirits more than the others?*

B: Not any more than others. Sometimes you know the situation fairly and you know which spirit would be good to take care of the situation. Or why two or three or four spirits could take care of the situation. You address yourself to them. But other times, if it is just a general situation and you are not sure who could best handle it, you address all the spirits in general. And say, "Please hear me. Whoever can take care of this. This is what I need."

D: *That sounds like a very good belief.*

B: We are happy with it—that's what counts. And it works.

D: *Yes, just as long as it is good for you. But you're getting older now?*

B: Yes. My hair, for the most part, has turned white.

D: *And you don't do the hunting any more?*

B: No. I am too old for it. The one that I trained does the hunting now.

D: *Do you have someone who takes care of you?*

B: (Indignant) I do not need anyone to take care of me.

D: *I mean to give you food and things.*

B: I have no problem getting food. I hunted for so long, I get all the food I want.

D: *You have earned it.*

B: That is what they say. I gave the village all the meat that it ever needed. They say it is nothing for me to get the food that I need. It is only fair.

D: *And the one you taught is a good hunter and he supplies food for the community now. Then what do you do with your time now?*

B: I go for many walks in the woods. I am always out in the woods wandering around when I am not with the children.

D: *Are there any particular children that you like to be with?*

B: All of them.

D: *All right. Well, let's leave that scene. Let's go forward to another important day as you are growing older. I will count to three and we will be there. One, two, three; it's another important day in your life. What are you doing?*

B: I am walking through the village, seeing what has changed and what has stayed the same. I have the feeling this will be the last time I see the village, so I am really *seeing* it. I am really looking at it to see all the details.

D: *Why? Do you think something has changed? (I didn't really understand what he had just said.) Have you been away?*

B: Oh, things gradually change over the years. And I am comparing the way the village looks now with my earliest memories.

D: *Do you see any changes?*

B: Well, there have been a few, you know. There used to be a house over there that was lived in, but it was torn down by the winter storms. And there is another one over there that has been built, and things get shifted around. The children are different because, well, children always grow up. And so, no big changes —just the small changes. The new wise man is doing very well.

D: *Did the old wise man die?*

B: Yes. It was too cold one winter. But the new wise man remembers everything and so we are in good shape. We are in good hands.

D: *He has passed on the memories to him, the legends and everything. Are there more people than there were, that you can remember?*

B: Oh no. Not really. Sometimes it seems so, but I think it is simply because I am old.

D: *Do you still have the large building that they use for the gatherings?*

B: Yes.

D: *Didn't you tell me one time there was a sign or something on that building?*

B: Yes. It has a picture on it that tells what type of building it is for, although everyone knows it. This thing of designs, according to the Wise Man, says what the building is for. It was supposedly put there by the Old Ones. The sign is made of the metal, and you never can tell that it has been out in the weather.

D: *Could you draw the designs that are on the sign for me?*

B: That would be difficult. I do not see as well as I used to.

D: *But you could remember what it looked like, couldn't you?*

B: Well, I never paid much attention to it. I knew what the building was for. The sign just happened to be there. I would look at it, but the designs do not look like anything. They do not look like trees. They do not look like animals. They are meaningless scrawls. Any child could do it in the mud. And so, I just never bothered to remember what they all looked like because there was no reason for it.

D: *Well, I would really like it if you could look at it and see if you could copy it for me. Do you think you could do that?*

B: I could try. It would not be what it looks like because I cannot see that. They are too far away.

D: *Could you go closer?*

B: (Exasperated) I am standing under it now! I just do not see well any more. I do apologize.

It was a good attempt, but it was obvious that if he couldn't see the sign he couldn't draw it.

D: *Why do you think this will be the last time you will go through the village?*

B: Because of the way the spirits are singing to me today. The song has changed. And I can tell by the way is has changed that I am perceiving it differently, which means it is getting close to my time to cross over.

D: *Well, you are getting old, but are you still in good health?*

B: Yes. When the weather is cold, and today it is cold, my joints ache, and are stiff. I cannot move quickly. I have to move slowly, and I cannot see. But other than that my health is still good.

D: *These are things that come naturally with aging, don't they?*

B: For some people. Some people get to where they cannot hear, some get to where they cannot see—it depends.

D: *That is the way life is.*

Upon awakening Beth told of what she remembered of the session.

B: I remember about his apprentice. He started playing a more important role. I remember that. And I remember something about journeying. I seemed to see lots of mountains.

D: *Was there anything else you remember?*

B: I think I had a feeling of something happening that was solemn. You know: good, positive, but still solemn.

D: *That was probably when Tuin's apprentice was getting the official nod from the wise man that now he could take over his duties. It was a ceremony thing. And during that time he was turning over his duties to his apprentice. Then they had a happy festival afterwards.*

B: I get the feeling of being more contemplative, like spending more time thinking about things, instead of with normal everyday things.

D: *That was as he was getting older.*

Beth also described a short out-of-body trip she made right at the end of the session, just before I counted her up from her deep trance. In her astral, spiritual body she went to a nearby city and into her friend's trailer home. She had been thinking about this young man before the session, and wishing there was some way to get him to call her for a date. I had made a joking remark about her sending him mental vibes or suggestions to call her. Apparently it was the last thoughts on her mind as she went under hypnosis, and she utilized the last part of the trance to take a side trip to see him and try to influence him.

This incident demonstrated that the topic of the session was not the most important thing to her at that point. She was more concerned about her present-day private life than she was about Tuin's life that occurred thousands of years ago.

An interesting thing happened as I was counting her up from trance. Usually by the count of five and six, the subject's body has begun to respond and is showing signs of returning to consciousness. She was still lying motionless until I reach the count of seven, when her body jerked uncontrollably all over. Then she began to respond. She said later that while she was standing (or floating) in the trailer and telling her friend to call her, she heard me counting seven, eight, in the background. She thought, "Whoops, I've gotta go!" and was zapped back into the room. This was probably when the body contraction occurred, as she reentered it. She said normally she could hear me counting, getting slowly louder, and she usually followed my voice, waking up slowly. This was the first time she waited so long to respond to it. But she was preoccupied. It is amazing how quickly she was able to accomplish the out-of-body trip and return, all in that short space before awakening. It also demonstrates the effectiveness of the hypnotist's voice to draw the subject back, and shows how the subject perceives the procedure from their vantage point. This side-trip was an interesting experience.

Incidentally, her friend did call her within a few days and asked her for a date. Whether it was coincidence or whether she actually did mentally communicate with him, we shall never know.

Chapter 13

Death of Tuin
and the Aftermath

WHEN WORKING WITH A SUBJECT on a past life, you eventually come to the point where you feel you have explored the main highlights of that life, and there is only one facet left, the death of that personality. When this point is reached, my usual procedure is to instruct the subject to move ahead to the last day of their life in that lifetime so they can tell me what happened. I give them the choice that they can view the incident as an observer if they wish, so they will not experience any physical reactions or trauma. Many unusual reactions have occurred at this point, depending upon the type of death (violent or natural). But the subject always experiences a feeling of detachment afterwards, and they can give an impersonal account. All physical sensations are left with the body. They never carry them over to the spirit state.

B: I have left the village and I am walking through the woods towards one of the mountains. There is a cave there that I like to go into to think. It has been raining. The weather is cold. I go to the cave, and as I get to the mouth of the cave ... I do not know if it is an avalanche or a cave-in, but I am caught in the rocks and I am crushed. The rocks bury me. The village, knowing that I am old, thinks that I walked directly over to the other side. They never found my body.

D: *This was a cave that you always went to?*

B: Well, I was getting older when I discovered the cave, and I never told anybody about it. And I would go to it fairly often.

D: *Then it's very unlikely they knew where you were going anyway.*

B: True.

I have witnessed so many hundreds of subjects go through the death experience that I no longer find it startling or unusual. But I am always curious about their description of the transition from the physical to the spiritual state.

D: *What was it like whenever you died? I mean, spiritually, what was it like to leave the body?*

B: Have you ever dived into a deep pool, where it is dark and murky at the bottom? Then as you come back up towards the surface of the water, it gets lighter and lighter. Then when you break through the surface of the water, there is sunlight all around. It was like that.

D: *Do you think it was like that because of the rocks that fell on you?*

B: No, it was like that because I was going from the physical plane to the spiritual plane. As I left my body, it was like coming up through the pool. And then when I reached the spiritual plane, it was like breaking the surface of the water and coming out into the sunlight.

D: *Many people worry about what it's like to die.*

B: If you die in an accident, physically it is painful just before you lose consciousness of the physical plane, because your body has been injured. But after you lose consciousness it is very easy and natural. It is as natural as anything else in life: making love, walking, running, swimming. It is just another part of life. There is no such thing as dying. You just go to a different stage of life.

D: *This is what I want to tell people, because some of them worry about it. That's why I like to get the information on what it's really like.*

B: It is pleasant. If they are worried about it, tell them to go to a place in the river that has a deep pool. Tell them to dive down to the bottom of the pool. And then at the bottom push up vigorously with their feet and come plunging up to the surface. Tell them it is like that.

D: *That was your experience then.*

B: I am looking down at the Earth and at the place where I died. I am thinking about my life. I feel that it was good. It was full. I was in harmony with the spirits. I was a hunter and I did a good job hunting.

D: *I think it was a good life. You were a good person and you did things for the people.*

B: Well, that is ordinary. In the village most people do things for other people.

D: *But you lived a useful life.*

B: I am looking down on the Earth now. Across the woods and the mountains.

D: *It was a beautiful place where you lived.*

B: Yes, the Earth is beautiful. And yes, the place where I lived is special to me. It is very wondrous. I see and understand things that I never dreamed possible. (Suddenly) Greetings!

D: *What?*

This remark was unexpected. I was startled.

B: Greetings.

D: *Greetings? (Laugh) What are you doing?*

B: Watching you. You are from a far stranger place than I had imagined.

D: *Oh? Tell me what you think.*

B: I see how you are gaining your information. That is so strange. That black box. It is like the things that the Old Ones had. (He was referring to my tape recorder.) And I can see that you like to ask questions.

D: *Uh-huh. But does it bother you?*

B: No. I find it amusing.

D: *Why is it amusing?*

B: It just is. No particular reason.

This was a very strange feeling, thinking that he somehow was watching me or looking over my shoulder. An invisible someone or something observing what I was doing. I felt a little uncomfortable and kept looking behind me. I don't know what I half-expected to see. Tuin the hunter in ghostly form floating in the air? It was just a normal reaction to the surprise statement, but it gave me a prickly sensation down my spine. I tried to continue as though nothing had happened. Although I now had the eerie impression that I was speaking to a ghost which was in the room with me.

D: *Do you know what the black box is used for?*

B: Well, since you are not doing any writing or any recording of information, I assume that it has information in it. Rather like some of the things the Old Ones had.

D: *It has ways of capturing information. There are many strange things, aren't there?*

B: Yes. The song of the universe never ends.

D: *What else do you see as you look at me?*

B: I see you are surrounded by many things.

D: *Can you tell me what you mean?*

B: I do not see them clearly. I mainly see your face. I look around and I see the song of the universe. The dancing of the spheres.

D: *But you can see now why I asked the questions. I wanted the knowledge to be remembered. It's very important that it not be lost.*

B: Because it has been lost totally.

D: *Yes. You realize that now, don't you? And I am trying to get it back.*

B: I am glad that I was cooperative when I was down there hunting.

D: *Yes. Oftentimes when I talk to people, they don't want to answer my questions.*

B: That is foolish. They have small spirits. They do not sing.

D: *Well, sometimes the knowledge is secret and they are afraid to tell me.*

B: They are not singing well. They are out of harmony with the Earth. The Earth has no secrets. The knowledge and the song is there for all.

D: *Oh, you were most cooperative. You were very eager to tell me. And I liked this.*

B: Good. One should be. Knowledge should not be lost. Keeping it secret is not wise.

D: *I think they were afraid some people wouldn't understand, or ...*

B: If they are in harmony with the Earth, they should understand.

D: *Sometimes they were afraid they would be in danger, too. They were afraid that they would be harmed if the knowledge was revealed.*

B: Well, among my people that would not happen.

D: *Yes, I know. They were a very good people, very gentle people. But this was why I was asking the questions, and when I discovered it* had *been lost, I wanted to try to get it back. And I put it in my little black box.*

B: When it is in the little black box, will other people have the information?

D: *Yes. For when I take it out of the black box, I will put it on paper and they can read it.*

B: Paper? (He seemed confused.)

D: *Well, it will be like writing. Do you know what writing is?*

B: All right, yes.

D: *Paper is just a material to write on.*

B: Ah! I understand.

D: *It will be written down and then many people can read it and they will know about your people.*

B: Good.

D: *They will know about your history and where you came from. And it will not be lost anymore.*

B: For another age or so anyhow.

D: *That's why I asked so many questions. I was trying to think of what people would want to know about your people.*

B: That explains some of the questions.

D: *Because things have changed. That's why I wanted to know the way it used to be. And sometimes I think Tuin would get a little aggravated. He didn't know why I was asking so many questions.*

B: He was not aggravated, just puzzled.

D: *He couldn't see why I didn't know these things.*

B: True.

D: *But as you look at the Earth now, you can probably see that many things have changed.*

B: Yes. Poor Earth. Man is not in harmony with the Earth. It aches.

D: *That's true. This kind of information might help us to get back into harmony.*

B: I hope.

D: *That's why I am always searching for knowledge. I thought it interesting that your people didn't have a God concept. Do you know what I mean? They believed in nature spirits?*

B: Yes. The oneness of the universe. There is no room for a god when you are one with the universe. That takes care of all that needs to be taken care of. A god would be childish and superfluous.

D: *But many people like to think of one being or one god over all.*

B: That is stifling for your song. That makes your song out of harmony with the Earth. For it stifles you from what you should be.

D: *Then it's better to think of many different spirits, or what?*

B: No. Everything is united in one, and together in one large entity where everything is in harmony. I suppose in a way you could think of it as many spirits, as many aspects of the same thing. As long as you remember that you are in harmony and part of the whole of everything. This idea of *separating* things into god and not-god and anti-god is out of harmony. It is not the way it should be. It is not the way it is.

D: *That's what they think: the being they call "God" is supposed to be one over everything.*

B: But that is not the way it is. Everything is together. Nothing over anything else. Everything is together.

D: *Yes, to have one above the others would be separating them, wouldn't it? What are you going to do now?*

B: Rest and learn. And go back. I see now that there are other people. Living in the village we never saw any. I see the immensity of space. I am looking around at things that I could never see when I was alive.

D: *How do you feel about it?*

B: It is beautiful. The harmony and the song of life is much more intricate and much bigger than I had ever dreamed.

D: *What are you looking at now?*

B: I am looking at the whole planet.

D: *As you look at that, can you tell me where your village was? On what part of the planet? You didn't know whenever you were living there.*

B: That is true. Shall I use your labels or mine?

D: *Whatever. I like your labels. Tell me those and then we could compare.*

B: Well, it does not matter.

D: *What would your labels be.*

B: Oh, descriptions of shapes mostly.

D: *Tell me those first.*

B: All right. There is a land that is like a horn and it is hooked to another land by a narrow neck. And this other land is like a bowl. It has mountains on both sides and it is flat in the middle. And it stretches from one pole almost to the other. That is one description. Another description would be of a land like a shield with islands all around. And there is a land that is like a horn with extremely high mountains on it. Your labels would be: this last one would be India, with the mountains and land like a horn. The land like a shield with islands all around it would be China and Russia, Asia. The one like a horn is South America connected by a narrow neck to the land like a bowl, which is North America.

D: *On which one of these pieces of land was the village located where you lived as a hunter?*

B: North America. In the mountains of western Canada.

Finally we had found the answer I had been searching for.

D: *I kept wondering where it was. Could you look at the planet today and be more specific?*

B: Northwestern Canada, in the mountains—close to Alaska.

D: *That was where the village was located. As you look at it, can you see what happened to the people that lived in that village? Did they ever leave that valley?*

B: They did not leave but some people came in eventually. At first there was a clash, but then the people who lived in the village lost their sight of being in harmony. They had to be able to survive the other people. When they married into the other people they were gradually absorbed.

D: *What kind of people were the other ones?*

B: They were Eskimos.

D: *The people that wore the furs and lived in snow houses?*

B: Yes. Or in wood and skin lean-tos in the summer.

D: *How did they discover your people?*

B: A hunting expedition. They had been gradually spreading. They were multiplying and moving out and taking up more room. And eventually they came to that valley.

D: *But they didn't understand these people, did they?*

B: Well, they did learn from the village. It helped their spiritual development to where they became aware of the spirits and tried to stay in harmony with the spirits. They were like children that had never been taught. And they did not know what to do to stay in harmony. They did not do as good a job, but they tried.

D: *Were there more of these Eskimos than the villagers?*

B: Eventually, yes. The hunting expedition, no, but later more of them came.

D: *You said there was a clash. Do you mean there was a fight of some kind?*

B: Not really. There was just suspicion on both sides. And some verbal arguments took place.

D: *I can imagine the people in the village must have been very shocked when they saw other people.*

B: Yes. By this time what I had told them had become a legend about the crazy hunter who said there was other people. And then when the Eskimos came traipsing down the valley they were surprised to see that it was true.

D: *But there was nothing they could do, was there?*

B: No. You cannot hide forever.

D: *And eventually the Eskimos interbred. Whatever happened to the legends of the villagers?*

B: They were gradually forgotten or absorbed by the Eskimos and changed and blended with their legends. Some of them were passed down. Some of the underlying concepts mainly were absorbed by the new people and were passed down, but the details were lost.

D: *The new people would have had their own legends, wouldn't they?*

B: True. But the concept could still be absorbed into their legend structure.

D: *They combined the two that way. Can you see what happened to the things in the Wise Man's hut?*

B: They eventually ended up being buried.

D: *The people didn't understand what they were? Is that why they buried them?*

B: Some of them, yes, because the legends associated with them had been forgotten. And some of them were buried deliberately, particularly after the first contact with the Eskimos. They thought, "We do not want these people to have this. This is for the spirits." And so they buried it.

D: *What about that large thing that had all the little knobs on it.*

B: Yes, that was buried with one of their wise men.

D: *After the Eskimos came in they buried that one especially?*

B: No, it had already been buried with one of the wise men.

D: *The old Wise Man?*

B: No, another one. I do not know which one. They did not know what it was for. And the wise man had been well loved, so they did it to honor him.

D: *What about the things like the hat and the pieces of metal?*

B: The hat accidentally became broken and could not be repaired. Since no one knew what it was for any more, it was thrown away. Very careless, those descendants.

D: *I didn't think it would break.*

B: Neither did I, but ... I do not know what happened.

D: *And the other things, the pieces of metal and things like that were buried whenever the ...*

B: Either buried or used up.

D: *They didn't want the Eskimos to have these things.*

B: Well, pieces of metal were not any big problem because there was hardly any metal left when the Eskimos came.

D: *Was this many generations after Tuin lived there?*

B: Yes, several generations.

D: *Then the legends were either forgotten or were changed.*

B: Both. Some were forgotten; that happens. And when the Eskimos came, they started swapping legends. Some were different, some were similar, and the children blended them all together and they gradually changed. Then some were forgotten. It is a natural cycle.

D: *Then the Eskimos did adopt some of the habits of your people. What do you think of those legends now that you're on the other side and can look at it like this?*

B: They were amazing.

D: *Do you think there was truth behind it?*

B: Yes, there was. That is what makes them amazing, that they were able to keep so much intact for so long.

D: *Yes, Tuin's life was very narrow, very limited in what he could see.*

B: All he had was his five senses. But his people saw a lot with their spirits. They could have closed themselves off, but they didn't. This was good for their karma.

D: *They developed that to a high degree, didn't they?*

B: Yes, they did. One aspect they deliberately shut off was being able to hear the animals. But it was best. They had to shut that part off for survival.

D: *I thought that was what happened. The legend said they didn't want to hear the animals speak any more, because at one time they could speak? Did he mean it was mental?*

B: Yes, they could hear the animal pleading that they wanted to live. And it put too much mental stress on them.

D: *That's what I thought he meant; that they had shut off that ability.*

B: But that was a matter of survival, so that did not count against their karma.

D: *He still used a great deal of psychic ability in order to locate the animals.*

Chapter 14

The Origin of the Old Ones

*W*HEN A REGRESSED SUBJECT relives the time of their death and they cross the portal to the other side of our reality, an interesting phenomenon occurs. I have watched this happen so often that I come to expect it when this point in a regression is reached. When they are once again in the spirit state they shed the physical body like a suit of old worn-out clothes, and with it go the inhibitions and limitations that the physical has imposed. When a person is alive in the physical world they are only aware of those events and that knowledge that is presented to them through their physical senses and experience. Tuin's world was extremely limited and he did not know the knowledge that might lie behind the legends he had heard all of his life. With the shedding of the physical body there was also the shedding of these limitations. I knew that if Tuin followed the repeated pattern which I had observed, that he would have access to expansive knowledge in the spirit state. And the origin of the old ones could finally come forth from its hiding place if that font of knowledge could be tapped.

I had made many deductions on my own, but there were still many unanswered questions. I felt a compelling need to find the answers, so I turned my search in that direction.

D: *Where you are now, you have much more knowledge, don't you?*

B: Yes, I understand a lot more. One is always gaining more knowledge. That is part of life.

D: *Well, I was wondering about the old ones, and about what really happened. I thought maybe you could see more now than you knew from your legends. I believe the legends were very accurate though, weren't they?*

B: Yes, they were surprisingly accurate. They were vague in several places but that is to be expected, because of the length of time they involved. My people placed great emphasis on trying to keep things accurate. And I believe they did a good job considering that nothing was written down.

D: *There was such a long distance of time. That's amazing that they were able to keep it all together.*

B: Yes. The emphasis was there which gave extra impetus to keep things accurate. I see that there are some peoples who like to embellish their stories and change them and after a few centuries they have been so simplified that they make no sense any more.

D: *Yes, many people do that. They try to make them more interesting. Your legends did contain a great deal of the truth.*

B: Yes. They were vague. Some details were lost through time, but it's unavoidable on the physical plane.

D: *Is there anything that you could tell me about the Old Ones that you didn't know then?*

B: Perhaps. I could tell you what I see.

D: *Did they come from this world?*

B: (Emphatic) No! They came from another world, from across the void. They came from another part of the galaxy. There was political upheaval. That was the reason why they had to leave. They knew they would not be going back, so they left with the intention of finding another place to live. On the planet where they came from, there was much political unrest. They had a planet-wide government, and they were on the verge of going into a civil war. They had weapons capable of destroying the planet and all life. But they decided, "No, we do not want to do this. We want to live. What shall we do?" And they reached a compromise. One of the parties in this political unrest, the party that was somewhat in the minority, loved their planet so much they didn't want it to be destroyed. So they agreed to leave, and they had the technology to do this. The basic underlying problem of the political situation was whether or not to establish colonies on other planets. The ruling majority did not want to do this, and there was a minority who did. And the situation was rising to fever pitch. So they decided, in order to cool down the situation and save their planet, that the minority would leave and establish a colony. But with the understanding that they would have no contact with the home planet, since the home planet did not want colonies. And they agreed to do this for they did not want their planet to be destroyed. They felt they would have the best of both worlds this way. Their home planet would not be destroyed, plus they would be able to establish colonies.

D: *If they were having all this unrest with the capability of destroying the planet, why would their leaving stop that?*

B: Because the main ones who were agitating for colonies would no longer be there to agitate. The general populace, like most general populaces anywhere, were neutral and didn't really care one way or the other.

D: *And the ones who were going to migrate, so to speak, to go off in the ships, were the ones that were causing the trouble?*

B: Yes, they were kind of rubbing the government the wrong way. The main government could have decided, "Yes, we'll do this." But they were somewhat bureaucratic and they were saying for some abstruse reason, "No, that's impossible. We need the people here. We need to keep the technology here." It would not have hurt the planet because the planet was prosperous and they had a high standard of living. And indeed, it would have eventually benefited the planet to establish colonies. But the ones that were in the government were narrow-minded about it. The group who were agitating for colonies had some rich supporters. And they got together and built some ships, and decided they would go off on their own anyway. And the government gave their unspoken consent thinking that ...

D: *Thinking they would get rid of the agitators that way.*

B: Yes. To save them a lot of trouble, because they had been a thorn in their side for quite some time. So they left. There were five large colony ships. In all it was about ... um, how many people was it? (He paused as though thinking.) Altogether it was close to 5,000 people that left.

D: *Had this planet done space travel before?*

B: Oh, yes.

D: *Then it was something that was common. They just didn't have colonies?*

B: Right. They had extensively explored their system and they had mining operations on some of the moons that were mostly composed of minerals. One of the reasons why the planet was prosperous was because the land that was not being lived on was mostly agrarian. Most of the industries had moved out into space. The mining companies were on some of the small rocky moons of some of the other planets. And it worked out very well. They just didn't establish colonies because the government felt that people would not want to be permanently marooned away from their planet. The miners and the people who worked out in space had rotating shifts. A certain number of days on a job, and then a certain number on the home planet. There would be several thousand working in space, but they were rotating back and forth to where there would only be, say, a couple of thousand out at any one time. And the rest would be on the home planet for their ground shift. But it was continuously rotating, so they had steady traffic back and forth.

D: *This was the first time they had ever gone so far away.*

B: Yes. They were going to be leaving their solar system. It was a time of great turmoil on that planet, and probably everyone involved had mixed reasons for going. Many were probably not sure themselves exactly why they were leaving. There were many scientists that went with the group, and they were excited about it. There were other scientists who wanted to go but couldn't. The main stumbling block was the government, which was somewhat planet-bound, through no fault of their own. They just didn't have as much foresight as they could have had.

D: *But it sounded as though they expected never to come back.*

B: Yes, they knew they would never come back.

D: *You said there were five ships that left. What happened to the others? Did only one come to Earth?*

B: Yes, it malfunctioned and could not make it any further. The ships were geared to be multi-generation-type ships. Each generation between the succeeding generation had to pass down all their skills, so that the ship could keep running and the knowledge be continued. And so the descendants would know what was involved and what was trying to be done, without losing the purpose of the journey.

D: *Do you mean that the people who ended the journey were not the same ones who began it?*

B: No. Their distance was several light years and they did not have faster than light travel yet. They were trying to develop it, but they had not accomplished it yet. The speed that they could travel was close to the speed of light, but it would still take many, many years to get from one star to another. The star they were aiming towards was similar to their own star. It was towards the red end of the spectrum, so they were heading for it. They had strong evidence that there would be a planet habitable for them. And as they journeyed through the years in space they set up each ship as a city in itself. There were families. People were married and had children. They had facilities for learning, and as the children grew up they were educated as they had been on the planet, even a university-type of training. Each child could decide what field he wanted to go into, and he would be trained for that. All the children were given extensive cultural training so they would not forget the type of culture they sprang from.

D *If the ship was in flight for so many years, what kind of power source did it operate on?*

B: Nuclear fusion. Not fission like you have, but fusion.

D: *What is the difference?*

B: Your scientists are trying to develop fusion. Nuclear fission is when atoms are split apart to release energy and hence, a lot of radioactivity and such. Somewhat messy. On the other hand, once the technology is developed for fusion, it is more easily controlled to where you are binding atoms together instead of splitting individual atoms into fragments.

D: *Oh, it's the opposite.*

B: Right. And when you bind them together it also releases energy, but you don't have to contend with such high radiation from it. And as long as you have material to feed it, it can continue combining atoms. It doesn't matter what the fuel source is. Anything physical: air, water, wood, metal, cloth; anything that has matter to it can be used as fuel. Because the way they had their system set up, they had an energy field that would split things up into individual atoms, into a kind of energy plasma-type of thing. I don't know the technical words too well. And it would feed the atoms together at a predetermined rate, so that they would combine and release a certain amount of energy at the required rate. They had these ships set up so they would be self-sustaining. In an enclosed environment like that the main problem is usually excess water, from condensation and such as that. So they would often feed water to the process to get rid of the excess water.

D: *This was one of the materials they used?*

B: Yes, they could use anything that is matter. And so they had no problem with energy source. They had brought material on hand for this.

D: *I thought they would have to carry a great deal of material if they were traveling over all those generations.*

B: They didn't need that much. Nuclear energy is efficient and compact, and the combining of atoms creates a tremendous amount of energy. It is much like your atomic bombs but it is controlled and not explosive. It is the same amount of energy but it is being used for thrusting and nothing explodes and nothing is violent, but you get a sense of the amount of energy involved. Instead of being uncontrolled as in a bomb, it is controlled as an electric current.

D: *I figured that all these people had to have food supplies, and they wouldn't have a lot of room for energy supplies to feed the motors or whatever it was.*

B: That is correct. There was some material that was more efficient than others, and so naturally they carried these. But they knew that if they happened to get low, they could feed anything into the engine and still be able to travel.

D: *I've heard that sometimes crystals were used in propulsion and energy sources on space ships. Did they use anything like that?*

B: Yes. Their nuclear fusion devices weren't exactly what your scientists would call nuclear fusion devices, but these are the closest words in your language. The energy involved was not purely atomic. There were other planes of energy, of finer levels than atomic. Subatomic-type energies that had to be focused through crystals. And various crystals with different matrices were used to focus the energy in different ways for various specific purposes.

D: *What about their food supplies? Could they replenish that?*

B: Yes. They had hydroponic gardens, and they had places on the ship set up for growing grains and such as that. Their food was continually replenishing because they were growing it. They had a section of the ship designed for this.

D: *It must have been a large ship.*

B: Yes, they were huge.

D: *The picture that Tuin drew of the design for the blankets—was that the accurate shape of the ship?*

B: That was somewhat crude. It actually represented one of their shuttles that they used for going from ship to ground. Instead of landing the larger ship every time, they would merely use a shuttle to go back and forth from the ships that were rotating.

D: *Then the main ship that crashed didn't look like that?*

B: No. The ships had been constructed in space because they were so large. They could land but ideally they would only have to land once or twice. They were basically designed to stay in space, and so they were shaped differently.

D: *What shape was the main ship?*

B: It was shaped like a teardrop-shape, a drop of water. The front of it was the rounded part instead of the sharp point. And surrounding the slender part of it was struts and landing gear. Along the sloping sides of the teardrop shape were the exit ports for the thrust of the engines.

D: *The pointed end was toward the back. And there were no wings or anything?*

B: No. Their entrance and exit port was in the back. Somehow they had an energy field to shield it from radiation so they would enter and exit through the back, for they had loading ramps.

D: *Did the ship have many floors?*

B: Oh, yes. Many. Some floors, like the one used for gardening and such, was very high to accommodate the machinery they needed to support the plants. The living quarters were of regular size, but somewhat taller than your average story because they tended to be a taller race of people. They were taller and more slender, so their ceilings were somewhat higher to accommodate this.

D: *Then they had everything they could find in a city. Is that correct?*

B: That is correct. And they kept everything carefully balanced because it was an enclosed environment.

D: *Did they use light on the ships?*

B: Yes, to see and to function they used light that was similar to their sunlight. It would appear dimmer and reddish to you, like a lamp that's on half power with a light orange bulb in it instead of white.

D: *I was thinking that we use incandescent or fluorescent types.*

B: I observe that you have clock faces that glow in the dark due to an internal radiation source. That it doesn't have to have any power source, and it glows from chemical reaction. This was the type of lighting they had. It was lighting that would last for centuries simply because of the nature of the materials involved, due to atomic or chemical reactions. They were glow panels located sometimes on the ceilings, sometimes on the walls, depending on how and where they were needed. And for specific works in the various places, like in the laboratories and such, there would be other types of light sources for the various functions. You have a similar light source that can function for years, but you've not made extensive use of it. You just use it for small things, like for indicator panels and dials and such as that.

D: *Then what happened to bring their ship to our planet?*

B: This trip continued through different generations. It was in between the second and third generations when the ships were coming past this solar system. One of the ships had developed a malfunction and it had been gradually getting worse. I don't know if it was by accident or by sabotage.

D: *Do you think someone on the ship sabotaged it?*

B: Or possibly by someone before they left. Delayed action damage.

D: *I wonder if they might have done something like that to all the ships.*

B: I don't know. It is possible.

D: *They may have wanted to keep these people from succeeding.*

B: One cannot tell when it comes to political upheaval, or religious upheaval. People will do things in the name of ... whatever. They had been trying to repair it but it continued to malfunction again, and became a little worse each time. By the time they got to this solar system this one ship was just barely functioning. They were frantically trying to find a place to land so they could repair their ship. According to their standards they considered the Earth to be marginally habitable because they considered the sun to be too bright and hot. But they thought that perhaps this one ship could make an emergency landing, and in the planet's conditions be able to repair the ship and then continue. They thought they could live there only under very careful conditions, because the sun was too strong for them and had too much radiation. But they thought if they wore protective clothing in the daytime and did most of their activities at nighttime, they would be able to land there long enough to repair their ship. While they were repairing, the other ships would orbit the Earth and send down help as it was needed, for they were wanting to all stay together. They thought there was strength in numbers. This ship, as it began to land, malfunctioned again and went out of control. By the time they regained control it was too late. They were able to soften the blow of the crash but the ship was then beyond repair. So the other ships had to leave them, because they felt they would not be able to live there. The radiation would kill them, or cause their crops not to grow. So the other ships went on towards their destination. I really cannot see where it was. And the survivors on this ship—there were several who were killed, but many of them survived—went ahead and made the best of it. Thinking, "Well, we were planning on being a colony anyhow. We'll go ahead and make this our colony."

D: *Even though it was not the conditions they wanted?*

B: Right. And so they went ahead and set about building a colony. It was smaller than originally planned since it was only one ship instead of five. But they had everything they needed to be self-sufficient and to start their new lives. And so they did this and coped the best they could with what they considered to be harsh conditions.

D: *This must have been very difficult on them.*

B: Yes, but they lived.

Chapter 15

Survival

D: *The legends said that the old ones had difficulty having children when they first came here. Did that have something to do with the crash?*

B: They healed from the effects of the crash, because those were short-term injuries. But the main problem was the sun. It was hotter, and the radiation band covered a different part of the spectrum. It was very different from the sun of their old planet. Theirs was a dimmer, cooler sun. Their planet was not quite as far away from the sun as Earth is from her sun, but instead of being a yellow-white star of medium size like our sun, it was a smaller, cooler star, more towards the red end of the spectrum. And so the radiation of their sunlight was different. The spectrum lines were totally different from this sun's emission lines.

Incredibly, this statement regarding the temperature of the various stars in our galaxy is correct. It seems to be the opposite from what we are taught, but the coolest stars are red and the hottest are blue. Thus their sun was one of the cooler types (red), and Earth's sun is in the medium range as a yellow-type. The temperatures change as one goes from one spectral class to another, and the color of the star appears to depend on its temperature.

D: *You said they also had a fascination with our moon.*

B: Yes. Although other planets in their system had moons, they were mostly small rocky ones that the mining companies were mining. Their home planet did not have a moon. The scientists

were fascinated that Earth had such a large moon in relation to
the size of the planet. Because they had formulated theories, due
to the observations in their home system, that this was not possible. They had theories based on the ratios of the moons' paths,
the size of the moons and the mass of the moons in relation to
the size and mass of the planet. And the moon of this Earth
broke all those rules. They were fascinated to see that such a
small planet could have such a large moon and the stress not
affect them adversely. They did form a theory that the size of the
moon was one reason why Earth has so much tectonic plate
shifting and earthquakes and such. It was due to the stress from
the moon, but they saw it was not anything drastic. It might
shorten the life of the planet by a few million years in the long
run, but not enough to affect life on the planet for several billion
years to come.

D: *Was the Earth's gravity different from theirs?*

B: Earth gravity was slightly stronger but it was not enough to
really affect them. They felt tired because their muscles were not
used to it. They discovered they were developing more bone
problems like arthritis and such, because the gravity was a frac-
tion stronger. But in a few generations they had adjusted to this.

D: *Being in an enclosed environment on the ship for so long might have
made it harsher, too, whenever they landed on Earth and were
exposed to the air and the sun.*

B: That is true since it was during the third generation that they
landed. Some of the first generation were still alive. They were
very old and they remembered what it was like on a planet.
They were able to help out some. But still, since it was totally
new to their experience, the younger ones had to go through
their individual adjustments to it. They had never seen open sky
before in their lives. That was the biggest shock of all, the large
horizons. They practically had agoraphobia (fear of open spaces)
because they were used to enclosed spaces.

D: *You also said that they did most of their work at night and they
stayed inside.*

B: Yes, particularly the first few years they were here. They were trying to become acclimatized to things. At first they were just trying to adjust to the heavier gravity, and the sun. And so they did most of their work at night when it was cooler. It made it easier to work with the extra weight. Meanwhile, they'd go out in the daytime some, but they were trying to figure out ways to adjust to the sun. The scientists were researching this, and they developed special sunscreens and such to help protect them from the radiation. They also wore protective clothing in the daytime. This was their white clothing that Tuin mentioned, which they started burying them in.

D: *The kind of shiny material. What did they normally wear?*

B: It's hard to say. They always had the protective clothing on. They had other materials underneath, not like what we have, but it was a flowing-type of clothing that they wore during the night.

D: *You said that when they first began to have children, the genes were affected?*

B: Yes, in the way that radiation normally affects genes. It was difficult and they mutated. It was quite a while before they were able to take the proper precautions. And they had to continue taking these precautions for several generations.

D: *What kind of precautions do you mean?*

B: Not to let a woman of child-bearing age outside during daylight hours. When she became pregnant, to protect her in protective clothing at all times, day or night. To be very careful about the food she ate, and so forth.

D: *I believe Tuin said that some of the first babies were either born dead or were deformed in some way.*

B: Yes. And many of the deformities were so bad that they died because they could not live in that condition.

D: *That must have been very distressing for these people. You said they had ways of replenishing their food while traveling on the ship. Did they carry animals?*

B: A few. They planned on making use of the animals that were native to the planet. But they knew they would need a few animals to start with. And so they mainly brought three different animals. One animal was basically a food source. Another animal was a food source and a source for making cloth from its fur, and a third animal was basically a draft animal. They didn't carry many, just breeding stock, because it was difficult to maintain extra lives on the ship.

D: *I suppose that over that long length of time they would have bred until there would be too many on the ship.*

B: They had ways of restricting it through controlled breeding. Basically they would just breed enough to replace the old stock that died, to keep the number constant until they could get to a planet. They planned to let them breed more numerously when they knew they were approaching a planet and it was proven to be habitable, so they would have more animals when they landed. And they would then carefully tend the animals until they bred into the safe-number range.

D: *There was an animal that Tuin called "oxen." Was that one of these?*

B: Yes. That was the draft animal. They were not true oxen as you know them, but that was the closest word he could find in your language to relate to the animals. They were used like oxen and they *vaguely* resembled them, in that they did not look like horses and they did not look like elephants. And they did not look like water buffalo, which are other draft animals on your planet. But they vaguely resembled oxen so that was what he called them. They were built differently. (He paused as though trying to think how to describe them.) Their general framework, their skeletons, were different. Their joints were hinged somewhat differently so they had a different gait. And their skull was shaped differently. Some of them had horns and some did not; it depended on the genetics. Their ears were set well back on the head and faced backward. The eyes tended to be gray in color and were set higher on the head than oxen's eyes. And the dentition (teeth) was different.

D: *I believe he said that the horns went straight out to the sides. Is that correct?*

B: Yes. And they did not have cloven hooves. It appeared like bony toes—three in the back and four in the front. They were four toe-like appendages that were very bony and ended in miniature hooves on each toe. (All this description was emphasized with appropriate hand motions.)

D: *That would be different. But he said they never had many of these animals.*

B: That's true. The radiation of the sun made it difficult for them to propagate and many times the males tended to be sterile. So whenever there was a fertile male, he didn't have to do any work. He was very pampered and was used strictly for breeding. It was hypothesized that because the testicles were more exposed than the ovaries, they received a larger dose of radiation and hence tended to be sterile.

D: *And there was nothing they could interbreed with?*

B: No, their genes were too different from the other animals on Earth. If they could have found some true oxen they could have developed so-called "mules"—hybrids that would have been sterile but would have been able to function. They considered using caribou but the bodily chemistries and structures were too different to develop viable crosses.

D: *You said there were two other types of animals that they carried. Did these survive after the crash?*

B: One did; one did not. The one that *did* survive was an animal remarkably similar to the domesticated goat.

D: *Was this the animal that Tuin said someone in the village took care of?*

B: Yes. They had lost the details of where it came from so he assumed that it had been bred from the wild mountain goats, because there was a close similarity. But there were plenty of differences, too. They were considerably smaller than the mountain goats. They had a similar type of fur and bone structure, but the horns were different. They were not as big. The horns were more slender and just went back a little ways, much like your dairy goats. At first the scientists were able to interbreed the animals they brought with some mountain goats, for amazingly there was a viable cross. They did that to help acclimatize the animals to the planet and still keep the characteristics that they had been brought for. And so they went into a very specialized selective breeding program. The other animal which was brought mainly as a food source did not survive. The animal had difficulty breeding and its offspring were usually deformed. And so it was decided that, since they had found the animals native to the planet were edible without any harm being done, they would go ahead and slaughter those animals they had brought and use them for that first winter.

D: *They didn't really need the ones they had brought anyway.*

B: Right. For they discovered that, although the sun was different, the bodily chemistries of the animals on the planet were not poisonous to them and they could receive nutrition from them.

D: *Did they experiment to find these things out, or did they do tests of some sort?*

B: They did tests.

D: *You said the oxen died off. What about the goat animal? Did that survive to our times?*

B: Yes. The goat ended up interbreeding with the mountain goats and it survived. But after so many generations of breeding it cannot now be differentiated from the mountain goats. Perhaps scientists may consider it a different breed of mountain goat. And any irregularities that may be observed could be explained away as differences between breeds rather than between species. Basically that's what it is today.

D: *You talked about them bringing seeds and things like that, too. Did any of those plants survive?*

B: They have crossbred so much with plants that were already here that you really couldn't find them. One plant that is a possibility is what you call "corn."

D: *Corn? The Native Americans called it maize. Do you think this is directly descended from the seeds they brought?*

B: Corn has also blended with native plants, but it has more predominant genes from the home planet than other Earth plants.

D: *I was wondering if there might be one plant that we could trace back to their seeds.*

B: No, it was so long ago. Many ages.

D: *What about the trees he spoke of? There were some that had fruit.*

B: Yes, one of them survived. It is known to you as persimmon.

D: *(Surprised) Persimmon?*

B: One of them. The persimmon that is found on this continent that is different from that found on the Asian continent. The other tree didn't survive, but was very similar to apricot. It didn't survive up there in that land because it had to be pampered; but the persimmon survived.

D: *Then the persimmon would be something that could be directly traced back to them. And he talked about the plant they made their cloth from. Do you know which one that is?*

B: That plant thrived here on Earth and it branched out into many different types of plants. It's difficult to say which one it was since there are so many plants that could be traced back to it.

D: *I was thinking of flax, because I know flax has been used for thousands of years for the making of cloth.*

B: Flax is one. Another adaptation of the plant is yucca or bear grass. There are many adaptations from the same plant.

D: *Then they have just split off into different kinds. I'd like to know a little bit more about the first people who were there. Tuin said there was a small group of people there whenever the ship crashed.*

B: Yes, the natives. They were aborigine-type people, distant ancestors to the American Indians. On the chain of evolution they seemed to be Stone Age people, in development between Neanderthal and Cro-Magnon humans. Although I do know Neanderthal and Cro-Magnon were not related directly in the line of evolution, so far as knowledge and cultural development. They wore skins and usually lived in caves or built shelters— usually out of sticks and mud.

D: *They didn't have any form of agriculture?*

B: No, they were hunters and gatherers. They hunted for game, and as the appropriate time of the year came around they would gather whatever fruits and nuts that were growing wild.

We were finally getting closer to dating the arrival of the Old Ones. Geologists state that there were four major advances of ice during the Ice Age, which included periods when the ice melted back. The last ice sheet disappeared from North America between ten and fifteen thousand years ago. With the retreat of the ice many forms of animals became extinct, to be replaced by modern animals. The scientists say that it was during the last glacial period that humans first appeared on Earth. Earlier species of humanoids, such as Neanderthal man, is supposed to have existed in the last inter-glacial period. The modern species of humans developed during the last advance of the ice (or roughly 15,000 years ago) and with its retreat (10,000 years ago) has populated the Earth.

According to this historical information the Old Ones crashed during the last interglacial period when modern man's predecessor was living in that region. The aliens (or their descendants) were living there when some type of cataclysm occurred, because it is recorded in their legends. Did the drastic event trigger the last advance of ice?

D: *Were they gentle people or warlike people?*

B: It's true they had weapons for hunting, but they were gentle. They didn't really have contact with other people because of their location. They were somewhat isolated. They were extremely psychic so they had almost no need for speech. They had a very small vocabulary, because there was simply no need to develop it.

D: *What about the people on the ship—were they psychic?*

B: Yes, they too were highly psychic, but since they were aliens it was ... well, a different wavelength, so to speak.

D: *This is what Tuin meant about being out of harmony.*

B: Yes. Yet as they adjusted to living on the Earth, their psychic powers also adjusted to be in harmony with the Earth's energies, which made it easier for them to be in contact with the natives. At first it was very painful for both groups since they were sensitive and psychic. They both realized what the problem was, but they knew there was nothing that could be done about it to rush the process. Thus the natives basically left them alone. And the colony worked on adjusting to the planet and coming into harmony. Since they were both basically gentle groups of people, the natives really didn't have that many problems with the clashes. There were a few misunderstandings but they were straightened up. The main problem was culture shock, which is to be expected.

D: *I wonder what the colony people thought when they landed and saw this type of... human.*

B: They rejoiced to see this, for they knew if a human species had developed in the support of the planet, they had a greater chance to live. If one human-type species could survive on a planet, that increased their chances of survival. Because it meant that ecological niche already existed and they would just need to fit themselves into it.

D: *But the natives were so backward intellectually, by their standards.*

B: Well, they were backward technologically, but not intellectually or psychically. They were at that stage of technological development where they only had stone tools and such. But because of their psychic ability and being in harmony with the Earth, their religion and philosophy was as advanced as the colony's philosophy. In that way it made the contact easier. At first the younger members of the natives wanted to worship the colony as gods. But then they came to see the error of their ways, and understood that they were not gods but human creatures like themselves. It was just a matter of adjusting to them. And the natives helped the members of the colony to find which plants and animals were edible and which were not.

D: *I'm assuming that they eventually interbred, and that was how they were able to survive.*

B: Yes. Although they had begun to adjust to the planet, the scientists knew they would never be able to fully adjust to the radiation of the sun. And they did want to survive. They decided that the best way would be to interbreed with the natives, and therefore take on some of their stronger traits in regards to the tolerance for the sun. The natives were shorter and stockier than the colony people. They were what you would consider of normal height and build, but they were attractive people. And so if the young people of the colony wanted to be sexually interested in the natives, they were allowed and even encouraged to do so.

D: *Then the natives were not really repulsive to them.*

B: No, not at all. Different but not repulsive. It was just a matter of introducing them to more modern standards of hygiene.

D: *I wondered if the interbreeding might have been difficult for them, because it was something that they* had *to do in order to survive.*

B: It was not that difficult. They had to do it in order to survive in general, but it was left to each individual to make his own choice about the matter. Some did and some did not. Some of the colony members bred among themselves, and some interbred with the natives. But eventually after two or three generations everyone had some native blood in them. Naturally this changed their appearance,and it also helped their psychic abilities to adjust to the energy fields of Earth.

D: *I guess they were never as light-colored after that.*

B: No. For the natives had the typical Native American coloring: brown-skinned, blue-black hair, heavily-lidded eyes. And the colony people were tall and slender. Their hair was blond; their darkest hair was ash blond. Light blue was also a common hair color (that was a surprise). It was kind of a pale, pastel type of blue. And their skin coloring was of a silvery-type color. When they died it looked like a light gray. When they were alive, with the secretions of their skin and the energy of life, it looked silver. Not that it would shine particularly, but it looked silver in a general way. In direct light the oil on the skin would make it shimmer a little bit, but nothing flashy. Because the natives were bronze colored, when they mated with the aliens their children would basically be of a lighter bronze color. It would still have the metallic type of tint to the color due to one parent being silvery-colored and the other one being bronze. There would not be a paler brown like what happened when the Native Americans bred with white people. With this, the bronze remained bronze, it was just a lighter bronze.

D: *Then the silver color was drowned out right away.*

B: Yes, it receded. It wasn't drowned out immediately, because for several generations one could tell who had descended from the aliens. Those who had some colony descent would be a lighter skin shade than the people who were strictly native descent.

D: *But the majority of the aliens were blond. Was there any white hair?*

B: Some. The colors ranged through ash blond to light blond to platinum blond and pale blue. And various variations of that range; sometimes someone might be platinum blond but with pale blue highlights. When they would be in direct light you would see pale blue glints in this platinum blond hair. And other people would be directly pale blue so that, regardless of the light they were in, it was obvious it was pale blue.

D: *Those colors would have been genetically drowned out right away, I suppose.*

B: Yes indeed. The blue aspect of it took longer to be bred out because the natives had blue in their hair from it being so black. You've seen the color. It's black when you look at it, but when the sun shines on it just right you see blue highlights because it's so dark. Some of the first and second generations had interesting hair colors. Usually when an ash blond would breed with a native, the hair would be red; not your spectrum red but the normal orange-red color or more of an auburn—a very pleasant color. And sometimes whenever someone with pale blue hair mated with a native the children tended to have bright blue hair. They found this very amusing.

D: *(Laugh) Bright blue!*

B: Because the darkness of the native's hair would have darkened halfway between the two. But since both of them had blue highlights it would be intense blue instead of brown or something like that.

D: *(Laugh) So that was the color that took the longest to disappear.*

B: Right. Usually if someone with bright blue hair mated with a native, it would come up with a dark color and you couldn't really decide if it was black or blue. But there were a lot of blue

variations for two or three generations. The blond characteristics bred out right away. Occasionally, particularly from the
ones who had red hair, about one in four children would be
born with a variation of blond hair. But that particular branch
of genetics with the red hair group tended to go towards brown
and black since the black gene was so dominant.

D: *I suppose the eyes must have been different, too, for a while.*

B: Oh yes. The natives had deep dark or golden-brown eyes. And
the colony had violet eyes. So the eyes would usually be violet
or dark brown in the children. Occasionally there would be a
couple of recessives that would come together and produce
someone with silvery-gray eyes, but that was extremely rare.
With all these various hair colors, for a while it became a fad
with the children, whenever someone would get a haircut they
would collect the hair and make different types of cloth with
designs in it, using the different colors of hair.

D: *(Laugh) That would be interesting. I guess they could have fun
doing that.*

Chapter 16

The Artifacts

D: *Apparently there are people on this continent today who are descended from the colony.*

B: At this point in your time, anyone who has any American Indian in them would have a little bit of the Old Ones' blood because it was eventually spread throughout the American Indian peoples. There were thousands of years of interbreeding involved here. That was long enough for their genes to be spread among all the American Indians, thus they are descended from the Old Ones.

D: *Would that mean the Native Americans came from the Eskimos?*

B: Oh, partially. The Eskimos interbred with the other Native Americans, too, and so it eventually spread. One of the traits of the Old Ones that has survived pretty much intact is a low tolerance to alcohol, because normal, pure earth-strained stock can have a high tolerance to alcohol. But on their planet the old ones had a different chemical combination for their recreational drug. They didn't have alcohol, so there was no tolerance to it. That is why Native Americans can go crazy when they drink. Their bodies cannot handle the alcohol.

D: *Are there any other traits that have been carried down?*

B: There are some blood factors, but they are so rare and difficult to find that they don't really make that much difference.

D: *Do you mean blood diseases or what?*

B: No. Factors in the blood that doctors and researchers know about when they factor down the blood in the centrifuge, and do chemical analysis on it. The doctors have labeled them as being very rare. They are just little offshoots of Old Ones' genes that still survive, because the old ones had different blood than we did.

D: *Was the radiation just normally higher during that time period, or was it because they were not used to it?*

B: They were from a different sun that had a lower radiation count, and so they did not have any natural defenses for it. That's one reason why people in your time get skin cancer from the sun. They have some of the genes of the Old Ones.

D: *Then they are still very sensitive to the sun now?*

B: Not as much as they were, but it still crops up some in your time.

D: *Are there any other traits that are still carried?*

B: There is Lupus Erythematosus. That is a condition where the skin is sensitive to the sun. I believe the word you use is "allergic." The person gets in the sun, their skin breaks out in a rash and the body starts aching and malfunctioning. It causes the body's natural immune system to attack the body itself. Particularly in the joints. That is another trait from the Old Ones.

Lupus is a chronic inflammatory disease that can affect various parts of the body, especially the skin, joints, blood and kidneys. The body's immune system normally makes proteins called antibodies to protect the body against viruses, bacteria and other foreign materials. These foreign materials are called antigens. In an autoimmune disorder such as lupus, the immune system loses its ability to tell the difference between foreign substances (antigens) and its own cells and tissues. The immune system then makes antibodies directed against "self." In other words, the body begins to attack itself, hence the name Lupus which means wolf.

Lupus is a rather mysterious disease because it is difficult to diagnose, and its cause is unknown. It is believed that environmental and genetic factors are involved. They have found that there is a genetic or hereditary predisposition to the disease, and environmental factors play a critical role in triggering flare-ups. One of these factors is an unusual sensitivity to sunlight.

The disease occurs more frequently in women than men, thus it is believed that hormones may play a part. And Native Americans develop the disease more frequently than Caucasians. Certain Native American tribes (Sioux, Crow, Arapahoe) have a high predisposition toward the disease.

This is a simplified description of a very complex disease, but it is amazing how the symptoms show that it could possibly be connected to a defective gene passed down through thousands of years from the Old Ones.

D: *It goes along with their sensitivity to the radiation?*

B: Yes. It doesn't necessarily crop up in the same person at the same time, but it is related to the problems they had with the radiation. But there were some good traits passed on, too. Many of the psychic abilities that people have. Some people have night vision or "cat eyes," as some people call it. They can see in the dark very easily. That is a trait from the old ones.

D: *Yes, they would have had to see in the dark if they worked at night, or in the dimmer light on their craft. You said the North American Indians were all descended from them. Is that where the blood stopped—just in North America?*

B: That is hard to say. It is predominantly in North and South America because that is where the Native American peoples are. And people who are related to the Indian peoples are mainly in the Western Hemisphere. Some of the blood has spread a little into other races, when people from this hemisphere went to other places to live and have children. But it is not as generally widespread as in the Western Hemisphere.

D: *Then the genes are more predominant here. (Another idea suddenly occurred to me.) I wonder, would you be able to draw the sign that hung on that building? The one that had the symbols on it?*

B: I can see it. I don't know what is says.

D: *Could you draw the design for me.*

B: I can try.

I had Beth open her eyes again and handed her the paper and marker. She began drawing the shape of the sign.

B: The sign is not a very unusual shape, and it's supposed to be straight. The background is dark, and the lettering on it is light. And the lettering ... I don't know if I'll be able to accurately reproduce the lettering because the sign was somewhat faded in Tuin's time, although he did not realize this.

D: *Just make an attempt anyway.*

She drew all the strange-looking letters.

D: *Are those all of them?*

B: Yes. At one time apparently there was finer print under those.

I took the paper away and had Beth close her eyes again.

D: *From your position now, can you tell what those symbols mean?*

B: Yes. It was a sign from the ship indicating a combination of the captain's quarters and bridge where the main computer area was located. In the ship the captain's quarters and the bridge and much of the research was combined in one facility, and that was the sign labeling that.

D: *And they saved the sign and put it on the building.*

B: Yes, they had signs on other buildings, too, when they were first built. They were eventually discarded, or rather given to the Wise Man for their metal content.

D: *These were signs for other compartments on the ship?*

B: Yes. And for labeling different people's quarters.

D: *Do you think there is a chance that any parts of the ship will ever be found?*

B: It is a remote possibility. Parts of it are still buried and have survived because of the intense cold.

D: *You would have to know where to look.*

B: Yes. It's in a very remote area. Perhaps someday.

D: *Is there any civilization in that area today?*

B: There are what are called "Eskimos" living in that area.

D: *No cities or towns?*

B: Well, nothing large or major. Small towns—population, say 44: population 14.

D: *I thought if it was near a large town or city, someone might find it someday if they were digging for construction or something.*

B: No, it would not be found that way. It would only be found by groups specifically exploring.

D: *There was a river running through there. Do you know what river that would be?*

B: It was one of the feeder streams to the Yukon.

D: *It would be pretty hard to find that place in such a large area. One thing Tuin talked about. When everything changed? Did he mean there was a shift in the axis?*

B: Yes.

D: *Do you know if this was before or after the time of the dinosaurs?*

B: This shift in the axis came just after the time of the dinosaurs. There was another shift earlier during the time of the dinosaurs. But this was already into the age of the mammals.

D: *I thought so, because he didn't mention any dinosaurs.*

B: He did not know of any.

D: *Then there was a large shift. And this second one was during the time of the Old Ones.*

B: Right. It was not as major of a shift, but it was still traumatic.

D: *Then the first shift was the one that created the ice ages, or am I correct?*

B: All the shifts contributed to the ice ages. That first major shift mainly altered the climate flow to where many animals died suddenly and drastically of violent means. The second shift caused much of the planet to turn colder and thereby enter an ice age.

D: *Because it moved the poles. But where he lived, did it get colder?*

B: It was extremely cold. It was just that he took it for granted. Where he lived had basically been cold for a long time anyhow. And when it got slightly colder it just meant more ice, more snow.

D: *I was thinking of an ice age and glaciers. I don't think he mentioned anything like that.*

B: No.

D: *Whenever the Old Ones crashed there, was the climate different than it was in Tuin's time?*

B: Yes, it was. There was an axis shift during the intervening centuries.

D: *What was the climate like when they first crashed?*

B: It was subtropical, much like southern North America—the area that you call the "deep south." It was warm, humid, much greenery, many plants, many animals, very fertile.

D: *Then it became arctic after the shift. One thing I've been wondering about was that strange animal Tuin found. Can you see anything about that?*

B: Yes. That was a rare occurrence. There are many, many separate universes existing in the same space as yours. They are normally invisible because they are vibrating at different speeds. These different universes intersect with each other but usually the points of intersection are not compatible, so inhabitants of the two different universes are not aware of the intersection. There may be some minor changes that one or two people might notice, but it will be nothing major. In this case there was one particular point that was a rare occurrence of a compatible intersection. When Tuin was out hunting he was in two universes simultaneously but was not aware of it. The animal he killed was an inhabitant of the other universe. But since it was a compatible intersection he was able to transport the animal into this universe without destroying its basic matrix.

This was very confusing to me. I had never encountered the idea of parallel universes before in my work. In my book *Keepers of the Garden*, we discussed other universes composed of energy, and I assumed these were located somewhere out in space. I had not heard of ones composed of similar earth-like physical properties, and occupying the same space as ours.

D: *Do you mean the other universe was also a physical universe?*

B: Yes. It was a physical universe built along a different basic matrix. But since the intersection was compatible the animal's matrix was not destroyed when it was brought across to this universe. That's what makes that occurrence so rare. If the intersection is not compatible, the basic matrix of anything from the other universe is destroyed and it no long exists in this universe.

D: *How do you mean, it is destroyed? It would just disappear or what?*

B: Yes. It would just dissolve into nothing and release the energy into the ether.

D: *Would somebody see it like a mirage or something?*

B: Perhaps. Under certain circumstances they would see it, then it would shimmer and fade away into nothing.

D: *You mean, this other universe is living, existing side-by-side with this one?*

B: Yes, there are an infinite number of universes existing side-by-side with this one. And they're all interwoven like a cloth. (Sigh) The terms of this language are not sufficient.

D: *I've been told that before.*

B: In order for there to be a compatible intersection, like at this one incident with Tuin, there has to be a very unusual set of variables existing at the same time. Since it happens so rarely, it cannot be expressed with percentages; the number is too small.

D: *Well, he did say that whenever he came across this animal he had a strange feeling with his senses.*

B: Yes, he was very highly developed psychically and so he was aware of the fact that he was in two universes simultaneously, but he did not know how to state this verbally. He knew what he knew without really knowing what he knew.

D: *Yes, he didn't know exactly what it was. But do you mean this was very unusual for him to be able to bring the animal back to the people?*

B: Yes. To be able to bring the animal back fully into his universe without the animal dissolving into nothing is *extremely* unusual. It rarely happens. It *does* happen, but just not very often.

D: *Of course, the people were very hungry at that time too. This might have been part of it.*

B: Yes. Their psychic abilities undoubtedly helped the animal to make the transition.

D: *For many years afterward the animal's head and skin was used by the Wise Man, so it was definitely something physical. And they did eat it, and it apparently didn't harm them in any way.*

B: True.

D: *The concept is very interesting, but it's also very complicated.*

B: Yes. I feel that I have perhaps left some mistaken impressions in your mind due to the inadequacies of this language.

D: *Well, that's possible. But other people I've spoken to like this have also said the language is inadequate to explain things. Sometimes they must draw analogies for me.*

B: True. But they are most inadequate, too. It leaves rather simplified notions in your mind.

This idea was so new and complicated to my mind that I just wanted to briefly touch on it in this book. I did not want to confuse the reader or distract from the story I am trying to tell. The concept of parallel universes will be more fully explored in my book, *The Convoluted Universe.*

D: *Tuin spoke of some things that were in the Wise Man's hut. One picture he drew looked to me like an instrument panel.*

B: It was. It was the panel that linked up with the central computer. They left the computer intact for several generations after the crash. And the main panel was put into the leader's hut, so he could consult with the computer when he needed to. When they were building the colony they used parts of the ship. And they ended up using all of the ship. Eventually they had to cannibalize the computer as well, but they kept the panel intact to remind them of their heritage.

D: *Where was the main computer located?*

B: All the archives and knowledge were stored in the ship. They used it as an educational device and for schooling and such as that. They did have a communication device set up, but it was not as powerful as they would have liked. So they did not count on contacting anybody elsewhere.

D: *Tuin said they spoke to a wall and also to something like a rock. Is that correct?*

B: When the people were first building the colony they were still living in the ship as well as living in separate buildings. In the library of the ship one could speak to the wall as part of the ship's intercom system and be speaking directly to the computer. The wall could be used to show information, much like a movie screen, as computer-generated images. The crystal that he spoke of was one of the specialized crystals they had. The science of crystallography was extremely advanced, and it was a very delicate science. They could develop a crystal for almost any purpose. And one they developed could be used the way you would use radios. If one person needed to contact another person they'd have a crystal they could speak through. It would be attached to an instrument so you could fine-tune it to the energy field and matrix of a particular crystal belonging to somebody else.

D: *Then they were speaking to each other and not speaking to people in the other ships?*

B: Before the ships left they spoke to the other people through a crystal like this. But after the ships had to leave, they used it for communicating with each other.

D: *Then when they were speaking to the wall, they were actually speaking to the computer on the ship. They had no way of contacting anyone outside after the other ships flew away?*

B: They had a radio-type device where they could broadcast, but no one ever came within the range of their broadcast.

D: *He also drew a picture of a strange-looking hat or helmet-type device. I was curious what that was used for.*

B: That was used for many things. It was a very delicate instrument, but basically it was a learning device. Whenever one wanted to learn about a particular subject, one would put this helmet on and the fine wires on the inside would, from the energy generated, extend outwards until they were barely touching all over the head. The energy would keep the hat suspended so you would almost not feel it. This hat was linked up to the central computer so you could learn about anything you wanted, or see anything you wanted. This was because the hat could generate images within your mind and give you knowledge directly. It was a more concentrated way of learning. They did not use it exclusively, because you could get brain burnout from it. If it were used in limited doses it was very therapeutical and very handy. It was an extremely complex device.

D: *It had all those protuberances on the outside. Were these connected to the wires or hairs on the inside?*

B: Yes. The protuberances on the outside were crystals and they were connected through microcircuits to the wires on the inside. And these crystals were tuned into the computer, hence one could control what one was learning just through thinking. One didn't have to really work any devices. The crystals were attuned to the brain so they could shift their polarities and their fine-tunings to respond to what your brain wanted, and obtain the information from the computer.

D: *Was it used with that instrument panel-type thing?*

B: It could be used separately. The panel was mainly a device in the library. The central library was like a chamber within the computer. But all the walls and the ceiling and floor were directly linked to the computer, so it was like an extension of the computer.

D: *Was this hat used to teach children, or to teach anyone something they wanted to learn quickly?*

B: It was usually used on young adults and older. The children were taught by different methods. Quicker than your methods, but still similar to your conventional methods of learning so they would learn discipline. They had to learn how to discipline their thoughts and how to concentrate, because you needed mental discipline to be able to use the helmet, and the library, properly.

D: *So you wouldn't have this burnout-type thing?*

B: Right. The helmet also helped with enhancing certain psychic powers as well. That's why it was only used on young adults, approximately 15 or 16 of your years on up. There were some safety devices built in. Normally they were not needed because, as a safety factor, they would make sure the person had the proper mental discipline before they would allow them to use the helmet. When you had the proper mental discipline you would know how much you could handle, and when you reached your limit, common sense would tell you to stop. And most of the time the majority of them did. Sometimes a few would try to go further. But there was a cutback device in it that would warn them that they were approaching their limit, in case they had not been concentrating or paying attention. If one ignored this cutback, after a certain length of time it would shut down before any permanent damage was done. One might have the equivalent of a headache for a few days, and might need to be doctored for it, but it would not be permanent damage. It would just be a temporary thing like a mild sunburn from the sun.

D: *They used this until they had to cannibalize the main computer?*

B: Yes, they used this for several generations. But they eventually had to use the materials in the computer for other things in order to survive.

D: *That must have been traumatic for them to shut it down and lose all that knowledge.*

B: Yes, it was. They spent much of their time trying to record the knowledge in other means, like in writing, because they knew they would eventually have to cannibalize the computer. And when the time came, they knew they did not have *nearly* all the knowledge from the computer recorded in another means. But they had done the best they could to record the essential parts, like their science and technology and basic things like that.

D: *What kind of materials did they write it on?*

B: In an effort to be self-sufficient and in tune with the planet they made paper-like products and they printed it on that. They stored this paper in specially constructed metal boxes to protect the paper from rotting.

D: *Did any of that pass down?*

B: Oh yes. It was all passed down for many, many generations. But eventually the paper started to wear out and they no longer knew how to make more paper. Thus through the centuries, they gradually lost their technology. At this point it passed into oral form, in the forms of their legends. Hence their emphasis to keep it accurate, because they knew they were passing down information that had once been printed, but they knew they would not be able to print it now. And they did not want misinformation to be passed down.

D: *This was one reason why it survived so long. But Tuin said the Wise Man knew how to write.*

B: Yes. Eventually it became harder to educate everybody to read and write, as those types of materials became scarcer. Eventually through centuries it developed to where the people in general felt they really didn't need reading and writing for their normal living. So they did not go through the trouble of learning as much as they could. It was felt that the head man should do this since it was part of his duty to keep track of the legends anyhow.

D: *Was the type of writing similar to the type you copied for me?*

B: Yes, it was. Since I was copying that from one of the plaques of the ship, that was the type of writing. Through the years the written type was altered a little bit. And by the time it got to Tuin's day most of the writing was used as symbolism rather than what it was originally intended for. The head man would use it on his headdresses and such for the symbolic meaning, rather than using it to form words and such.

D: *Did any of that come down to our time?*

B: No, it was lost.

D: *I'm trying to remember all these things he talked about. He mentioned something in the Wise Man's house, that I thought must have been glass tubes.*

B: They were crystal tubes. Everything of that sort was made of a type of crystal rather than glass. Since they had ways of forming crystals into anything they needed, it was very efficient and economical. They really didn't feel the need to go through the trouble of melting down crude crystal into glass.

D: *He said that the wise man had liquids in them. Was this a form of making medicines?*

B: Yes. The bulk of the laboratory type of knowledge that was passed down came under the head man's jurisdiction. And it was mainly concerning necessary medicines and essential things such as that.

D: *It was mostly the things for survival. And the other technology wouldn't have been important enough to remember.*

B: Yes. They had to stick with the essentials. There was medicine and also some specialized fertilizer for their crops, to help them be resistant to some of the sun's radiation.

D: *I think those are all the questions. I wanted to get a different viewpoint than his. His viewpoint was very restricted by what he knew at the time. I was curious about the true story of these people that came here. I have often believed that we were descended in some way from the people on other planets.*

B: Yes, that is true. There have been many explorers here. This was just one case.

D: *Maybe someday we can speak of others, and you can give me more information.*

B: Yes. You are the asker.

D: *Is there anything else you would like to say about that time? About the legends or about the people?*

B: They were a good people. Their emphasis and life was closer to what it should be. The people in your situation and time have lost the true emphasis of what they should be working for— their further spiritual advancement.

As I was counting her up, Beth reacted the same way she had before. She showed no signs of response until I reached the numbers seven, eight, and I had given her instructions about becoming aware of her surroundings. Then her body jerked in one spasmodic motion and she awakened on signal. From the similar experience she had earlier, I knew she had taken another side trip before awakening. She described a quick visit she had astrally taken to a friend's house. She had seen him and the house in great detail. Then she heard the numbers "seven, eight" in the background and the noise of the fan in the room, and was pulled back into her body. She said for a little bit she felt out-of-breath, as if she had been running. She certainly didn't look out-of-breath; she looked very refreshed and relaxed.

She stated: "Sometimes when I come back to consciousness, I feel, not really dizzy,but a little bit light-headed,momentarily,like I need to stretch,as if I'm just waking up. But this time I felt alert immediately."

I explained this was normal even among people waking up from a normal sleep. She seemed to take advantage of this near-waking state to take these little out-of-body trips. Often she would remember virtually nothing from the session, but she remembered these side trips in great detail. Maybe this was because they occurred just before awakening when she was coming out of the theta level, and also because they had more importance to her than the purpose of the regression. This is very similar to people remembering the last remnants of their dreams before they awaken.

Beth was definitely not influencing the information that Tuin was giving because she did not have much interest in it. Sometimes she wanted me to extend the session and ask her subconscious about health questions. When she awakened she asked about that in detail, but did not mention Tuin. I came to know that gentle hunter very well, but he remained only a shadow to Beth's mind. She was not even interested in listening to the tapes.

Chapter 17
The Magic of the Old Ones

THREE YEARS PASSED between the time I gathered the information about the legend of the Old Ones and the time I began to put it together in book form. I was never idle during that time. I was involved in hundreds of normal regressions with people who wanted the experience, either out of curiosity or for help with problems in their daily life. I also spent much time writing other books about the adventures I had encountered along the way. When I began to arrange the data from these transcripts I realized there were still some unanswered questions. These would have to be answered before the book would be complete. I had visited Beth, but we had not worked on this material for three years. Even though I had not spoken to Tuin in all that time I did not think it would be a problem to call him up again. In a sense the people in these reincarnation experiments never die. They can be resurrected as many times as necessary. They are in this sense eternal, immortal; they are always living their lives in their respective time periods, and can be easier contacted. This is an amazing part of this phenomenon for which I have no answer. I only know that it is possible, because I have accomplished it many, many times. The entities appear to live forever in the subconscious minds of the subjects.

I phoned Beth and told her that I needed to contact Tuin again. She had not consciously thought about him during the ensuing years, but was willing to reopen the experiment so I could tie up the few loose ends. On the day of the appointment I used her keyword.

It worked perfectly, as though there had been no interruption in our sessions. She entered immediately into a deep somnambulistic trance, and we began. I knew that the information I needed would not be found during Tuin's lifetime because of his narrow focused physical viewpoint. I would have to speak to his spirit after his physical death in the avalanche. I counted her back to that time, and she immediately began to describe a scene of ethereal beauty which she was watching on the spirit plane.

B: Everything exists on multiple planes, and I'm looking at the Earth and at all the various planes it exists on. The picture is very beautiful, but it's also very complicated. I can see that not only is there the physical Earth that I was familiar with when I was hunting down there, but there are also other Earths that are occupying the same space, but on a different level of energy.

D: *That sounds complicated.*

B: It's very beautiful. They're all linked together and related to each other. But as you go from one type of energy to another, as well as from one *level* of energy to another, there are subtle changes that differentiate the different types of Earth from each other, and the different levels of Earth from each other.

D: *Do these different levels and different parts look alike?*

B: They look similar, but there are subtle changes. As an example I will use an apple tree. In the springtime when it's blooming on the regular physical Earth that one sees when one is on the physical plane, you see the grayish-brown bark, and the white blossoms with a touch of pink to it. It looks like a regular apple tree. But on the next level up, when the same apple tree is blooming in the springtime, the blossoms will be more of a gold color instead and the bark will be darker. It will still be the same concept, an apple tree, but you're on a different energy level. As you go up through the different energy levels, you keep seeing subtle changes like that. There's one energy level where apple trees have dark brown bark, silver blossoms, and blue leaves. But not just any shade of blue; it's a particular shade. I'm trying to think of a way to describe it for you. You know how it is at sunset when the sun has set all the way and it's twilight, and you still have some gold at the horizon. But straight above you is this pure shade of blue. That's the shade of blue the leaves on the apple trees are on one of these energy levels. The leaves have gradually changed from green to blue-green to turquoise to this blue color, as you go up through the different energy levels.

D: *It is the same form. It's just changing in color.*

B: Right. The landscapes stay similar, but they alter a little from one level to the next. If you go up through levels in order, you can see the landscape *shift* slightly, but you can see where it's related. But if you would start at one level and skip several levels in between, it will look different because you haven't seen the shifting process. It would be different colors, different shapes, different locations. But it all shifts very subtly from one level to the next. For example, you're standing in a field on Earth on the physical plane. There's a river over here to your left, and a mountain to your right. You shift up to the next plane, and the mountain is sloped just a little differently. It might have slightly more gradual slopes or slightly steeper slopes, but it will be shaped just a little differently. It's still at the same location, so you can tell it's the same mountain. And the river might be wider, for example, but it's still the same river. It's just a little different. And if you go up to the next plane, the river might still be the same size, but it might be a little bit closer to the mountain. And so it's just subtle changes like that. If you go up through the levels one at a time you can see these gradual shifts, but you can see where they're related to everything on the level below it. If you were to skip from the Earth level and go up five or six levels, and hit that without looking at any of the levels in between, you might find a level where the grass is bluer in color, the mountain is quite a bit different in shape, and the river has moved to where it's right next to the base of the mountain. And it has now turned into a small rushing mountain stream. You might think you were at a different location, when you're actually still standing at the same place.

D: *That does sound complicated, but I think I can understand that.*

B: As you go up through the higher energy levels, the relationships of the colors to each other change. Somehow the *light* changes when you go up, so that the colors appear differently to you. The light apparently affects the colors of everything.

It sounded like a very beautiful scene and it was an interesting concept, but it was time to get down to the business for which I had contacted Tuin's spirit in this other-worldly state.

D: *I wanted to ask some questions about things in Tuin's life, that he couldn't understand in his time. I thought you might have the answers, because you have much more knowledge now. You've already given me explanations about other things he saw and experienced that he couldn't understand. He talked about the wise man's strange pot which he called a cauldron. I was curious about that. It was a strange pot that he said changed colors, and it had a handle which turned. All he knew was that the wise man used it for something. He had a hard time explaining it. Do you know what I mean?*

B: Yes. This pot that he referred to is a very ancient relic. For you see, Tuin's people were descended from galactic travelers who came there long ago and colonized that part of Earth. And since they weren't planning on flying their ship again, they cannibalized it. They used everything that they could convert for everyday purposes. But as the centuries passed the things wore out, became broken, lost or taken away as groups moved away. By the time of Tuin's group, one of the artifacts they still had was this pot that the wise man used, and it was from the galactic travelers'ship. It was not originally designed as a pot, *per se*. It started out as a part of a device that helped to control the flow of energy that ran the ship. By Tuin's time they no longer had the source of energy that was available for the ship. All they had was fire and running water. The keepers of these artifacts were traditionally the wise men of the tribe, or the wise women, whatever the case would be. And they passed this artifact down from generation to generation. They also passed down instructions for its care and its use, what it was for and what it was supposed to do. But since they knew this was a precious thing and the information was precious, they were very careful about who they told about this. The original source of energy to activate what was left of this device was no longer available, so they had learned to partially activate it through the application of heat. They would set it over a fire to start the activation, because this device would take the heat of the fire and convert it into the energy it needed. It could not operate the way it was supposed to, because it did not have enough energy. It could partially work. And by this time so much knowledge had been lost, that although it was only working partially, the pot was considered to be very impressive and very special.

D: *But on the ship it was part of the controls that ran the ship?*

B: No, no, no. It was part of channeling the energy system. The controls were something else totally. It was part of a device that helped shape the energy. They had a different concept of energy. On this Earth in your time period energy is pictured as something that flows through something, like electricity through wire, or water through a dam to produce energy. These galactic travelers had a different way of dealing with energy. Instead of energy just flowing where it wanted to, energy was shaped. It's hard to explain. I'm not sure I understand, but they had devices that would shape the energy. And depending on what form the energy would take it would do particular things, or it would react in particular ways. So according to what they needed to have done on the ship, the device would shape the energy. The controls were a separate device that would let this device know what shape it needed to mold the energy into.

D: *So it was not always the same shape. It was shaped for what it was needed.*

B: Exactly. There were an infinite number of shapes it could be. But it took a particular amount of energy to do it the way it was supposed to be done. By Tuin's time, part of this artifact, the energy shaper, was missing. Plus they didn't have a steady source of energy for it, so it really couldn't operate properly. But the things that it did and the color changes that it went through, were part of it trying to shape what energy it received.

D: *He said he thought there might have been more than one pot because he saw it as different colors.*

B: It was the same artifact changing colors as it tried to shape the energy it was receiving. But it was not receiving enough to complete the process.

D: *He said it had a strange type of handle or something on it.*

B: Yes. The pot, this device, was not all there; part of it was missing. And this handle was a part that used to connect with the missing part. It was kind of an in-between part to connect the piece they had into a larger device that could have come closer to doing what it was supposed to do. But as it was, they had only part of it, and so they never could—even if they knew how—make it do what it was supposed to do, because they didn't have the entire device.

D: *He said the handle could be moved around.*

B: That was part of shaping the energy. The part they had could be used to do some things, but they couldn't realize its full potential.

D: *What did the wise man use it for?*

B: The wise man used it for applying energy. If someone was sick or injured, the pot could direct enough energy to aid with the healing process. Also, if the wise man applied some of this energy to himself while in a meditative state, it would cause him to have visions.

D: *Tuin said sometimes if the farmers found rocks or things in the field, they would bring them to the wise man. I don't know if he used the pot for this or not.*

B: If they found a rock or something in the field that seemed to have a high metal content, they would bring it to the wise man. He would apply fire and sunlight or what-have-you to the pot to give it as much energy as he could. And it would be enough so that whenever he inserted this rock it could purify it into a purer metal content, and perhaps shape it in a particular shape that was needed. Similar to what the complete device would do to energy, the partial device could do to material things. It could either purify them some or change the shape or what-have-you. But it would only work with certain things. It wouldn't work with wood, for example, but it would work with certain types of rocks, certain types of metals.

D: *It sounds like he couldn't do very much at a time.*

B: No, it was a specialized thing. Another useful thing that the pot did, was that it was good for making medicines. They knew that when you chewed on the leaves of a particular plant that the juice would help you in a medicinal way. If you placed these leaves in the pot and applied energy to it, it would extract this liquid from the leaves. You'd have concentrated medicine, rather than having to chew a lot of leaves to get the medicine value.

D: *It was in the wise man's house, and it seemed like no one else knew how to use it.*

B: This was very specialized knowledge, because some of the details had been lost. They had been passing it down from person to person across many centuries, so it was difficult to keep track of everything.

D: *Can you see what eventually happened to that artifact?*

B: Yes. More centuries pass, and eventually enough knowledge is lost so they're not able to use it any more, and for two or three centuries it's used as a status symbol. Whoever the pot is passed down to is designated as the spiritual leader of the tribe. And finally at one point in time there was one particular spiritual leader who was very charismatic. When he died, as a gesture of respect they found a cave that would make a good tomb. They placed him in there, and put the pot and some other things with him. Then they put a boulder and some rubble in front of it, and blocked the cave to protect this particular wise man's body and the artifacts.

D: *It seems it would be very unlikely that it would be found then.*

B: It is somewhat unlikely unless there happens to be an earthquake or something that would knock loose the boulders and the plants and such that have grown over the cave opening. It would have to tear or knock them away to expose this again. Or if, with modern machinery, one were to apply sensing devices such as radar, sonar or what-have-you, to the mountain range one could find the hidden caves and such. But, as you say, it is probably unlikely that it will come to light any time soon. It has been too long and it was a small cave to begin with.

D: *I was curious about a few other things that were mentioned in the legends. Tuin talked about the sun spear that the Old Ones used. I think he said they used it to kill animals.*

B: It was a device that would shoot out a ray of energy. It appeared like intense light, but it had other energies in it as well. You would aim this device like one would a firearm, and press the activating button. The light would shoot out and hit whatever animal or what-have-you you wanted to hit, and it would kill them on the spot. It appeared as a straight beam of light, or a spear of light. It's one of those devices that survived down through those years and some of the knowledge was lost. They started calling it a sun spear. After a while the device wore out so it did not work any more, and then it became lost.

D: *I thought it sounded like a laser beam or something similar.*

B: There was visible light in the ray of energy, but there were other energies in there as well. It had a particular balance of energies. So that if you shot it at an animal, it would kill it instantly without causing the animal pain, and without doing excess damage to the body. It was assumed that you wanted to use the animal to eat, and so you didn't want to damage the body, because that would be damaging what you could eat.

D: *He also talked about a box that cooked food. It was supposed to have been very miraculous.*

B: Yes. This box that cooked food was actually quite simple, but the technology involved was far beyond anything Tuin's people had at the time. This box ran by solar energy. You would set it out in the sun, and the energy it absorbed from the sun would be converted to energy to cook with. It was similar to micro-wave but not exactly, because the people who designed this box had a different concept of energy, that I mentioned earlier. It was different concepts with different principles involved, but most basically, the equivalent would be a solar-powered microwave oven.

D: *It was powered by the sun.*

B: Right. Just set it out in the sun, and it would cook things.

D: *It ran off the type of energy they were familiar with. It wouldn't be the same thing if we put a box out in the sun.*

B: Right. Because the people who invented and built the box had a different concept of energy use.

D: *He talked about a round ball that could be held in the hand, and he also mentioned a rock that could talk back. I don't know if these are the same things or not, or if they were related to each other.*

B: They're two different things. The round ball that could be held in the hand was a nearly perfect sphere. The material it was made out of was a special kind of crystal that does not exist on this Earth. Now as humankind expands into space exploration, sooner or later they will run across this material. This particular material is actually a crystal, although it appears metallic. And when you held this crystal sphere in your hand, the energies that flow through the Earth—the magnetic and gravity energies, plus the energies from your body—would cause the crystal to react. As a result it could do many wonderful things. One could channel energy through it and use it for all kinds of things. For example, one very common side effect was that whenever someone used the crystal things would start levitating around them, or it would accidentally teleport things. Something would pop out of existence here and then pop back into existence over there. It would be a side effect of the energies being channeled through this sphere. Now the rock that could talk back to you was actually not a rock, although that was how Tuin perceived it. Through the retelling of the tales and legends across the centuries it had been corrupted. The rock that could talk back to you was actually or basically a metallic device, and it had its own self-contained energy system. It could be used for transmitting and receiving messages, rather like radio, but there was a different level of energy involved. They would use it to communicate with people in the ships in orbit around the Earth.

D: *Do you mean the others that were there whenever they first landed?*

B: Yes. They were in communication with the ones that were still orbiting, to let them know whether or not they could live on this planet. And this device had other uses as well, because they could use it for analyzing types of energies. For example, it could analyze the type of light the plants were absorbing. The type of energies being used by the ecosystem on the Earth. It sent the information back up to the ship in orbit, where they could analyze it, and determine whether or not they could live here.

D: *So it was a radio-type device. I think I only have one more question. Do you remember the drawing Tuin made of the blanket design? I think you said one time that this was not a drawing of the main ship, but it was like a shuttle or something, a smaller ship. The way the picture was drawn, there was a star-shaped object above the doorway. I thought it looked like a six-pointed star. Only it was standing on two legs with two legs up in the air and two out to the side. That's the way Tuin drew it anyway. Can you tell me if that star had any real significance, or was that something they made up for the blanket?*

B: The star had significance because of where it was positioned. It represented an actual object on the shuttle ship.

D: *In that area above the door?*

B: When you first entered the door the ceiling was right above your head. But above the ceiling was a lot of instrumentation and such. And the central part of this instrumentation was this huge and very complex crystal. The star design that they drew in that position was their simplified representation of this crystal. This crystal was very complicated with many fingers and branches and such. It was similar to a gigantic and complicated piece of quartz, for example, with all the fingers of crystals sticking out all over. But every bit of this crystal was used. Each finger of crystal, each size, each angle and each shape did particular things

to the type of energy they used. It was used as a central channeling of the energy, to apply it particularly to the automated
devices, so they would basically run by themselves. It ran the shuttle,
plus it kept the shuttle systems coordinated with the ship systems.

D: *When I first saw it I thought it looked like a six-pointed Star of
David, except that it was not shaped the same way.*

B: There is a similarity, particularly when the Star of David is
drawn so that the various branches seem to weave in and out
with each other, as for the Seal of Solomon. That is another
representation of this crystal I have mentioned.

D: *Do you mean that is where the Seal of Solomon and the Star of
David came from?*

B: Yes.

D: *I thought it looked similar. But if this was a craft that landed in
North America and was related to Tuin's tribe, how did the knowledge of it get to Asia? I probably could be wrong on the history of
where the Seal of Solomon came from.*

B: You are correct as far as you have taken it, because this group
landed in North America and established their colony there. But
this was not the only group of space travelers to land on your
planet. Since several of the other peoples were not very
advanced yet, whenever any of these groups landed their ships
in other parts of the planet, the people would take it as a miraculous event. There have been many stories of this type of visit
that were put into legends and passed down, particularly in the
Middle East. The people who were living there at the time were
very superstitious and took notice of anything out of the ordinary. Since they had reading and writing they recorded it and
the event would be preserved in that way. As a result, in several
holy writings around the Earth you have these descriptions of
miraculous visits and voyages. For example, in the ancient king-
dom of Mesopotamia we have *The Epic of Gilgamesh* which
gives us the story of Gilgamesh and his friend, Enkidu. (The
encyclopedia lists this as one of the very earliest epics and was
written on Babylonian clay tablets in cuneiform. It also refers

to Utnapishtim, an equivalent to Noah.) The epic describes a voyage that Gilgamesh takes, to where the sea that he looks at becomes a pond and then a mud puddle and then like a porridge bowl. What he is describing is that he was able to take a trip in one of these ships. There are other descriptions that have been preserved in what you would call the *Bible*. There are several descriptions of the landing of this type of ship and the people who came out of it. For example, the man named John who wrote "Revelation" saw a ship land, and they broadcasted greetings and such. The people who were listening to this were very frightened of what was happening. In another place Ezekiel described seeing the ship land in the desert. Ezekiel had been out in the desert for a while, and as part of his meditation he indulged in hallucinogenic substances, so he was accustomed to strange things happening. Thus he was not as afraid as other chroniclers had been, and so he could be a bit more objective about what he was writing. But it was still very wondrous to him, because he did not have enough knowledge of technology to give as accurate a description as he would have liked.

D: *This is getting a little confusing to me. I thought the only group of people to land on Earth were this small group that landed in Tuin's area. Do you mean there was this group that stayed there, and then other people that might have landed somewhere else?*

B: You're thinking too narrowly. You're not thinking of a broad enough picture. A small group landed and lived there in Tuin's area, because they had no choice. But they weren't the only people coming to Earth. There's a galactic civilization and since Earth was not at a very high technological level, they were not very careful about where they landed in the past. They knew the natives of Earth could not harm them, because they did not have the weapons. So this ship that landed with Tuin's ancestors was not the only ship that ever visited the Earth. When that group landed they basically settled down where they were and just lived their lives in that isolated area. The other people from the same galactic civilization are as complex as we are. Different people have different motivations. And others would come in their ships, and they didn't care if the people saw them or not. They wanted to land and maybe do some exploitation, or some exploration. Other groups have come at different times in the history of the planet. This group which Tuin spoke of had designed their ships so they could take them apart and use them on the planet's surface, so they dismantled them and just stayed there.

D: *Then the other groups that came were either before or after. They were coming to different parts of the Earth. They all seemed to use this same type of crystal energy. And this was where the designs for the Star of David and the Seal of Solomon came from.*

B: This crystal energy was one of the most common forms of energy in this galactic civilization. They used the crystals for focusing the energy. For example, in your civilization you use electricity. To get that electricity into your home you have a wire carrying it into a breaker box where it is split up into many wires going to many different directions, coming out as light sockets for light and electrical outlets for plugging in various machines. This galactic civilization, instead of having a wire carrying electricity and a breaker box to split it up and send the electricity in its different various directions, used something that is similar to what they call "coherent energy." Very pure, very solid forms of energy focused through crystals. Depending on how many different forms of energy was needed and where it was needed, this would affect the shape of the crystal. The crystal would focus the energy and then send it wherever it needed to go.

This is similar to the description given in my book, *Keepers of the Garden,* of how crystals were used by other civilizations for different types of energy. Their shapes also affected their functions.

B: They had crystals of all sizes. The larger, more complicated ones were for running ships and running buildings and such. And then they had smaller, portable, hand-held ones, for doing other things. For example, if the ship landed somewhere in the desert, and the crew decided they needed water, they would take a hand-held crystal outside. They would hold it in their hand and focus the energy from the sun either towards a rock or towards the ground. This would cause one of the underground streams of water to alter its course and come up to the surface to form a spring where they could have water. They could do things like this without going through a lot of physical labor. The concept is similar to the sphere that Tuin described. The round ball worked in similar principles, but different things happened because it was a perfectly round crystal rather than a faceted one. It had a different function, but it was still the idea of holding the crystal where it could absorb the various energies and focus them in certain ways.

D: *So the blanket design was really just a simplified version of the crystals that they saw, and this was passed down.*

B: Yes. When they tried to draw the crystal, they would draw it in the stylized design to symbolize the power that the crystals used. It became a sacred symbol. There are many ways that all this connects, even with your present time. There is the Seal of Solomon and the Star of David, plus any of the various specialized triangles and such, also. All of these go back to these ancient pictures of trying to describe what the crystals did. For example, the swastika was the attempt to picture the crystal as a central point and the energy branching out performing these different functions.

The swastika is an even cross, the arms of which are bent at right angles. Since all four bars point in the same direction (either clock- or counterclockwise) the form creates an impression of perpetual rotation. The origin of the symbol is unknown. It has been used for thousands of years as a symbol of the sun, of infinity, of continuing re-creation, as well as a decorative motif in the Americas, China, Egypt, Greece, Scandinavia, and elsewhere. It has been found in the catacombs of Rome, on textiles of the Inca period, and on relics which were unearthed on the site of Troy. It had always been considered as a sacred symbol until the time of the Second World War. Adolf Hitler corrupted it when it was transformed and defamed into a symbol of a horrific regime.

B: This type of knowledge is needed, and it will be useful for you and for those of your present time. It will remind your people of their origins.

Chapter 18

Research

ONCE I HAD COMPLETED THE REGRESSIONS, the next step was research. The purpose of this research would be to find similarities between the beliefs and the stories of Tuin's tribe, and present-day Native American beliefs. I had to discover if some of the lore of the Old Ones may have crept into the modern rituals and customs in such a manner that the natives are unaware of their origins. Tuin said the blood of his people and that of the Star People have descended and have been incorporated into the blood of most Indian tribes. My task would be to attempt to trace this theory and see if any remnants of his stories have survived. The logical place to center my research would be the Eskimos and the Native American tribes of Canada. That was where I began, with the help of inter-library loan at the University of Arkansas.

I decided to confine the majority of my research to very old books and magazine articles. During the last four or five decades UFOs and extraterrestrials have become household words and are certain to influence any modern person. But if there are suggestions of such things in very old records then it would have more validity. Thus I chose to concentrate my research on old records before the Native Americans were influenced and contaminated by European culture and missionary's beliefs. Some of this information was from books so old and fragile that they were only available on microfilm. At one point I borrowed a portable microfilm reader from the library. I became bleary-eyed from hours of trying to read archaic print on faded pages, but the results always justify the search.

The task of tracing the beginning of human life on our planet is beyond the scope of this book. It will probably be gone into in depth in a future book, as I continue to explore our origins, as connected with our alien ancestors. It will be sufficient to say that the accepted theory of our beginnings is that humanoid types started in Africa, and spread outward from there to all corners of the globe. This chapter will focus on my research concerning the origin of the North American Indian, and the relationship to Tuin's story.

I found there is much debate about the origin of the Native American tribes in North America, and I suppose the debate will not be settled any time soon, as there are still several theories. One of the oldest, and since discredited, is that the Red Man is the degenerate descendant of the lost Ten Tribes of Israel. It is generally conceded that the Indian did not originate on the North American continent, but came from somewhere else.

Anthropologists are positive that no type of prehuman remains have been found on the northern or southern continent of this hemisphere. *Homo sapiens* (or modern man), as far as present knowledge stands, is the only humanoid species that has occupied the Americas. This fact, that only remains of biologically modern man have so far been discovered in the New World, indicates that the migrations which populated it took place in the last, or at least the latest, stage in the development of humankind. Humans had become one biological species before the migrations began.

Scientific observers have noticed the striking resemblance between the natives of America and northern Asia. The most popular belief is that they migrated across the Bering Strait during a time in the ancient past when a land bridge (the Miocene bridge) existed in the area. The great glaciers of the Ice Age captured and held so much water that ocean levels dropped hundreds of feet, exposing land bridges that tied Siberia to North America. At its widest this bridge stretched 1,000 miles north from the present-day Alaska Peninsula. It was a land that the migrants had to share with mammoths,

saber-toothed tigers, and giant bears. Stone tools were found in
Siberia that were identical to those found in Alaska and western
Canada. Scientists believe the immigrants came in three waves. Two
moved inland, the ancestors of the Native Americans. A third wave,
including Eskimos and Aleuts, rimmed the coast. Warming
periods—the last beginning about 13,000 years ago—melted the glaciers and put the bridge back under the Bering Sea. When the
bridge disappeared the people were confined to the Western Hemisphere, and became the first Americans. Cut off from the rest of
mankind they developed their own unique cultures. They survived
and thrived by adaptation.

The estimated dates for the arrival of the first of a long series of
migrations have varied from 12,000 to 18,000 years ago. Some isolated sites hint at peopling 30,000 years ago and earlier. It is believed
that the human migrations from Asia probably continued into the
4th century B.C.

The entire biological journey occurred against the backdrop of
the Ice Age, with alternate periods of warm and cold. About 18,000
years ago the last major glaciation reached its maximum, creating
climate and vegetation very different from today's warm interglacial
period. This causes me to speculate that Tuin's ancestors must have
been firmly established before the Ice Age. The legends indicated
that during the time of the Old Ones the climate was warmer,
milder. Something very dramatic occurred at that time (it sounded
like a comet strike), the Earth moved and caused tragic changes.
The original inhabitants of the valley, the First Ones, seem to be
descendants of aborigines who had journeyed there long before the
migrations of men from Asia. Or (for the sake of argument) had
been deposited there by aliens after the original seeding and development of humans. As indicated in my other books the humans
were distributed throughout the world so they could multiply in
various areas. Investigations in archaeology have made it clear that
man was distributed throughout the habitable earth at some very
remote time, in the very lowest stage of human culture. A study of
the languages of the world leads to the conclusion that probably man

was distributed before the development of organized or grammatic speech. This was true of the First Ones, because they communicated with their minds.

The Eskimos now occupy the entire northern fringe of the American continent. Archaeological excavations in Alaska and Canada show that their culture was not an original condition, but the result of relatively recent population movements and contacts. Migration about 1,000 years ago carried the culture from its place of origin in northern Alaska eastward through northern Canada to Greenland. Excavations indicate there was continuous cultural growth and change over a period of more than 2,000 years, especially around the Bering Strait area. This area was one of the finest hunting territories of the world, and living conditions in general were better there than in any other part of the Arctic. Excavations also show that, although the Eskimos were in all practical respects a Stone Age people, they had some knowledge of metal.

According to Norse sagas describing the visits of 10-century Scandinavian voyagers to the eastern coast of America, the people they encountered did not resemble the present-day inhabitants. The Vikings nicknamed the American natives "Skraelingr" or "Chips," because of their puny appearance. They were described as small and dwarfish in appearance and possessing Eskimo characteristics. The area where the Vikings settled seemed to be farther south than Tuin's people. These "chip" people were also extremely violent, repulsing any attempt at settlement, so they do not sound like Tuin's gentle people. But they may have been aborigines similar to the First Ones that the Star People found in the valley.

In the December, 1912 edition of *National Geographic* there was the story of the remarkable discovery of a group of blond Eskimos. They were found in the Arctic area of Victoria Island, which is actually further north than Tuin's valley, but it could be speculated that some of his ancestors could have migrated there. The area had been considered to be uninhabited, and the natives had never seen white men. Many of them had blond hair, blue eyes, and a few had reddish beards. The first explanation was that they were a mixture of European and Eskimo blood, because many such hybrids were found eastward to Greenland. Yet the history of this area did not substantiate this theory. These tribes were so isolated that most of them could not have had contact with white men.

There were reports that in the 1700s, when missionaries established Christianity in the areas to the east, natives were seen who were quite distinctive from the Eskimos. These people were about six feet fall, quite handsome and white-skinned. In the 1600s when the area was still reportedly free from modern European contact, a sea captain reported two distinct types of natives living peacefully together in the coastal area. One type was very tall, well built, and fair complexioned. The other type was much smaller, of olive complexion, well proportioned, except their legs were short and thick. In 1821 Sir Edward Parry came ashore in Lyon Inlet and found people who had Native American features and complexions as fair as Europeans. They in no way resembled the Eskimos. These natives had never seen Indians or Europeans. More small isolated groups were reported in Repulse Bay, Point Barrow, and Boothia Isthmus during the 1800s. Many similar reports from the time showed the existence of hybrid individuals among various Eskimo tribes. Their distribution was proven to be in unbroken continuity along the entire northern coast of North America, prior to the general corruption of the Eskimo by contact with whites during the past century.

There was speculation and suggestion that some of these people could be descendants from Norse explorations in the new world, extending from the 10th to the middle of the 15th centuries. These expeditions were believed to have covered the Greenland coast south of the Arctic Circle, and the shores of the American continent probably from Baffin Island south to Nova Scotia, and probably Labrador. It is believed that the Norsemen were not exterminated by the Eskimo, but were gradually absorbed by them. It was thought that when some of these groups were rediscovered in the 15th–16 centuries they had adopted the Eskimo way of life completely, and thus did not know of their ancestry.

It was speculated that if the blond Eskimo are descendants of Norse-Greenlander ancestors of five centuries before, the Norse strain would have been overwhelmingly diluted through pure Eskimo intermarriages. If such was the case then one must consider the "blonds" as a remarkable instance of occasional reversion of types, whereby a passing race gradually resumes the general form of its ancient ancestors.

It could also be a case of atavism—the recurrence in a descendant of characteristics of a remote ancestor (or a "throwback")—instead of those of an immediate or near ancestor. This explanation could apply whether those ancestors were Europeans, Vikings, or aliens.

It was remarked in the *National Geographic* article that this discovery presented an intricate racial problem that may well tax the acuteness of American ethnologists for some time. I think if they were aware of the even broader scope of the interbreeding with aliens, it would further confuse them.

During the summer of 1991 an accidental find by a group of hikers in the Italian Alps led to the discovery of the oldest and best preserved intact human body ever found. Estimated to be 5,300 years old, the description of the man's clothes and tools sounded as though it could have been our friend Tuin, except that the ancient hunter was found on the wrong continent. Trapped in the ice for all these centuries the frozen corpse was almost 2,000 years older than King Tut, and gave the scientists an amazing insight into the time period that I estimate Tuin lived. This is considered the most important discovery in modern archaeology. He was assumed to have been a hunter, and died wearing his buckskins and grass cape. His bow and arrows, a copper ax, and other tools were recovered nearby.

Very little is known about the people who farmed and hunted in the forests of Europe during the late Neolithic Age. Farming communities spread through Europe 7,000 years ago. The people farmed the clearings and pastured their sheep and oxen in the woods. There was also a seminomadic group skilled in hunting, fishing and tracking. The two cultures merged and the practice of farming spread throughout Europe.

The scientists were amazed because the Ice Man's clothes and tools clearly showed an unexpected high technology from the late Stone Age. No leather work had ever been found from this period. His deerskin clothes were tanned and expertly sewn. His shoes were cleverly made with many eyelets. And he wore a unique waterproof grass cape that showed considerable skill in the weaving, knotting, and splicing of the grass. (Tuin enjoyed weaving and knotting as a solution to boredom during the winter months.) The four-inch blade of his copper ax was cast from molten metal poured into a mold, and worked with a hammer. Besides his metal tools, the sheer size of his bow surprised the archaeologists. They said the strength required to pull the bowstring back to firing would have been the same strength needed to lift 90 pounds with one hand. When a similar bow was tested the arrow blew a hole through a deer's chest cavity from 30 yards away. It exited out the other side and continued going. The amazing thing about this find was that it now gives scientists insights into an era where man was considered to be primitive. They are finding that man has had technology for a much longer period than previously thought. I believe the similarity to Tuin is remarkable, and shows that if such development occurred in Europe it was also possible on the North American continent during the same time frame.

Tuin's people developed from the interbreeding between the Old Ones and the First Ones. They remained isolated in their valley until the coming of early Eskimos, probably during or after one of the several migrations onto our continent. Over the centuries the absorption and diversification continued, and all these races merged, resulting in many different Native American tribes.

By the 1500s two million people were living on the North American continent, speaking some 300 languages. When America was "discovered" by Europeans it was inhabited by great numbers of distinct tribes, diverse in languages, institutions, and customs. This fact has never been fully recognized and writers have too often spoken of the North American Indians as a body, supposing that statements made of one tribe would apply to all.

Several tribes spoke distinct languages that were wholly different from any known in any other part of the world. This fact led to the conclusion that these tribes had occupied their lands for very long periods without contamination. Some were highly civilized, and showed influences from other cultures. The prehistoric Mound Builders of Kahokia, in eastern Missouri, had their own Stonehenge, an astronomical observatory consisting of a circle of upright poles. Among the prehistoric ruins of Chaco Canyon in New Mexico, a large, partially underground, circular ceremonial chamber was discovered. It was so constructed that on the day of the summer solstice, and on that day only, a shaft of light shone through a slit in its stone wall. Burial mound builders like the Natchez practiced an elaborate death cult with pyramids for the dead. The ruler was buried with material treasures, as well as women and servants, dispatched to serve him in the next world.

Most of these wonderful cultures were destroyed by methods similar to those employed in the destruction of the ancient Mayan and Incan civilizations. The early missionaries and explorers in the late 1500s set out to destroy the old cultures. In converting natives to the new religion they had to eliminate the old. Some myths and traditions were absorbed and Christianized, while others merely went underground. Entire tribes became extinct or were absorbed through 16th–18th centuries. The effects of European culture on many regions was devastating, with whole bodies of Native American literature erased, or warped beyond recognition. Where legends endured, they did so fiercely.

When Tuin drew the picture of the type of houses his people lived in, I thought it was very similar to log cabins used by early settlers. I discovered during my research that this type of construction was widely used by certain Native American tribes before the coming of Europeans. Englishmen finally settled on the Virginia coast in 1607. They admired the practicality of the log structures and adopted this type of construction. Log cabins then became the favorite habitations of English-descended frontiersmen.

The rapid progress in the settlement and occupation of the

country resulted in the gradual displacement of the Native American tribes, so that a great many were removed from their ancient homes. Some were incorporated into other tribes, and some were absorbed into the body of civilized people. Many (the majority) were removed from their traditional lands and resettled in an area totally remote from their homelands. This has led to erroneous confusion and the combining of tribe names and traditions. It is very difficult to follow any tribe through post-Columbian times, let alone pre-Columbian. Centuries of intimate contact with modern man has had much influence on the pristine condition of the tribes. Speedy and radical changes occurred. (For example, the introduction of the horse in the Native American cultures made some dramatic changes in the way the Plains tribes hunted and conducted their warfare.) Migrations and enforced removals placed tribes into strange environments where new customs and adjustments were necessary. It soon became difficult to discriminate between what was primitive and what was acquired from civilized humanity.

By the 1700s trade was occurring between the Native Americans and the Europeans. The price was dear, for besides the new goods, there came new and fatal diseases—measles, smallpox, cholera, and a variety of fevers—wiping out hundreds and even thousands of people at one blow. Whole tribes that had lived in the region for hundreds of years were wiped out or left in such a fragmentary condition that they joined with other tribes and lost the knowledge of their past identity.

The marauding Navahos and Apaches, Athabascan-speaking tribes who had come out of the Northwest into the Southwest in the 13th century, were at first less affected by the Spanish invasion. These people were drifting and remote, and there was apparently nothing in the desert and mountain country they occupied that anybody else wanted at that time. Athabascan culture was influenced by Spanish horses, burros, and sheep, but not by their religion and culture. This explains why so much more of their religion, ritual, and mythology has survived to this day. Many other tribes incorporated elements of Christianity. A few fortunate isolated tribes had less direct contact with Europeans and could preserve their sacred myths into the 20th century.

As white settlement continued to move into the more remote areas (often attracted by gold and other "valuables"), tribe was pushed against tribe, with resulting outbreaks of hostility between them. (There were some traditional enemies; for example, the Dakotas (Sioux) nation and their neighbors, but they were in the minority. A prime example of traditional animosity between Native Americans cultures would be the Navahos and the Hopi tribes which was not only instigated by the U.S. politicians hungry for their land, but which is still perpetuated to this day!) Some groups were exterminated; some merged for protection with stronger tribes. But there were always some tribes, downfacing all enemies, who have maintained their identities even to the present day.

No one at the time paid any attention to the Native American religion, art, music or ritual except to label it pagan and primitive. The U.S. government created a Bureau of Indian Affairs (BIA) to "protect" the Indians. Yet at the same time white men continued to urge Native Americans to throw the old ways aside, and to replace them with faiths and skills of the Euro-Americans. These culture traits of the invaders, because they were of European origin, *must* be superior to those of the aborigines. Many shamans were probably killed during these times before they could pass on the treasured legends of the tribes. When things settled down again after the relocation of tribes onto reservations, ceremonies and rituals and legends became once again an integral part of their life, and these things were revived. Because the records were not preserved in writing, but were kept orally, there were undoubtedly many missing pieces. During this time much Native American knowledge and literature was lost and gone forever.

Then a curious thing happened. Curiosity about the Native Americans was aroused among the intellectuals in the cities and universities in the eastern United States. For the first time, in the 1830s, scholars realized that these Indians were *people*. They were human beings. Surely they must have beliefs and knowledge, as other peoples had. Certain scientists and early anthropologists became concerned that a unique way of life might disappear before it could be studied. These people were a small minority and they went to live among the Native Americans to learn about these vanishing species, and began recording their findings. Most of my research came from their data because it was the most thorough. But by the time of their studies in the late 1880s and early 1900s the damage had already been done. Their work was highly scholarly and professional, but was complicated by the fact that, since the majority of the Native Americans lacked writing, most of the lore was verbal. These men often had to laboriously wind their way through phonetic jungles, trying to record half-forgotten tales, told in bits and pieces by men and women grown too old to remember the myth's ramifications, entirety, or context. What we now know of Native American religions, myths and legends, was recorded by these men of intellectual curiosity because it *was* curious. But it is fragmentary at best and much slipped by them unrecorded. The researchers of the late 19th century are invaluable to present-day scholars. Yet much of what was recorded early in this century still remains in musty field notebooks, untranscribed.

Much to my disappointment the Eskimos have little tradition that can be considered old or to have been influenced by anything of the nature of Tuin's story. The Church's efforts caused the Eskimo to become secretive about practicing their religious rites in the vicinity of white men. Yet they all still believed implicitly in the power of the shamans and in the religious rites handed down by the elders.

Their tribal stories and legends are mostly about the adventurous feats of their ancestors, dealing with survival against great odds in a hostile atmosphere: *i.e.,* the weather, animals, *etc.* They have an active belief in monsters, evil spirits and such strange tales, but these seem to have arisen from their extreme isolation and their fear of the hostility of their environment.

In a general way, it may be concluded that the Eskimos are more interested in earthly matters than heavenly or celestial matters. One author thought it strange that there were not more tales trying to explain the absence of the sun from the sky during long periods in the Arctic, the amazing display of Northern Lights, or the sudden and furious Arctic storms. There are a number of Eskimo stories which deal with the stars and the sun and moon, because astronomy was most important for a hunting people. People who live close to nature are keen observers of the stars. Their position in the sky told them of the time of the migration of the caribou, or the appearance of the fish. They also told them when the freeze-up of the long winter nights was coming, and when the ice would be breaking up in the spring. The struggle for existence was not always successful, and whole tribes simply disappeared from history after an unsuccessful hunting season.

The old tales are best known by certain old men who entertain their fellow villagers by repeating them before the assembled people. Some of the tales are long, occupying several successive evenings in their recital, and sometimes require two narrators. The tales are heard with pleasure over and over again, forming the unwritten lore upon which they draw for entertainment during the long winter evenings. In addition to the more important tales, which are the property of the men, there are many children's stories which the women relate. These are short, simple stories used for entertainment for themselves and children.

The ancestral spirits as well as the supernatural powers of Earth and sky are still implored to bring the animals to the hunter. The shamans were always a special group among all the North American cultures.

I found more similarity to our story in the lore of other Native American tribes. I will attempt to coordinate it and trace the origins of their beliefs. It is obvious that many Native American traditions have changed through the evolution of several generations. The myths and stories have been embroidered and added to over a long period of time, to the point that it is difficult to know what the root story was. But in some there is the whisper of Tuin's people, and I am confident their long-protected stories have not totally disappeared, but have undergone major distortion and incorporation.

The links between the historic past and the present through

myth are strong. Legends, of course, vary according to a people's way of life, the geography and the climate in which they live, the food they eat and the way they obtain it. The nomadic buffalo hunters of the Plains tell stories very different from those of Eastern forest dwellers. To the Southwestern planters and harvesters, the coming of corn and the changing of seasons are of primal concern, while people of the Northwest who make their living from the sea fill their tales with ocean monsters, swift harpooners, and powerful boat builders. All tribes have spun narratives as well for the features of the landscape: how this river came to be, when these mountains were formed, how our coastline was carved. Rather than being self-contained units, the legends are often incomplete episodes in a progression that goes back deep into a tribe's traditions.

Legends as well as cultures overlap and influence each other, not only when people of different tribes live in adjacent territory, but even when they encounter each other through migration or trade over long distances. Artifacts have been found that originally came from another tribe or culture many hundred or thousand miles distant.

Yet with all their regional images and variations, a common theme binds these tales together—a universal concern with fundamental issues about the world in which humans live. We encounter again and again, in a fantastic spectrum of forms, North and South, East and West, the story of the children of the sun, of the culture bringers, of the sacred four directions, of worlds piled on top of each other, of primordial waters, of perpetual destruction and re-creation, of powerful heroes and tricksters.

According to one author all mythological systems spring from the same fundamental basis. The gods are the children of reverence and necessity, but their genealogy stretches still farther back. The following are the main basic belief structures:

Animism: Savage man believed that every surrounding object possessed life and consciousness. Trees, the wind, the river, *etc.* He believed that they spoke to him, warning him, guarding him. Even such things as light and darkness, heat and cold were given characteristics. The sky was seen as the All-Father and by cooperation with the Mother Earth all living things had sprung forth.

Totemism: A step higher than the belief that inanimate objects and natural phenomena were endowed with the qualities of life and thought (animism). This concerned the high opinion placed on animals for their qualities and instinctive abilities. Various human attributes and characteristics were personified and even exaggerated in certain animals. If the Native American or the tribe coveted a certain quality they would place themselves under the protection of the animal or bird which symbolized it. A tribe even acquired the nickname of the animal, thus the animal was considered to be a guardian. In return that animal was not killed by the tribe. After many generations the tribe could consider that animal as their direct ancestor, and all members of the species as blood relations. These rules eventually influenced the laws and customs of the tribe, thus the animal was considered a powerful guardian being.

Fetishism: The belief that an object, large or small, natural or artificial, possessed consciousness, volition, and supernatural qualities, and especially magic powers (such as protection). It would seem that our belief in lucky charms *etc.* have descended from this belief, and thus modern man is not exempt. As has been said, the Native American intelligence regards all things: animals, water, the earth, trees, stones, the heavenly bodies, even night and day, light and darkness, as possessing animation and the power of volition. It is also the belief that many of these are under some spell or potent enchantment. The rocks and trees are confidently believed to be the living tombs of imprisoned spirits, so it is not difficult for a Native American to conceive an intelligence, more or less potent, in any object, no matter how uncommon—indeed, the more uncommon the greater the probability of its being the abode of some powerful intelligence. Fetishes could be small objects, such as small quartz crystals or feathers, and were often placed in tiny bags. Things that seemed unusual in any way were accepted as supernatural and lucky for the finder. Is this any different from the belief that a rabbit's foot is lucky? Nearly all the belongings of a shaman, or medicine man, are classified as fetishes. The idea in the mind of the original maker of the fetish is usually symbolic, and is revealed only to one formally chosen as heir to the magical possession, and pledged in his turn to a similar secrecy.

This could explain Tuin's reverence for the objects in the wise man's hut. He assumed they possessed magic and were secrets guarded by the wise man. He felt he should not even be allowed to see them. The secrets of these objects, as well as the stories, were passed on only to the wise man's successor and not to the general populace. Tuin said this was because the knowledge had to be committed to memory and could not be distorted.

Among the Algonquins a peculiar type of fetish consisted of a mantle made from the skin of a deer and covered with feathers mixed with beadings. It was used by the medicine men as a mantle of invisibility, or charmed protective covering. This sounded similar to the wise man's costumes that he wore for the different festivals—especially the skin of the strange animal which Tuin had killed. This could have been considered as a fetish for the wise man because he knew it was unusual and thus might possess some special power.

Fetishes could easily evolve into a god, but this was not the original intent. An idol is the abode of a god. A fetish, on the other hand, is the place of imprisonment of a subservient spirit, which cannot escape, and must serve the owner by bringing luck, protection and good fortune (hunting was included in this). Fetishes which lost their reputations as bringers of good fortune usually degenerated into mere amulets of talismanic ornaments.

It is agreed that certain Native American tribes have been using fetishes since prehistoric times, but the actual age of the oldest fetish is unknown. Nevertheless, it is known that the Zunis, for example, were making fetishes before the arrival of the Spanish missionaries. It is suspected that fetishes may have undergone a reduction in size during this period (1692–1800) because of Spanish (Christian) intolerance of idolatry. It is a matter of record that the first Spaniards, attempting to stamp out "heathen" rituals, outlawed the Zuni's fetishes. As a consequence, the Zuni were forced to conceal them, with the result that the size was reduced to smaller objects that could be more readily hidden.

It would appear that Tuin's tribe possessed some of these beliefs, but not all of them. They believed in animism because they thought all inanimate objects possessed a spirit, and that this spirit could talk to them and guide them. They also were careful not to offend these spirits or to call them up for frivolous reasons, as they believed they were very powerful. He was very reverent of the Mother Earth and the Moon. He also had a fetish, the stone that he carried in a small bag around his neck. He had been told by the wise man that it contained a spirit because he could see a spark within the stone.

His tribe did not have the belief of totemism. During other regressions to Native American lifetimes, which I have preformed with other subjects, I have encountered this belief. The person, while under the influence of drugs, would spend several nights alone in the wilderness until they encountered their protective brother: an animal or bird. This belief would seem to have evolved later than Tuin's time, or to have been incorporated from the beliefs of the people who came later and interbred with his tribe. At that time the beliefs of the newcomers were incorporated and the legends of the Old Ones began to be contaminated and distorted. It would appear that the beliefs of animism and fetishism were basic, and totemism was added later, although Tuin did have the belief of apologizing to the animal before it was killed. There may have occurred an incorporation of this belief into the one about totem animals.

I found that the Indian had no clear conception of a supreme deity. The Great Spirit, or the Great White Spirit, occasionally referred to by today's storytellers seems to be a blending of aboriginal concepts with the Christian idea of God. Each division of the race possessed its own word to signify "spirit." This original Native American concept was practically the same as those among the primitive peoples of Europe and Asia. The Native American had a different view of "good" and bad." That which was "good" was everything that was to their advantage. "Evil" was that which injured or distressed them. Thus their gods had the same functions; there were no "good" or "bad" gods. It was as though the savage did not believe divine beings could be fettered by such laws as he himself felt bound to obey. This applied to the deities of all primitive races; they possessed no ideas of good and evil. The gods were only "good" to their worshippers inasmuch as they ensured them abundant crops or game, and only "bad" when they ceased to do so. The idea of the "devil" is foreign to all primitive religions. Early translators of the Bible found it was impossible to find any native word to convey the idea of a spirit of evil.

The mythologies of the Native Americans also contain no place of punishment, any more than they possess any deities who are clearly malevolent toward humanity. Should a place of torment be discernible in any Native American mythology at the present day it may unhesitatingly be classed as the product of missionary influence.

When these myths were recorded most of the American Indian tribes were already dispersed. Only among the Eskimo, Pueblo, and the Navajo peoples did the mythology represent a living religious cult. A few centuries of change had largely altered the religious observances of the other tribes into either social observances or folklore. In particular the traditions of the Native Americans of the southeastern states had become the heritage of only a few old people. At the present day the process has continued much further and many Native Americans have found that the traditions have only been preserved through the work of the white ethnologists at the turn of the century, who made records of what survived. This does not mean that the myths have totally lost their power; but they are assuming more and more the nature of folktales. Some tribes still sing some of the ancient chants and the religious dances are publicly performed, though probably largely for the benefit of the tourists. On the whole the modern Native American thinks of the ancient traditions as echoes of a past which is no longer important. But the impact of the new culture has not totally destroyed the past.

It seems to be a curious occurrence that in the early days of Christianity whenever the Christians or missionaries came upon other beliefs in their travels and their early conquering, they felt a compelling need to destroy the prevailing culture and religious beliefs and replace it with their own. This occurred many times throughout history. Most notably was the destruction of the vast Alexandrian Library, and the total destruction of the Mayan and Aztec history and written languages. It may have been spurred on by the belief that Christianity was the only true religion and source of knowledge. But was it also a suspicion or a fear that something similar or greater might also exist in ancient or primitive cultures? When the first missionaries came to America they were startled to find stories of Creation and the Flood that were too similar to the Biblical accounts to be coincidence. Rather than accepting this as confirmation that the stories might have widespread historical basis, they considered them a threat and labeled them heathen. If others had a similar belief system, then theirs could not be unique. Their solution was to destroy anything they saw as conflicting. Most of this ancient knowledge was then destroyed or corrupted in the name of religion. Thus through the centuries great storehouses of irreplaceable information was lost forever under the mistaken cover of the Christian conversion of (so-called) primitive cultures.

I was amazed to find an abundance of Creation myths among the Native American folklore. The mythologies of the Red Man are infinitely more rich in creative and deluge myths than any other race in the two hemispheres. Many of these are similar to European and Asiatic myths of the same genre, while others show great originality. The creation myths of the various American Indian tribes differ as much from one another as do those of Europe and Asia. In some we find the great gods molding the universe, in others we find them merely discovering it. Still others lead their people from subterranean depths to the upper earth. In many myths we find the world produced by the All-Father Sun, who thickens the clouds into water which becomes the sea. In many other Native American myths we find the wind brooding over the primeval ocean in the form of a bird. In other stories amphibious animals dive into the waters and bring up sufficient mud to form a beginning of the new earth. This is a theme that has a common connection with the Hindu myths.

The theme of primeval water covering a not-yet-created earth is perhaps the most prevalent, found in every area except that of the Eskimo.

In all the creation myths the order of creation is always the same: the world covered with water, then land, plants, animals and finally humans. A creation myth may involve the mere statement that the creator "made all the animals." Repeatedly the legends say man was created from the soil of the earth. In a Yuma creation legend there is even an episode where a trickster appears to the first woman and tries to get her to disobey the Creator. These myths closely resemble the story in "Genesis."

Many of the Native American flood legends center on a man and his wife building a raft and taking animals onboard. Another example is of a number of animals escaping in a canoe. In some tribes the people escape the deluge by climbing onto the back of a giant turtle rather than a boat. Some of these tales relate that it rained for 40 days, and toward the end of the time a bird (usually a raven) flew out to see if it could locate land. Several tribes have their own version of Mount Ararat (using different names) where the people and animals landed. In several traditions, the flood came because of the wickedness of the people.

These are the types of legends that greatly disturbed early missionaries because they could not logically explain the similarity to Biblical accounts. It would appear that the more complicated Creation stories of Tuin's time were put aside in favor of the simpler and more entertaining children's stories—apparently because they were easier to explain and understand.

When these traditions of the North American Indians are compared with those of Middle and South America, as well as the traditions and records of the Eastern Hemisphere, it forms a very strong argument in favor of both the truth of the Biblical account and the unity of the race.

Some scientists have objected that perhaps these traditions were not handed down from former ancestors, but were received from early traders and teachers. But many tribes will even now distinguish between the traditions of their ancestors and the teachings of the first Europeans who came here. Although the Aztecs (cousins of the Navajos and latecomers to the Mexican mid-valley), Olmecs and Mayans did not have a system of writing as we know it when Cortez invaded central Mexico, they had a way of representing events by pictographs (similar to the Egyptian hieroglyphics), and this flood event was recorded.

Hence we must either conclude that all the traditions had little or no foundation, which would be absurd, or that there were a large number of floods which would be almost as absurd. For in that case the tradition of one flood in each tribe could not have been preserved so distinctly, especially when a bird of some kind, and a branch of some tree, are often mentioned in connection with it. The other conclusion is that there was one great flood, one so great that most of the descendants of those saved have preserved a tradition of it. If this is so, all must have descended from the few who were saved.

Another common belief in the legends is that in the beginning the animals, fish, insects, trees and rocks could talk. People could understand and converse with them. They could understand each other because they had a common language and lived in friendship. Some of today's medicine men still claim to understand the language of certain animals.

Just as trees, ponds, clouds and rocks are thought of as living beings, so the sun, moon, and stars in their firmament are depicted in Native American mythology as alive and endowed with human passions and yearnings to anthropomorphize. The sun, the father of light who begets all living things upon Mother Earth, the illuminator of the primordial darkness, is life giver as well as destroyer. The great Earth Mother concept is common to all mythologies.

There are many legends about the bringing of light and fire. Another version of this concerns the coming of the sun. The people apparently had lived in darkness, and when they first saw the sun they were afraid and cowering from the light they turned away from it. This is also similar to the story in the *Lost Books of the Bible* when

Adam and Eve first saw the sun. They were terrified and thought that it would surely burn them and they could not live in its light. These stories give the impression that the first people came from somewhere where the sun did not exist, or perhaps did not exist as fiercely as it does here. Could these legends have a connection with the Old Ones' spaceship and the aliens emerging into the light of the sun after being closed up in the craft for generations?

Native American tribes had various ways of computing time. Some of them relied upon the changes in season and the growth of crops for guidance as to when their annual festivals and seasonal celebration should take place. Others fixed their systems of festivals on the changes of the moon and the habits of animals and birds. It was, however, upon the moon that most of them depended for information regarding the passage of time. Most of them assigned 12 months to the year, while others considered 13 a more correct number. The Kiowa reckoned the year to consist of 12½ moons, the other half being carried over to the following year. Some of the Dakota tribes reckoned their years as consisting of 12 lunar months, observing when 30 moons had waned to add a supernumerary one, which they termed the "lost moon." There was no division into weeks. Days were counted by "sleeps," and times of the day were determined by the movement of the sun.

The chief reason for the computation of time was the correct observance of religious festivals. These were often of a highly elaborate nature, taking many days in their celebration. They consisted for the most part of a preliminary fast, followed by symbolic dances or magical ceremonies, and concluding with a gluttonous orgy. Most of these observances bear great similarity to one another, and visible differences may be accounted for by circumstances of environment or seasonal variations.

When Europeans first came into contact with the Algonquian race it was observed that they held regularly recurring festivals to celebrate the ripening of fruits and grain, and more irregular feasts to mark the return of wildfowl and the hunting season in general.

The winter was when the old people told again all the tales of glory, the wonderful traditions of the past, which have been handed down from generation to generation. In the winter the long, dark nights would be whiled away in song and story. The medicine man was trained in his youth to memorize and fast for days at a time to conjure his visions. His memory became very retentive, and by these men and women old legends were carried down through generations.

There are many Native American legends dealing with the stars. They usually involved people traveling up to the sky and being transformed into stars. This is a common thread weaving through many legends. Occasionally the legends speak of the star people returning to Earth to see their families or for various reasons. This may be parallel to the Greek stories of the gods who came down from the higher regions in order to help the poor shepherds at the beginning of their living experience—a story tradition later handed down to the Romans. At some time the gods, for one reason or another, saw their job as "done," and went elsewhere. Usually in the Native American legends they come to Earth because they are homesick, especially if they have been taken against their will to dwell in the sky worlds.

There seemed to be a fascination among several tribes with the constellation of the Pleiades, maybe because it is an unusual feature in the night sky. Maybe this was why they had to have a legend or myth to explain it, as they did for other star features. Or maybe it was because deeply embedded in their subconscious was the knowledge that their forebearers came from that distant place. The Pleiades were their favorite constellation and they took little note of the others except the Great Bear. The myths are varied, often dealing with seven girls who were taken to the sky by various means. Because the Native Americans saw the group of stars shimmering they describe it as the girls (or children) dancing. Among tribes along the Atlantic coast the Pleiades were called the "Seven Stars," or literally, "They sit apart from others," or "are grouped together." Onondagas: "There they dwell in peace." The Blackfoot call the Pleiades "The Seven Perfect Ones."

In South America the cult of the Pleiades was most highly

developed. Here this most wonderful group of stars was watched with constant interest and homage. It marked the seasons, the time to sow and reap, and the most important feasts and ceremonies. The ancient Mexicans, in a national festival kindled the sacred fire as the Pleiades approached the zenith. So did the Tuscayans of the southwestern plains. The Arapahoes, Kiowas, Yuncas and Incas regarded this constellation with reverence. The Adipones of Brazil and some other nations claim that they sprang from the Pleiades. In some California tribes it was deemed calamitous to look at them heedlessly.

The polestar or North Star (also called Polaris) was always the Native American's guide (called "the star that never moves"), and the northern lights (aurora borealis) were an indication of coming events. If they were white, frosty weather would follow; if yellow, disease and pestilence; while red predicted war and bloodshed: and a mottled sky in the springtime was ever the harbinger of a good corn season.

Many of the star legends claim the sun, moon or some other major star as the parent of various heroes, thus claiming celestial descent or origin. Instead of defining their origin as people from the stars, it was broadened into describing the parent or culture-bringer as the larger celestial object itself. This could indicate a deterioration of the stories over many generations, a simplifying of a more complicated story. A dropping away of elements in the story-telling that were confusing or considered unnecessary in the subsequent retelling.

Much North American Indian star lore has been lost, for several reasons: First, determination of ceremonies was dependent on secret knowledge, revealed only to the priests, and told by them only to the ones they trained to succeed them. Second, many constellations known to Native Americans did not have European equivalents. Third, many of the earliest recorders who worked with Native Americans were city people, unfamiliar with the astronomy of their own culture.

Strange unearthly figures often are featured in the stories. One of the Onondagas' myths concerns a very old man who came to them several times. They had never seen anyone like him before.

He was described as being dressed in white feathers, and having white hair that shone like silver. In this tale several children rose into the air, and upon reaching the sky they became the Pleiades.

A curious mention of a magic stone turned up in a book from the 1800s. The tribe supposedly had a magic transparent stone which the medicine man would consult. It was jealously guarded and even the people of the tribe were not allowed to see it. The writer could not describe it further, and he did not say which tribe had it. (*The Migration from Shinar*, by Captain G. Palmer [London], 1879.)

There are stories in several tribes about a supernatural canoe that flies and requires to be fed as it travels. **Tsimshian:** A legend about a self-moving canoe with a monster head at each end. These heads eat whatever cross the bow or the stern of the canoe. This idea of the feeding of a self-moving canoe occurs in many other connections, where the load is used for feeding the canoe. In one story the canoe had great magical powers, and was propelled by a certain song. When it was flown it would quickly rise very high into the sky. It was described as shooting upward like an arrow. The magic song could also make the canoe descend and stop. In another story when the canoe is taken ashore, it is transformed into stone. Could these legends be memories of the original spacecraft which was powered by feeding on the material it carried onboard? Also, could the magic song that propelled it be the memory of the propulsion system? When it came to Earth it was transformed and couldn't fly anymore.

In some cases there is a belief existing which stands alone and is not made a part of the folktales, such as: the thunderbird, whose awesome power ignited the lightning. Could the Thunderbird legends have originated from the Native Americans seeing spacecraft?

A favorite type of myth in America is one in which a culture-hero comes and teaches the people, for example, to make baskets—an art unknown till that time. Or, he teaches them how to plant crops. The Culture Hero stands for the strength, wisdom, and perception of humans. He is not the Power Above, but he is the intermediary between that Power and mankind.

Various tribes have the legend of Glooscap (or Gluskap) as the culture bringer. The tradition of Glooscap is that he came to this country from the East—far across the great sea; that he was a divine being, though in the form of a man. Glooscap was the friend and teacher of the Native Americans; all they knew of the arts he taught them. He taught them the names of the constellations and stars. He taught them how to hunt and fish, and cure what they took; how to cultivate the ground, how to plant, and trained them in all forms of husbandry. All that the Native Americans knew of what was wise and good he taught them. His canoe was a granite rock which turned into an island. In one of his travellings he found another tribe of people with a different language. He stayed with them five or six years to give them rules. When Glooscap went away, he went toward the West because his work was completed. It is believed he might return one day. He never grows old, so he will last as long as the world. The place where he lives is in a beautiful land in the West. The journey to that fair region far away is long, difficult, and dangerous. The way back is short and easy. There are many tales and legends of brave young men who attempted the journey. There are other personages in the legends with Glooscap, who are mighty, but Glooscap is supreme.

Many culture heroines are mentioned in the legends. They are known by many names, and they brought important things to the people: buffalo, salt, corn and the knowledge of planting, pottery and basketry, and flint to spark the first cooking fire.

In one legend Corn Mother gave the Native Americans maize to plant and taught them many things before she returned to the sky. One day a wonderful man was seen beside the lake, who taught them more things. Then Corn Mother stood beside him to teach them how to grow maize. She told them of the stars, of the planets, sun and moon and the gods in the sky. Then a dog was sent from the sun with medicine and told the people about the diseases of humans and how to cure them. Afterwards the man and Corn Mother left the people.

None of these cultural advances occurred spontaneously in the

stories. They were always brought to the people or given by someone. For example, the myth recounting the adventures and career
of some culture-hero may include the statement that "he taught the
people all the arts."

The legend of the Bahana, white brother, or white savior of the
Hopi, is firmly established in all the villages. He came up with
people from the underworld and was accredited with great wisdom.
He set out on the journey to the rising sun, promising to return with
many benefits for the people. Ever since, his coming has been
anticipated. It is said that when he returns there will be no more
fighting and trouble, and he will bring much knowledge and wisdom with him. The Spanish Priests were allowed to establish their
Missions in the Hopi country because of this legend, for the people
thought that at last the Bahana had come. Since that time they have
suffered many similar disappointments, but they are still expecting
the arrival of the "true Bahana."

The origin of the word Bahana is unknown, though there are
several theories. Today, this word is a term used to designate the
coming of the Spaniards.

The main features of this story bear a strong resemblance to the
ancient legend of Quetzalcoatl, Mexican culture-god of the Mayas,
Toltecs, and later adopted by the Aztecs. He is also associated with
the Sun and being originally a Mayan god he did not require human
sacrifice. Quetzalcoatl was the god of arts and crafts, of the calen-
dar, and of culture in general.

There was an ancient legend that the Great Culture God,
Quetzalcoatl, after instructing the people in the useful arts, departed
eastward over the sea, promising to return at a definite time in the
future. According to tradition, he was white-skinned and bearded.
The arrival of the Spaniards in the appropriate year, led Montezuma
II, who had been trained as a priest and been carefully sheltered from
the mainstream world, to welcome them. It was a policy that proved
fatal for the natives. The experience of the Incas in South America
with Pizzaro was very similar with the same devastating results.

CONCERNING MYTHS in Native American cultures, many of them have explanatory elements. This means the story uses ingenious ways to explain certain phenomena. Many are called "explanatory tales" which are used to explain things in everyday life (identifying marks on animals, birds, *etc.*). These bear a marked resemblance to Tuin's children's stories. Some researchers have concluded that there are a considerable number of cases where a definite tale is demonstrably older than the thing it is now supposed to "explain." As though the story is the original thing and the explanation an afterthought. This can lead to the conclusion that in North America tales do not originate as explanations.

Researchers found that a considerable part of the tales known to one tribe were known also, sometimes in slightly different forms, to all neighboring tribes. They found that a tale could travel for enormous distances. In some cases tales wandered thousands of miles from what was considered their "original" home.

This is particularly true of some tribes in the plain states whose origin was thought to be of the eastern forest Native Americans. They migrated from their old homes in the east with the encouragement of their culturally-related neighboring tribes and prior to the European invasion which got underway in the 17th century.

Another example are certain tales that were common to the natives of eastern Greenland and western Alaska in the early 1900s and were also known to tribes as far south as the Arkansas River. A given tale usually radiated out from some central point, losing its character little by little in direct proportion to the distance from this center. This helped the investigators to shed light on the problem of "dropping-off" of the explanatory significance of tales. It became evident that very profound discrepancies existed in the explanations attached to certain tales by different peoples. Some explained one thing, some another, and others nothing at all. While the various tales changed at the hands of different people, the explanations changed much more rapidly and radically. The absence of explanations were accounted for on the ground that they had dropped off. When they examined the tales in their various forms they concluded it was impossible to determine which was the original. They felt that the same complicated tale could not have been independently invented each time an explanation was needed, thus many of the tales were a corruption or reinterpretation of the original.

Later myths can be recognized as containing European elements, and some have been influenced by missionaries. These elements were not present in the original form. In some cases the natives were forbidden to recite the old tales because they were considered pagan and sacrilegious. In many of these cases the original tales were slowly forgotten or changed to fit in with the missionary requirements. The originals would be very difficult to find, especially in the form used before the coming and the influence of Europeans.

Considering these difficulties, I think it is remarkable that I was able to find one story that has passed down in an unpolluted form, and is exactly as Tuin told it to the children of his day. After much searching I found this one in an old book. It was recited to the author and explorer on the Six Nations Reserve in Canada in the late 1800s. It is part of a longer narrative centering around a fox.

How the Bear Lost His Tail

The cunning fox next met a bear who was also anxious to procure some fish. "Well," replied the fox, "down at the river you will find an air hole in the ice; just put your tail down it as I did and you can draw out the fish as fast as you wish." The bear followed the directions carefully, but the weather being cold, instead of securing a fish, his tail was frozen off. This accounts for the tailless condition of the bear.

It appears that the only way some of this ancient knowledge can be retrieved is through this unusual method of hypnotic regression. The knowledge is still there in the subconscious memory banks of people living on the Earth today. It is just a matter of regressing an excellent subject back through the corridors of time to a life when the information was common knowledge. Nothing can ever be totally lost or forgotten as long as the human mind survives. What is written in the subconscious cannot be erased.

To SETTLE AN ARGUMENT, as least within himself, the writer of an article written in 1900 asked, "What, then, and where, then, is the origin of the Indian? The Indian, what is he, whence is he? I know not—do you? What do I think? Since all of the theories appear to be true, at least in part, why not call them all true and be done with it? Could anything more strikingly indicate that the Indian belongs to the whole universal race of mankind, that the common blood of brotherhood leaps within our veins, that he is brother to the whole wide world? All signs point to the fact that he is the child of the ages, one of the numerous progeny of old Mother Earth, and that the secret of his primitive origin is locked up beyond our ken, together with the great mystery of the origin of life. Whence he came we do not know. But it is certain that he has inhabited this continent for a very long period of time, long enough to have established here a people, a race, well-differentiated, and concerning whose purity and antiquity there can be no question. It may be that the unity of the human race is a fact so profound that all attempts at a fundamental classification to be used in all the departments of anthropology will fail, and that the human family will be considered as one race. Many individuals of aboriginal and mixed bloods have disappeared, but they have disappeared not by extinction, but by absorption. It is very apparent that the Indian blood is not dead, it is not extinct; no, it is diffused, absorbed, assimilated—term it anything you will, save death. His race may disappear, but the blood will not die."

To this I can only add that this statement also applies to the blood of the aliens. It will live forever in the veins of mankind.

Chapter 19

The End of the Adventure

I DID NOT DO RESEARCH by travelling to the tribes and speaking to elders, because I did not believe this would yield the information I was looking for. I am aware that many books have been written in recent years by people who claim they are passing on ancient legends and prophecies of coming events. These are reported to have come from older members of the tribes who kept the sacred knowledge. In some cases these Native Americans were ostracized by their people for revealing this knowledge to the white man, who was considered their traditional enemy. It is possible these legends are genuine, but they would have had to survive orally through many years of persecution, annihilation, prejudice, separation and relocation. I could find no record of them in the annals of the early researchers.

It became obvious to me that I would never be able to find the legends of Tuin's people. That noble race had vanished many years ago and only their genes were passed along to our time. The bits that I managed to glean were as small crumbs of a once beautiful and whole loaf. A loaf that has crumbled, been devoured and disappeared. But according to Tuin the blood that flows through many Native American tribes contains a bit of the Old Ones. The memory is there still visible in the DNA. Maybe that will have to be enough, just to know that the Native Americans had a noble origin that is not acknowledged by the world as a whole. That some of their ancestors came from the stars and survived against great odds. As Tuin said, we have the wonderful story back—at least for this generation. Does this mean that it will disappear again into the sands of time? If it does, maybe the records of our own civilization will also be wiped from the face of the Earth, and no one will ever know that *we* existed. It is beginning to be accepted as fact that this has occurred many, many times in the ancient past. Other civilizations have risen, flourished and died, leaving nothing to mark their passing. *Except* the human being. If we believe in the reality of reincarnation we believe that this has not been our only life. Then it would be reasonable to assume that we may have lived in those other bygone civilizations that perished from the face of the Earth in cataclysms. We know our own death is nothing to fear because we have survived it countless times before. Thus we also know that we can survive the death of a civilization, a nation or a world. These things are motivated by cycles just as our own lives are. The immortal human soul can triumph over any catastrophe and return again and again to constantly rebuild and improve what has been destroyed. Just as humans shall rise again, the cycle can turn and civilizations and worlds can rise again. Such is the indomitable spirit of life. No destruction is permanent.

Humans have always been survivors and they will continue to be. They will rebuild and reshape their lives, but they will always remain. We are now discovering that the memories of these lost civilizations are contained in the subconscious of people living today. These memories are beginning to surface and thus the stories of these people will never die. This may be the uncharted space for scientists of the future to explore. This may be where lost history is to be unearthed, through the use of regressive hypnosis rather than the archeologist's shovel.

AFTER MY RESEARCH WAS COMPLETED, the story of Tuin and his ancestors was still just a story, almost impossible to prove. But I like to believe that it could have happened, that it is a forgotten part of our history. The story of the Old Ones is one of adventure, the indomitable spirit of exploration that founded our country, perseverance in the face of danger and the unknown, and the inextinguishable flame of hope. What better legacy to bequest to the human race, no matter where they originated.

I can imagine the sense of finality these people must have felt when forced to leave their home planet. Because of political conditions they could no longer safely remain there. They knew when they set out on the voyage across the void, that they would never see their planet again; they would never be able to return home. It was a final closing of the door, a cutting off from everything that had been familiar to them. But I suppose the sense of wonder, the curiosity of the unknown was also present. They would be breaking new frontiers, going where no one had ever been before. But they would also be unable to share what they found with their homeland because they would become people without a country. The home planet did not want any further contact with them. As far as they were concerned the pioneers would cease to exist. Drastic perhaps, but in their eyes it was better than death.

So they set out, their eyes on a far distant star. They had to look forward, there could be no looking back. Life aboard the ships might have been boring. They had everything they needed to survive. They had planned well, probably years in advance. But they knew that generations would grow up within the confines of the ship before they would once again touch solid ground. Many years of our time passed before they came close to the gravity of our planet while passing through our solar system. Earth was not their destination. They would never have stopped here if it had not been for a malfunction in the ship. Whether delayed sabotage or not, they were placed in a crisis situation. They knew they could not continue with the others, and the others could not wait and help them. They would have to land somewhere to make repairs, and hopefully catch up with the others later. They were confused when they saw the moon. According to their scientific theories it was too large of a solar body to be a satellite. At first they were uncertain whether to land on the moon or on the planet. Their technology must have shown them that the Earth had a compatible atmosphere, so they chose to land here. This was fortunate, because they had no way of knowing that repair would be impossible and they would be stranded forever. To land on the moon would have meant certain death.

I can imagine the wonder, awe and perhaps terror as they came out of the ship into the open air. Generations had been raised entirely within the walls of the ship; they had never seen the open spaces. The sight of such vast expanses of air and land must have been overwhelming in the beginning. But there was more immediate dangers. They found that the sun was not kind to them. Their bodies were not compatible to the harsh rays and the harmful radiation. They stayed within the safety of the ship, emerging only at night to try to make repairs. When it became obvious that they would never be able to escape from the planet, they began to adjust to the idea that this would be their new home. After all, they were intending to colonize a planet anyway, even though this had not been their first choice. They would have to learn to adapt and adjust. Their lives depended upon it.

They discovered there was a small group of original aborigines living in the mountainous valley. This gave them hope for their own survival. If a humanoid species could survive, then they could also. The aborigines were in awe of the space travelers in the beginning and considered them to be gods that had come down to Earth. But in time they came to realize these were only people like themselves. The adjustments were not easy. Both the Old Ones and the First Ones relied on telepathic communication, and because they were so different it was physically painful to be in close proximity with each other. But as time passed the Old Ones realized that the radiation of the sun was creating terrible genetic problems. Their only hope for survival was to mix with the First People. When it comes down to the alternative of living or dying, the human spirit will find a way. This could be another of the legacies that were passed down to us.

As time continued to pass they saw that the interbreeding was producing viable offspring, and their future here was assured. They gradually adjusted and cannibalized the dead ship to built houses. To me one of the most painful of their experiences must have been the loss of the knowledge that was contained in the computers.

They tried to save what they could by transferring it to writing. But there was so much, so much. The computer must have held more than several of our libraries. How does one decide what is essential to preserve, and what is to be thrown away? They decided that the portions of the knowledge pertaining to their survival would be the most important parts. Instruction that was needed to carve out a living in an alien surrounding. The portions that dealt with growing food, making clothing, medicine and healing arts. The knowledge that would have been important only on their home planet may have been the first to be discarded. It was a final cutting off, as they lost the history of their origin. Mathematics, other sciences, reading and writing survived for a while, but was gradually relegated to the care of one person as the pressures of survival became more important. Over time more and more of their artifacts disappeared and remained only in the memories described in the legends. It must have been difficult for them to let everything from the ship go. They wanted to hang on to some of the memories at least, so they kept and passed down some of the objects from the ship. The later descendants didn't understand the purpose of these artifacts and they took on a religious and revered quality. They were things that had belonged to the Old Ones and thus were protected.

It is remarkable that the legacy of these space travelers could have survived at all, let alone traverse the apparent thousands of years between the forced landing and Tuin's time. If his group had not been so isolated the knowledge probably would have been absorbed, diluted and changed many generations before his time. But they were completely cut off from any contaminating influence. They were the only people in the world. It was absolutely essential to their survival that all knowledge be preserved. Each person had a talent that had to be passed on to the descendants. The loss of any person's ability was unthinkable because it was essential to the welfare of the village as a whole. Thus the passing on of each one's trade was part of their life-style and greatly respected. The same thing was true of the legends. They felt they must be preserved, and as accurately as possible. There was almost a religious quality about this. Extreme

care was taken that the legends remain true to form. Nothing could
be added, and nothing could be taken away. It became a sacred duty
of the group to preserve and protect the purity of the legends, even
though they did not understand a great portion of them. It was only
the group's dedication and isolation that kept the tales intact for
such a long time. Our alien ancestors also passed down a true love
and respect for Mother Earth, their adopted home. This is deeply
instilled in the North American Indian cultures.

But eventually the inevitable happened, as it always has and
always will. Outside influences came into the valley. The group
must have been in absolute awe and terribly frightened to find that
they were not the only ones existing in the world. People like themselves had come into their homeland and life would never be the
same again. Tuin was not alive to see it, but he was one of the few
that knew it was true because he had seen other people during his
walking adventures outside the area. But the village had not believed
him; his stories became part of their legends. They did not believe
until they saw for themselves. After that it was only a matter of time
until the outside people would cause their way of life to deteriorate,
and the legends to be corrupted.

Tuin's life by itself was not remarkable. He lived a simple life free
from apparent worries. He had great psychic abilities and used them
to guide him in his hunting. He had strong religious and spiritual
beliefs, although he did not consider them as such. He lived his
entire life in service to the others in his village. By providing meat
he did the job he was meant to do and helped the village survive. He
did not consider this to be remarkable. It was what was expected of
him and he did it without question. He loved the outdoors and the
freedom of nature, and he respected all life. He lived among a
people who had learned to live without fear, and with complete
caring for their fellow creatures. He laughed and he loved, and
although he was ordinary by some standards, I believe he was quite
a remarkable untainted person. These are all wonderful qualities for
anyone to develop in their life upon this Earth. But I believe the
most remarkable service that he performed was one that he did not

consciously intend. A service that was performed through regressive hypnosis thousands of years after his death, long after all traces of his village and the artifacts were turned to dust. I think his greatest service was his ability to transfer his beloved legends through the barriers of time and space, and present them once again to our world. The Old Ones would have been very proud. They have not been forgotten. Their story has returned through the inexplicable mind corridors of humans. Our origins have been returned to us as a gift from the past. We are reminded that our legacy is from the stars. Let us not forget again.

About the Author

Photo by Richard Quick.

DOLORES CANNON was born in 1931 in St. Louis, Missouri. She was educated and lived in Missouri until her marriage in 1951 to a career Navy man. She spent the next 20 years traveling all over the world as a typical Navy wife and raised her family.

In 1968 she had her first exposure to reincarnation via regressive hypnosis when her husband, an amateur hypnotist, stumbled across the past life of a woman he was working with who had a weight problem. At that time the "past life" subject was unorthodox and very few people were experimenting in the field. It sparked her interest, but had to be put aside as the demands of family life took precedence.

In 1970 her husband was discharged as a disabled veteran, and they retired to the hills of Arkansas. She then started her writing career and began selling her articles to various magazines and newspapers. When her children began lives of their own, her interest in regressive hypnosis and reincarnation was reawakened. She studied the various hypnosis methods and thus developed her own unique technique which enabled her to gain the most efficient release of information from her subjects. Since 1979 she has regressed and cataloged information gained from hundreds of volunteers. She calls herself a regressionist and a psychic researcher who records "lost" knowledge. She has also worked with the Mutual UFO Network (MUFON) for a number of years.

Her published books include *Conversations with Nostradamus* (3 volumes) and *Jesus and the Essenes* which has been published by Gateway Books in England. She has written several other books (to be published) about her most interesting cases.

Dolores Cannon has four children and twelve grandchildren who demand that she be solidly balanced between the "real" world of her family and the "unseen" world of her work. If you wish to correspond with Dolores about her work, you may write to her at the following address. (Please enclose a self-addressed stamped envelope for her reply.)

Dolores Cannon, P.O. Box 754
Huntsville, AR 72740-0754